■ TREATMENT OF VERBS

In the dictionary, verbs are generally erb appears in the passive, causative, ca[...]rm in the story, a note to that effect (e.[...] The following chart provides a handy re[...]ans-mutations of Japanese verbs that a[...]old.

FORM / CLASS	DICTIONARY	PASSIVE SPONTANEOUS	CAUSATIVE	CAUSATIVE–PASSIVE	POTENTIAL	VOLITIONAL
Reg. I	思_{おも}う	思_{おも}われる	思_{おも}わせる	思_{おも}わされる	思_{おも}える	思_{おも}おう
	聞_きく	聞_きかれる	聞_きかせる	聞_きかされる	聞_きける	聞_きこう
	泳_{およ}ぐ	泳_{およ}がれる	泳_{およ}がせる	泳_{およ}がされる	泳_{およ}げる	泳_{およ}ごう
	出_だす	出_だされる	出_ださせる	出_ださせられる	出_だせる	出_だそう
	持_もつ	持_もたれる	持_もたせる	持_もたされる	持_もてる	持_もとう
	死_しぬ	死_しなれる	死_しなせる	死_しなされる	死_しねる	死_しのう
	遊_{あそ}ぶ	遊_{あそ}ばれる	遊_{あそ}ばせる	遊_{あそ}ばされる	遊_{あそ}べる	遊_{あそ}ぼう
	読_よむ	読_よまれる	読_よませる	読_よまされる	読_よめる	読_よもう
	乗_のる	乗_のられる	乗_のらせる	乗_のらされる	乗_のれる	乗_のろう
	ある					あろう
Reg. II	見_みる	見_みられる	見_みさせる	見_みさせられる	見_みられる	見_みよう
	食_たべる	食_たべられる	食_たべさせる	食_たべさせられる	食_たべられる	食_たべよう
Irreg.	来_くる	来_こられる	来_こさせる	来_こさせられる	来_こられる	来_こよう
	する	される	させる	させられる	できる	しよう
	愛_{あい}する	愛_{あい}される	愛_{あい}させる	愛_{あい}させられる	愛_{あい}せる	愛_{あい}そう

NOTE: The "spontaneous form" mentioned frequently in this book follows the same pattern of conjugation as the passive form, but not all verbs have such a form. The verbs that most often appear in the spontaneous form (at least in the stories presented in this collection) are 思う ("think") and 感じる ("feel"). The meaning is that the action—thinking or feeling, for example—happens naturally or automatically, irrespective of the subject's will. 聞こえる and 見える are the usual spontaneous forms of 聞く ("listen") and 見る ("see"), respectively, though 聞かれる and 見られる are also possible.

EXPLORING JAPANESE LITERATURE

Presented to

J R Trusted KS

Honoris Causa

Commended for Good Effort
L2012

Head Master

EXPLORING
JAPANESE
LITERATURE

Read Mishima, Tanizaki and Kawabata in the Original

GILES MURRAY

Kodansha USA

The original titles of the stories are, in the order in which they appear in this book, "Yukigunishō" (1972), "Yūkoku" (1961) and "Himitsu" (1911).

Permission to reprint the original Japanese texts arranged by The Sakai Agency, Inc., and Chuo Koron Shinsha (for "Himitsu" only).

New translation of "Yukigunishō," first published in English as "Gleanings from Snow Country" in *Palm-of-the-Hand Stories* by Yasunari Kawabata, translated by Lane Dunlop and J. Martin Holman (translation copyright © 1988 by Lane Dunlop and J. Martin Holman), published by permission of North Point Press, a division of Farrar, Straus and Giroux, LLC.

New translation of "Yūkoku" by Yukio Mishima, first published in English as "Patriotism" in *Death in Midsummer and Other Stories* (New Directions Publishing Corporation, 1966), translated by Geoffrey W. Sargent, published by permission of New Directions Publishing Corporation.

Map on back endpapers published by permission of Chouga Co., Ltd.

Jacket art by Tetsuji Kiwaki.

Published by Kodansha USA, Inc.
451 Park Avenue South
New York, NY 10016

Distributed in the United Kingdom and continental Europe
by Kodansha Europe Ltd.

"Yukigunishō" (Snow Country Miniature) copyright © 1972 by Masako Kawabata.
"Yūkoku" (Patriotism) copyright © 1961 by Iichirō Mishima.
"Himitsu" (The Secret) copyright © 1911 by Emiko Kanze.
English text and book concept copyright © 2007 by Giles Murray.
Illustration copyright © 2007 by Tetsuji Kiwaki.
All rights reserved.
Printed in South Korea through Dai Nippon Printing Co., Ltd.
ISBN 978-1-56836-541-1

First edition published in Japan in 2007 by Kodansha International
First US edition 2013 by Kodansha USA

21 20 19 18 17 16 15 14 13   6 5 4 3 2 1

The Library of Congress has cataloged the earlier printing as follows:

Library of Congress Cataloging-in-Publication Data

Exploring Japanese literature : read Mishima, Tanizaki and Kawabata in the original / Giles Murray.
    p. cm.
  Bilingual, parallel-text ed. of three short stories.
  Includes bibliographical references.
  ISBN-13: 978–4–7700–3041–2
  1. Japanese fiction—20th century—Translations into English. I. Murray, Giles.
  PL782.E8E97 2007
  895.6'3—dc22
                       2007002891

www.kodanshausa.com

CONTENTS

PREFACE

OVERALL AIM

This book is designed to help you navigate your own way through a selection of short stories by three of Japan's greatest writers: Yasunari Kawabata, winner of the 1968 Nobel Prize for Literature; three-time Nobel nominee Yukio Mishima; and Jun'ichirō Tanizaki, supposedly robbed of the award only by his ill-timed death. The stories are presented here unabridged, and I have tried to select classic works typical of the respective writers. Were you to encounter these stories first in translation, they would all make you long to read them in the original. *Exploring Japanese Literature* is designed to help make that wish come true.

THE THREE STORIES

The stories in *Exploring Japanese Literature* are arranged in a very rough order of linguistic difficulty, but this book is not designed as a graded series of texts. You should not feel duty-bound to start at one end and slog your way through to the other. With literature of this level, measuring difficulty objectively is next to impossible; far better to let taste be your guide. None of the stories are easy, but whichever of them you most want to read is the one that will be easiest for you.

The first story in the collection, "**Snow Country Miniature**," is one of Kawabata's palm-of-the-hand stories. It is placed first in the book because it is shorter in length and—superficially at least—less linguistically demanding than the two stories that follow it: its component sentences are relatively short, there is plenty of dialogue, and the kanji characters are relatively simple. "Some books are to be tasted, others to be swallowed, and some few to be chewed and digested," observed the philosopher Francis Bacon, and Kawabata definitely falls into the last category. The very spareness of his prose endows each individual word with greater weight and significance. Translating Kawabata's Japanese into English is only the first step; coming up with your own interpretation of what is really going on is probably the greater challenge.

Mishima's "**Patriotism**," the longest of the three stories, is conceived as the centerpiece of the whole book. Its opening two paragraphs are written in the formal style of an epitaph, but do not be misled into thinking the entire story is in the same rather archaic and impenetrable style. Ultimately, "Patriotism" is a straightforwardly linear account of a couple's lovemaking followed by their bloody self-inflicted deaths. The individual sentences are long and somewhat involved in structure, but the story itself has a compelling and hypnotic momentum that will trigger a psychochemical reaction in your brain, enabling you to move "into the zone" and read far beyond your natural powers, paralleling the elation of the protagonists that overcomes their fear of death.

Tanizaki's "**The Secret**" is the oldest work in the collection by a half century or so and undoubtedly features the greatest number of hard-to-decipher kanji words. In addition to place names from old Tokyo, "The Secret" features the detailed descriptions of beautiful objects—everything from fine fabrics to religious paintings—so typical of decadent fin-de-siècle literature. As if that were not challenge enough, the love letters (which take up only four pages in this edition) exchanged by the two central characters are written in ultra-polite classical Japanese. Should you start to feel out of your depth, do not be ashamed to make use of the dictionary and translation provided; that, after all, is what they are there for. Rather than squander your strength grappling heroically with obscure terms you are unlikely to ever encounter again, be pragmatic and conserve your energy for the relatively straightforward narrative passages where you stand a fighting chance.

ACCESSIBLE LAYOUT

Reading Japanese literature in the original can be a slow, frustrating business. *Exploring Japanese Literature* is designed to serve as your private tutor, tactfully stepping in to boost both your performance and your morale by minimizing frustration and maximizing enjoyment. Reducing the time you spend hunting down the meanings of individual words will give you the opportunity to appreciate the stories as complete works of art, rather than as thickets of semantic puzzles. The page layout has been designed for maximum readability and ease of use: the Japanese text is in large print with generous line spacing, and the paragraphs are numbered to help you locate words in the dictionary, which lists almost every single kanji as it occurs. Every double-page spread is thus a wholly self-contained unit, or "closed loop," with everything you need to create your own English version of the text from the "raw materials" of vocabulary to the "semifinished" translation on the right-hand page.

JAPANESE ORIGINAL

The Japanese texts are based on the Shinchōsha Bunko editions of Mishima's *Hanazakari no mori • Yūkoku* and Tanizaki's *Irezumi • Himitsu*. Kawabata's "Snow Country Miniature" is based on Rindōsha's *Chūshakuikō "Yukigunishō • Sumiyoshi" rensaku*. With Tanizaki and Kawabata, old-fashioned kanji characters were replaced by their simplified modern equivalents, and classical kana (only in Kawabata) were converted to their modern forms. With all three authors, we have added hiragana superscript to difficult words that even Japanese people would find puzzling and, conversely, to some simple words that you would probably have no trouble recognizing were they not in kanji.

FAITHFUL ENGLISH TRANSLATIONS

The primary aim of the English translations in this book is to help you figure out what the Japanese actually means. In cases where there was a conflict between style and fidelity to the original, then, nine times out of ten fidelity won the day. Although the translations may be a little on the literal side, they do nonetheless reflect the style of the Japanese originals. Kawabata is thus rendered into short sentences with simple, transparent language and haunting rhythms. Contrastingly, the English versions of Mishima and Tanizaki retain the long, elaborate sentences festooned with rich, baroque vocabulary that characterize the Japanese.

CUSTOM DICTIONARY

The dictionary running underneath the stories includes almost every kanji word as well as the more difficult hiragana words. If the same word appears more than once on the same page, it is listed only on its first appearance but marked with a ⊛ icon to alert you to the fact that it will recur.

What the dictionary does not include are basic particles like *wa* and *no, ko-so-a-do* demonstratives, the auxiliaries *-sō* (as in *sema-sō*, "looks narrow") and *-yō* (as in *okashii-yō*, "seems funny"), and the copula *da* (including *desu, dearu* and variants like *dearō*). It assumes knowledge of simple hiragana adverbs like *mada* and *mō* that students learn at beginner level, and omits some phrasal conjunctions such as *soko de* ("whereupon") and *sōshite* ("then") that can be understood from their constituent parts. It dispenses, too, with the basic expressions for giving and receiving, *-te ageru, -te kureru* and *-te morau*, as well as other elementary-level words and phrases, such as *-nagara* ("while").

The definitions provided fit the usage in the stories and are not comprehensive definitions for the word in all possible contexts. Direct

English equivalents rather than academic explanations have been given. As the number of words defined per page is generally on the high side, definitions have been kept short to save space. At the same time, when a long explanation is necessary—to explain the nuances of particle usage, say, or the background to some historical personage—then a long explanation is duly provided.

A guide to the dictionary, including abbreviations used therein and explanations of speech labels, is given on the front endpapers, while a map of the Asakusa area of Meiji-period Tokyo (described in "The Secret") appears at the back of the book for ease of reference.

EXTRA FEATURES

Exploring Japanese Literature includes a number of extra features designed to enrich your experience, taking it beyond mechanical translation and into the realm of literary appreciation. **Mini-biographies** place the three authors in the context of their times, provide an overview of their literary output, and sketch in the interplay between their lives and their works. **Mini-prefaces** position the individual stories in the context of the authors' overall oeuvre and offer helpful last-minute orientation. By appealing directly to the imagination, the **illustrations** stimulate you to engage with and understand the stories through empathy and intuition, rather than through reason alone.

My previous book, *Breaking into Japanese Literature*, offered audio files of the stories it contained over the Internet. This was possible only because the copyright for Akutagawa and Sōseki, the two authors it featured, had expired. As the three authors in this collection remain under copyright, regrettably audio was not an option this time around. What we have done instead is to establish **GroupThink**, a translation forum hosted on the website www.speaking-japanese.com. GroupThink gives readers a chance to critique the translations in this book, propose new translations and interpretations of their own, ask questions and exchange reading tips. When translating books professionally, I always make a point of soliciting second opinions. I am quite happy to acknowledge that it is difficult for any single person to hit upon the perfect word or the most suitable idiomatic expression all of the time. Translation may thus be one of the few human activities that actually benefits from being performed by committee, so I am looking forward to seeing what sort of alternative versions of the three texts our online symposium will come up with.

THANK YOU

This project would never have got off the ground had literary agent Tatemi Sakai not been kind enough to grant us permission to use these three stories. Once work got underway, Naoko Ito was, as always, the source of much helpful advice. Kazuhiko Miki created the book's elegant and functional page design—a crucial, if easy to overlook, part of the user experience—while Tetsuji Kiwaki provided the evocative illustrations for the cover and individual stories. Kay Yokota read through my original translations, pointing out errors and omissions, and proposing numerous improvements. Yoshiko Shimizu and Keith Learmonth proofread the book. Junko Uenishi's redesign brought the www.speaking-japanese.com website into the twenty-first century. Last, but by no means least, I owe an enormous debt of gratitude to my editor, Michael Staley, who took charge of everything from securing the initial permissions to seeing the book through the press.

ACKNOWLEDGEMENTS

Exploring Japanese Literature synthesizes information from a variety of sources. For the mini-biographies I am indebted to the works of Van C. Gessel, Charles Cabell, Dennis Washburn, Phyllis I. Lyons, Henry Scott Stokes, Christopher Ross and John Nathan. The pre-existing translations of the three stories to which I referred were by J. Martin Holman (Kawabata), Geoffrey W. Sargent (Mishima) and Anthony Chambers (Tanizaki). Further details are provided in the bibliography at the end of the book.

川端康成

YASUNARI KAWABATA
(1899–1972)

Yasunari Kawabata was born in Osaka to a family that was far from wealthy despite its aristocratic origins. His childhood was a litany of loss: his father, a frail and scholarly doctor, died when he was two, his mother when he was three. Going to live with his grandparents near Osaka, he soon lost his grandmother and his sister and was left alone with his blind grandfather.

A delicate boy who often missed school, Kawabata preferred to bury himself in the Japanese classics rather than to play with his peers. Despite a conviction that he, too, was destined for an early death, he resolved to become a writer in his early teens. Gessel (1993, 144) describes him as "determined to be a success, if only to restore to the family some of the dignity and property lost in his grandfather's day." When his grandfather eventually died in 1914, the teenage Kawabata was left with no close family.

Kawabata moved to Tokyo in 1917 to attend high school, then, in 1920, enrolled in the English Literature Department of Tokyo Imperial University. There he helped resurrect *Shinshichō*, the literary magazine in which Tanizaki had made his debut a decade earlier. Kawabata was to be actively involved with literary magazines throughout his life. He also sat on the first-ever jury for the Akutagawa Prize in 1935 and helped launch the careers of many writers, including the young Yukio Mishima.

Kawabata's own career started to take off in the mid-1920s. A 1925 account of his grandfather's last days was followed the next year by *The Izu Dancer*, the story of an unconsummated love affair between a high school student and a young dancing girl. Perennially popular, it established what was to be a recurring theme in Kawabata's oeuvre: "the discovery of a younger, impoverished, virginal girl by an urban, well-educated male" (Cabell 2001, 153). Kawabata also wrote the screenplay for *A Page of Madness*, a film set in a lunatic asylum, produced a number of prose vignettes called "palm-of-the-hand" stories, and serialized *The Scarlet Gang of Asakusa*, a collage-style portrait of life in the dancehalls and cafés of Tokyo's entertainment district.

In 1934, Kawabata began work on *Snow Country*. The story of the hopeless relationship between a wealthy Tokyoite and a geisha at a hot-spring town in the mountains of Niigata, it was published first in 1937, then in a revised version in 1948. Kawabata's method of producing his novels was unconventional. He would never write a book straight through; instead he would write a section, publish it, then add more when inspiration visited, only declaring it finished when he felt the work had finally achieved its proper form.

Kawabata's work is sometimes described as "expressing the essence of the Japanese mind" (Österling 1968), his oblique and fragmented mode of storytelling seen as more akin to haiku poetry than conventional prose narrative. One must, however, be careful about sentimentalizing him into no more than the frail and nostalgic exponent of traditional Japanese beauty. A pioneer of the Neo-Perceptionist school in the 1920s, Kawabata consciously tried to import the techniques of European modernism into Japanese literature, while spare dialogue, an almost total absence of exposition, and sudden shifts in time and place owe much to the techniques of the cinema.

During the war, Kawabata was called on to perform various duties by the militarist government: editing the writings of soldiers about to go into battle, touring Japan's conquests in China—even spending April 1945 in Kagoshima with the kamikaze corps. It has been suggested that Seidensticker's portrayal (1973, vii) of Kawabata as a man who would "have nothing of jingoistic wartime hysteria" may be more wishful thinking than fact.

As Japan crashed to humiliating defeat, Kawabata set up a publishing company to reissue prewar literary masterpieces and publish a magazine to showcase new writing talent. The early 1950s saw Kawabata himself publish *The Master of Go*, *Thousand Cranes* and *The Sound of the Mountain*. True to his famous remark that "after the war he could write nothing but elegies," these uniformly pessimistic masterpieces deal with death, deceit and the decline of tradition. Later works from the 1960s such as "The House of the Sleeping Beauties" address the emotional isolation and physical impotence that afflict men in old age.

Kawabata's works started to be translated in the mid-1950s and his reputation—bolstered also by his tireless efforts as an ambassador for Japanese literature—spread overseas. International recognition culminated in the award of the Nobel Prize for Literature in October 1968, but Kawabata's health was in decline, and the 1970 suicide of his protégé, Mishima, had hit him hard. In the evening of April 16, 1972, Kawabata went to his writing room in Kamakura and gassed himself to death.

Snow Country Miniature

雪国抄

ゆき ぐに しょう

Through a Glass Darkly

Kawabata's works are frequently described as disjointed, diffuse or lacking in finality, and his characteristic opacity is only exaggerated by the brevity of his 146 *tanogokoro no shōsetsu*, or "palm-of-the-hand stories," of which this is one. Completed only months before his death, "Snow Country Miniature" is a distillation of *Snow Country*, the novel Kawabata's translator Edward G. Seidensticker regarded as "his masterpiece" (1957, x). The story may have been inspired by Kawabata's experience of being jilted by a girl from Niigata, the "snow country" of the title, in his early twenties.

In this compressed version we meet (if not always by name) the key characters from the full-length novel: Shimamura, the feckless dilettante from Tokyo; Komako, his geisha lover; and Yōko, the mysterious girl whose death in a fire serves as the conclusion of the original work.

Kawabata prefers implication to explanation, leaving it up to the reader to catch the inferences of each brief, inconclusive episode and retro-assemble them into an interpretation of events. Look out for unannounced chronological leaps; be aware that the characters may often be talking at cross-purposes; and notice how nature, in mirroring the emotions of the protagonists, fulfills a role akin to the chorus in Greek tragedy.

Go to www.speaking-japanese.com to join an online discussion about this story and share your questions, translations and insights with other readers.

1▶ 国境の長いとんねる（トンネル）を抜けると雪国であった。夜の底が白くなった。信号所に汽車が止まった。

2▶ 向側の座席から娘が立って来て、島村（しまむら）の前のガラス窓を落した。雪の冷気が流れこんだ。娘は窓いっぱいに乗り出して、遠くへ叫ぶように、

3▶ 「駅長さあん、駅長さあん。」

4▶ 明りをさげてゆっくり雪を踏んで来た男は襟巻（えりまき）で鼻の上まで包み、耳に帽子の毛皮を垂れていた。

5▶ もうそんな寒さかと島村（しまむら）は外を眺めると、鉄道の官舎らしいバラックが山裾（やますそ）に寒々と散らばっているだけで、雪の色はそこまでゆかぬうちに闇（やみ）に呑（の）まれていた。

1

国境【こっきょう】border (between prefectures)

長い【ながい】long

とんねる tunnel

抜ける【ぬける】pass through

雪国【ゆきぐに】snow country (in Niigata Prefecture)

夜【よる】night

底【そこ】bottom, bed

白い【しろい】white

信号所【しんごうしょ】signal box

汽車【きしゃ】steam locomotive

止まる【とまる】stop

2

向側【むこうがわ】opposite side

座席【ざせき】seat

娘【むすめ】girl (NOTE: This is Yōko.) ⊛

立つ【たつ】stand up

〜て来る【〜てくる】indicates movement toward the narrator ⊛

島村【しまむら】Shimamura (surname) ⊛

〜の前【〜のまえ】in front of

ガラス窓【ガラスまど】(glass) window

落す【おとす】lower, push down

雪【ゆき】snow ⊛

冷気【れいき】cold air

流れこむ【ながれこむ】flow in

窓【まど】window

いっぱいに fully, completely

乗り出す【のりだす】lean out

遠く【とおく】far away

叫ぶ【さけぶ】shout

They emerged from the long border tunnel into the snow country. The night was carpeted with white. The train halted at a signal box.

Rising from the seat across the aisle, a young girl came over and opened the window in front of Shimamura. The snow-chilled air flooded in. The girl leaned far out of the window and shouted as though to someone far away:

"Stationmaster! Stationmaster!"

The man who came tramping slowly over through the snow held a lantern. He was wrapped in a scarf to the bridge of his nose and the fur flaps of his hat hung down over his ears.

So cold already, thought Shimamura. He gazed out at the sheds—probably housing for railroad workers—that straggled desolately across the lower slopes of the mountain. The white of the snow was swallowed up in darkness before it reached them.

3

駅長さあん 【えきちょうさあん】 Mr. Stationmaster (drawing out the last syllable) ✿

4

明り 【あかり】 light
さげる 【さげる】 carry
ゆっくり slowly
踏む 【ふむ】 tramp
男 【おとこ】 man
襟巻 【えりまき】 scarf
鼻 【はな】 nose
〜の上まで 【〜のうえまで】 to the top of
包む 【つつむ】 wrap up (in)
耳 【みみ】 ear
帽子 【ぼうし】 hat
毛皮 【けがわ】 fur
垂れる 【たれる】 allow to hang

5

寒さ 【さむさ】 coldness
外 【そと】 outside
眺める 【ながめる】 gaze at, look at
鉄道 【てつどう】 railroad
官舎 【かんしゃ】 housing for civil servants
〜らしい apparently, look like 〜
バラック makeshift building
山裾 【やますそ】 foot of a mountain
寒々と 【さむざむと】 bleakly
散らばる 【ちらばる】 become scattered about
色 【いろ】 color
そこまで to that point
ゆかぬうちに = いかないうちに before reaching
闇 【やみ】 darkness
呑む 【のむ】 [passive form in text] swallow up

6▶ 　もう三時間も前のこと、島村は退屈まぎれに左手の人差指をいろいろに動かして眺めては、結局この指だけが、これから会いに行く女を、なまなましく覚えている、はっきり思い出そうとあせればあせるほど、つかみどころなくぼやけてゆく記憶の頼りなさのうちに、この指だけは女の触感で今も濡れていて、自分を遠くの女へ引き寄せるかのようだと、不思議に思いながら、鼻につけて、匂いを嗅いでみたりしていたが、ふとその指で窓ガラスに線を引くと、そこに女の片眼がはっきり浮き出たのだった。彼は驚いて声をあげそうになった。しかしそれは彼が心を遠くへやっていたからのことで、気がついてみればなんでもない、向側の座席の女が写ったのだった。

6

三時間【さんじかん】three hours

〜前【〜まえ】before

こと event, matter, fact ❀

島村【しまむら】Shimamura

退屈まぎれに【たいくつまぎれに】to relieve boredom

左手【ひだりて】left hand

人差指【ひとさしゆび】index finger

いろいろに in various ways

動かす【うごかす】move

眺める【ながめる】gaze at, look at

結局【けっきょく】ultimately

指【ゆび】finger ❀

これから hereafter, later

会いに行く【あいにいく】go to meet

女【おんな】woman ❀

なまなましく vividly, freshly

覚える【おぼえる】remember

はっきり clearly ❀

思い出す【おもいだす】[volitional form in text] recall

〜（そ）うとする try to 〜

あせる fret, be impatient

〜ば〜ほど the more (one does something) the more . . .

つかみどころない difficult to pin down

ぼやける go dim, become blurred

〜てゆく indicates an increase in tendency

記憶【きおく】memory

頼りなさ【たよりなさ】unreliability

〜のうちに amidst

触感【しょっかん】feel, touch

今も【いまも】even now

濡れる【ぬれる】get wet, get moist

It had been three hours earlier that, in a fit of boredom, Shimamura had been watching the index finger of his left hand as he waggled it around. In the end, only this finger retained a vivid memory of the woman he was about to see. The harder he tried to form a clear picture of her, the more elusive and hazy she became in his inconstant memory. It struck him as extraordinary that this one finger, seemingly moist even now from her touch, should be thus drawing him to her from afar, and he brought it up to his nose to take a sniff of it. When he absentmindedly traced a line with the same finger on the fogged-up glass of the window, one of the woman's eyes suddenly loomed at him. In his surprise he almost cried out. But he had been daydreaming, and when he got a grip on himself he realized it was no more than the reflection of the girl in the seat across the aisle.

自分【じぶん】oneself, himself
遠く【とおく】far away ⊛
引き寄せる【ひきよせる】draw, pull
不思議に思う【ふしぎにおもう】think it amazing
鼻につける【はなにつける】put to one's nose
匂い【におい】odor
嗅ぐ【かぐ】smell
〜てみる to see what it is like ⊛
ふと MIMETIC suddenly, without thought
窓ガラス【まどガラス】windowpane
線を引く【せんをひく】draw a line
片眼【かため】one eye (of two)
浮き出る【うきでる】float up, stand out
彼【かれ】he ⊛
驚く【おどろく】be surprised
声をあげる【こえをあげる】let out a cry

〜そうになる almost 〜
しかし however
心【こころ】heart, mind
やる send
気がつく【きがつく】get one's wits together
なんでもない nothing
向側【むこうがわ／むかいがわ】opposite side
座席【ざせき】seat
写る【うつる】be reflected

外は夕闇_{ゆうやみ}がおりているし、汽車の中は明りがついている。それで窓ガラスが鏡になる。けれども、スチームの温_{ぬく}みでガラスがすっかり水蒸気に濡_ぬれているから、指で拭くまでその鏡はなかったのだった。

7▶　鏡の底には夕景色が流れていて、つまり写るものと写す鏡とが、映画の二重写しのように動くのだった。登場人物と背景とはなんのかかわりもないのだった。しかも人物は透明のはかなさで、風景はおぼろな流れで、その二つが融_とけ合いながらこの世ならぬ象徴の世界を描いていた。殊に娘の顔のただなかに野山のともし火がともった時には、島_{しま}村_{むら}はなんともいえぬ美しさに胸が顫_{ふる}えたほどだった。

外【そと】outside
夕闇【ゆうやみ】twilight
おりる come down
汽車【きしゃ】steam locomotive
中【なか】inside, interior
明り【あかり】light
つく come on (of lights)
窓ガラス【まどガラス】windowpane
鏡【かがみ】mirror ⊛
スチーム steam heater
温み【ぬくみ】warmth
ガラス glass
すっかり completely
水蒸気【すいじょうき】steam, vapor
濡れる【ぬれる】get wet
指【ゆび】finger
拭く【ふく】wipe

7
底【そこ】bottom, lower part
夕景色【ゆうげしき】evening landscape
流れる【ながれる】flow
つまり that is to say, in effect
写る【うつる】be reflected
もの thing
写す【うつす】reflect, mirror
映画【えいが】film
二重写し【にじゅううつし】double exposure
動く【うごく】move
登場人物【とうじょうじんぶつ】character (in a film, novel, etc.)
背景【はいけい】background
なんの〜もない no ~ whatsoever
かかわり relation, connection
しかも moreover

Outside twilight had fallen, and the lights had been switched on in the train, turning the window glass into a mirror. But the glass had been completely coated in water vapor due to the warmth of the steam heaters and had not been functioning as a mirror until he wiped it with his finger.

With the evening landscape flowing by in the depths of this mirror, reflected objects and the reflecting mirror moved in tandem like double-exposed images on film. The characters and the background scenery had absolutely no connection to one another. The people were transparent and fragile, the landscape a hazy flow, and as the two of them merged they created a universe of symbols that was not of this world. Particularly when the lights of the countryside shone within the girl's face, Shimamura's chest throbbed at the inexpressible beauty of it.

人物 【じんぶつ】 figure, person
透明の 【とうめいの】 transparent
はかなさ fragility, fleetingness
風景 【ふうけい】 landscape
おぼろな hazy, indistinct
流れ 【ながれ】 flow
二つ 【ふたつ】 two
融け合う 【とけあう】 fuse together
この世ならぬ 【このよならぬ】 not of this world
象徴 【しょうちょう】 symbol
世界 【せかい】 world
描く 【えがく】 depict, conjure up
殊に 【ことに】 particularly
娘 【むすめ】 girl
顔 【かお】 face
～のただなかに right in the middle of
野山 【のやま】 fields and mountains

ともし火 【ともしび】 light, lamplight
ともる burn, glow
～時 【～とき】 when
島村 【しまむら】 Shimamura
なんともいえぬ indescribable
美しさ 【うつくしさ】 beauty
胸 【むね】 heart, chest
顫える 【ふるえる】 tremble
～ほど to the extent that ～

8▶　遙かの山の空はまだ夕焼の名残の色がほのかだったか
ら、窓ガラス越しに見る風景は遠くの方までものの形が消
えてはいなかった。しかし色はもう失われてしまってい
て、どこまで行っても平凡な野山の姿が尚更平凡に見え、
なにものも際立って注意を惹きようがないゆえに、反って
なにかほうっと大きい感情の流れであった。無論それは娘
の顔をそのなかに浮べていたからである。窓の鏡に写る娘
の輪郭のまわりを絶えず夕景色が動いているので、娘の顔
も透明のように感じられた。しかしほんとうに透明かどう
かは、顔の裏を流れてやまぬ夕景色が顔の表を通るかのよ
うに錯覚されて、見極める時がつかめないのだった。

8

遙かの【はるかの】distant
山【やま】mountain
空【そら】sky
夕焼【ゆうやけ】sunset
名残【なごり】vestige, trace
色【いろ】color ✽
ほのかな vague, indistinct
窓ガラス【まどガラス】windowpane
〜越しに【〜ごしに】through
見る【みる】look
風景【ふうけい】landscape
遠く【とおく】far away
〜の方まで【〜のほうまで】in the direction of
もの thing
形【かたち】shape
消える【きえる】vanish

は（in 消えては）particle used for emphasis)
しかし however ✽
失う【うしなう】[passive form in text] lose
〜てしまう completely, fully
どこまで〜も no matter where
行く【いく】go
平凡な【へいぼんな】commonplace ✽
野山【のやま】fields and mountains
姿【すがた】appearance, shape
尚更【なおさら】all the more
見える【みえる】seem, appear
なにものも〜ようがない nothing at all would ~
際立つ【きわだつ】stand out
注意を惹く【ちゅういをひく】attract attention
〜ゆえに because ~

The sky beyond the distant mountains was still aglow with traces of light from the setting sun, and the shapes of things far off in the landscape outside the window had not yet faded from sight. But they had lost their color, making the endless expanse of banal fields and mountains look only more banal; and because nothing in the scene stood out and grabbed your attention, it was somehow like a great stream of indistinguishable emotions. Of course, that was because the girl's face was floating in it. With the evening landscape in continuous movement around the edges of the girl's reflection in the mirror, her face appeared transparent. But caught up in the illusion that the darkening landscape rushing past behind her face might actually be passing in front of it, he could not for a moment tell if it really was transparent or not.

反って【かえって】on the contrary, all the more

なにか somehow, for some reason

ほうっと＝ぽうっと MIMETIC indistinct, blurry

大きい【おおきい】big

感情【かんじょう】emotion, feeling

流れ【ながれ】flow, stream

無論【むろん】naturally, of course

娘【むすめ】girl ⊛

顔【かお】face ⊛

浮べる【うかべる】set afloat

窓【まど】window

鏡【かがみ】mirror

写る【うつる】be reflected

輪郭【りんかく】outline

〜のまわりを around

絶えず【たえず】ceaselessly

夕景色【ゆうげしき】evening landscape ⊛

動く【うごく】move

透明の【とうめいの】transparent ⊛

感じる【かんじる】[spontaneous form in text] feel

ほんとうに really

裏【うら】back

流れる【ながれる】flow

やまぬ not stop

表【おもて】front

通る【とおる】pass

錯覚する【さっかくする】[spontaneous form in text] be under an illusion

見極める【みきわめる】ascertain

時【とき】time, moment

つかむ [potential form in text] grasp

　　汽車のなかはさほど明るくはないし、ほんとうの鏡のように強くはなかった。反射がなかった。だから、島村は見入っているうちに、鏡のあることをだんだん忘れてしまって、夕景色の流れのなかに娘が浮んでいるように思われて来た。

　　そういう時、彼女の顔のなかにともし火がともったのだった。この鏡の映像は窓の外のともし火を消す強さはなかった。ともし火も映像を消しはしなかった。そうしてともし火は彼女の顔のなかを流れて通るのだった。しかし彼女の顔を光り輝かせるようなことはしなかった。冷めたく遠い光であった。

9

汽車【きしゃ】steam locomotive

〜のなか inside

さほど〜ない not very

明るい【あかるい】bright

は (in 明るくはない) particle used for emphasis ⊛

ほんとうの real

鏡【かがみ】mirror ⊛

強い【つよい】strong

反射【はんしゃ】reflection (of light)

島村【しまむら】Shimamura

見入る【みいる】gaze intently at

〜うちに while, as

こと fact, situation ⊛

だんだん gradually

忘れる【わすれる】forget

〜てしまう completely, fully

夕景色【ゆうげしき】evening landscape

流れ【ながれ】flow

娘【むすめ】girl

浮ぶ【うかぶ】float

思う【おもう】[spontaneous form in text] think, feel

〜て来る【〜てくる】indicates a condition coming into effect

10

そういう時【そういうとき】at that moment

彼女【かのじょ】she, the woman ⊛

顔【かお】face ⊛

ともし火【ともしび】light, lamplight ⊛

ともる burn, glow

映像【えいぞう】(reflected) image ⊛

窓【まど】window

外【そと】outside

It was not that bright inside the train, and the image was weaker than in a proper mirror. The window did not reflect much light, so in the course of peering into it Shimamura gradually forgot it was a mirror at all and it began to seem as if the girl was floating in the darkness outside.

It was then that a light gleamed from within the girl's face. Her reflection in the mirror was not strong enough to blot out the light outside, and the light did not obliterate her reflection either. The light streamed across her face. It did not, however, illuminate it. The light was of a cold, faraway quality.

消す 【けす】 extinguish, wipe out ⊛
強さ 【つよさ】 strength
そうして in that way, meanwhile
〜のなかを through
流れる 【ながれる】 flow
通る 【とおる】 pass by
しかし however
光り輝く 【ひかりかがやく】 [causative form in text] shine
冷めたい 【つめたい】 cold
遠い 【とおい】 distant
光 【ひかり】 light

小さい瞳のまわりをぽうっと明るくしながら、つまり娘の
眼と火とが重なった瞬間、彼女の目は夕闇の波間に浮ぶ、
妖しく美しい夜光虫であった。

11▶ 　スキーの季節前の温泉宿は客の最も少ない時で、島村が
内湯から上って来ると、もう全く寝静まっていた。古びた
廊下は彼の踏む度にガラス戸を微かに鳴らした。その長い
はずれの帳場の曲り角に、裾を冷え冷えと黒光りの板の上
へ拡げて、女が高く立っていた。

12▶ 　とうとう芸者に出たのであろうかと、その裾を見てはっ
としたけれども、

小さい【ちいさい】small
瞳【ひとみ】pupil, eye
〜のまわりを around
ぽうっと MIMETIC describes a spreading
　warmth or glow
明るい【あかるい】bright
つまり briefly, in effect
娘【むすめ】girl
眼【め】eye
火【ひ】light, fire
重なる【かさなる】overlap
瞬間【しゅんかん】moment
彼女【かのじょ】she, the woman
目【め】eye
夕闇【ゆうやみ】twilight
波間に浮ぶ【なみまにうかぶ】float on
　waves
妖しい【あやしい】bewitching

美しい【うつくしい】beautiful
夜光虫【ほたる】firefly

11

スキー skiing
季節【きせつ】season
〜前【〜まえ】before
温泉宿【おんせんやど】inn at a hot-spring
　resort
客【きゃく】customer, guest
最も【もっとも】most
少ない【すくない】few
時【とき】time
島村【しまむら】Shimamura
内湯【うちゆ】indoor bath
上る【あがる】get out of (a bath)
〜て来る【〜てくる】indicates the subject
　coming back to a previous location or
　condition, with emphasis on the com-
　pletion of the action

As it softly illuminated the area around her tiny pupils—at the instant, that is, when the light and girl's eyes had become perfectly aligned—her eyes became mysterious and beautiful fireflies floating on waves of twilight.

Guests of the hot-spring inn were at their fewest prior to the skiing season, so when Shimamura emerged from the indoor bath the place was already sunk in sleep. At every step he took along the old corridor, the glass doors would rattle faintly. The woman was standing bolt upright at the far corner by the reception desk, her skirts flowing icily over the black polished floor.

Had she finally become a geisha then? He was taken aback at the sight of her skirts.

全く 【まったく】 completely
寝静まる 【ねしずまる】 sleep silently
古びた 【ふるびた】 old, musty
廊下 【ろうか】 corridor, passage
彼 【かれ】 he
踏む 【ふむ】 tramp, tread
〜度に 【〜たびに】 each time
ガラス戸 【ガラスど】 glass door
微かに 【かすかに】 faintly
鳴らす 【ならす】 make a sound
長い 【ながい】 long
はずれ end, extremity
帳場 【ちょうば】 desk
曲り角 【まがりかど】 corner
裾 【すそ】 hem, skirt ⊛
冷え冷えと 【ひえびえと】 coldly
黒光り 【くろびかり】 black sheen
板 【いた】 floorboard

〜の上へ 【〜のうえへ】 onto, upon
拡げる 【ひろげる】 spread out
女 【おんな】 woman, she
高い 【たかい】 tall
立つ 【たつ】 stand

12
とうとう finally
芸者に出る 【げいしゃにでる】 become a geisha (NOTE: The subject is Komako. Previously she was a sort of stand-in geisha who entertained visitors to the resort only when it was exceptionally busy.)
見る 【みる】 look at, see
はっとする be startled

こちらへ歩いて来るでもない、体のどこかを崩して迎える
しなを作るでもない、じっと動かぬその立ち姿から、彼は
遠目にも真面目なものを受け取って、急いで行ったが、女
の傍に立っても黙っていた。女も濃い白粉の顔で微笑もう
とすると、反って泣き面になったので、なにも言わずに二
人は部屋の方へ歩き出した。

13▶　　あんなことがあったのに、手紙も出さず、会いにも来
ず、踊の型の本など送るという約束も果さず、女からすれ
ば忘れられたとしか思えないだろうから、先ず島村の方か
ら詫びかいいわけを言わねばならない順序だったが、

歩く【あるく】walk

〜て来る【〜てくる】indicates movement toward the narrator

体【からだ】body

どこか somewhere

崩す【くずす】relax (one's posture)

迎える【むかえる】welcome, greet

しな coquettish airs

作る【つくる】put on (airs)

じっと MIMETIC motionless

動く【うごく】move

立ち姿【たちすがた】standing figure

彼【かれ】he

遠目にも【とおめにも】even from a distance

真面目な【まじめな】serious

もの thing, something

受け取る【うけとる】receive, feel

急ぐ【いそぐ】hurry

〜て行く【〜ていく】indicates movement away from the narrator

女【おんな】woman, she ✖

〜の傍に【〜のそばに】beside, near

立つ【たつ】stand

黙る【だまる】say nothing

濃い【こい】thick

白粉【おしろい】face powder, make-up

顔【かお】face

微笑む【ほほえむ】[volitional form in text] smile

〜（も）うとする try to 〜

反って【かえって】on the contrary

泣き面【なきつら／なきっつら】tearful face

なにも言わずに【なにもいわずに】without saying anything

二人【ふたり】both of them, they

She did not walk over to him, nor relax her pose into any coquettish gesture of recognition. Even from a distance he could sense something serious in her rigidly immobile figure, and he hurried over and stood close to her, though he still said nothing. Her heavily powdered face attempted a smile which only ended up as tears, and in silence they walked off together to his room.

Despite what had happened between them, he had not written her any letters, come to see her, or kept his promise to send a book of dance movements. The woman must have thought he had forgotten all about her—meaning that the proper procedure would be for Shimamura to come up with an apology or an excuse.

部屋【へや】room
〜の方へ【〜のほうへ】in the direction of
歩き出す【あるきだす】start to walk

13

あんなこと that kind of episode
〜のに although, in spite of the fact that ~
手紙【てがみ】letter
出さず【ださず】without sending
会いにも来ず【あいにもこず】without even coming to see
踊【おどり】dance, dancing
型【かた】set form
本【ほん】book
送る【おくる】send
約束【やくそく】promise
果さず【はたさず】without fulfilling
〜からすれば from the point of view of

忘れる【わすれる】[passive form in text] forget
〜しか other than, besides
思える【おもえる】feel
先ず【まず】first of all
島村【しまむら】Shimamura
方【ほう】side
詫び【わび】apology
いいわけ excuse
言う【いう】say, utter
〜ねばならない ought to
順序【じゅんじょ】order, procedure

顔を見ないで歩いているうちにも、彼女は彼を責めるどころか、体いっぱいになつかしさを感じていることが知れるので、彼は尚更、どんなことを言ったにしても、その言葉は自分の方が不真面目だという響きしか持たぬだろうと思って、なにか彼女に気押される甘い喜びにつつまれていたが、階段の下まで来ると、

14▶ 「こいつが一番よく君を覚えていたよ。」と、人差指だけ伸した左手の握り拳を、いきなり女の前に突きつけた。

15▶ 「そう？」と、女は彼の指を握るとそのまま離さないで手を引くように階段を上って行った。火燵の前で手を離すと、彼女はさっと首まで赤くなって、それをごまかすためにあわててまた彼の手を拾いながら、

顔【かお】face
見る【みる】look at
歩く【あるく】walk
～うちにも even as
彼女【かのじょ】the woman, she ✻
彼【かれ】he ✻
責める【せめる】criticize
～どころか far from (doing something)
体いっぱいに【からだいっぱいに】throughout one's entire body
なつかしさ sentimental longing
感じる【かんじる】feel
こと fact
知れる【しれる】be able to know, know instinctively
尚更【なおさら】all the more
どんなこと～にしても whatever
言う【いう】say

言葉【ことば】word, remark
自分の方【じぶんのほう】he (rather than she)
不真面目な【ふまじめな】frivolous
響き【ひびき】sound, ring
～しか other than, besides
持つ【もつ】have
思う【おもう】think
なにか somehow, for some reason
気押される【けおされる】be overawed, be overwhelmed
甘い【あまい】sweet
喜び【よろこび】joy
つつむ [passive form in text] envelop
階段【かいだん】stairs ✻
下【した】bottom
来る【くる】come, reach

But even as he walked along without looking at her, he sensed that, far from reproaching him, her whole body was awash with joy at their reunion. He felt that no matter what he said, the tone of his words would only mark him out as the shallower of the two. He was enveloped in the sweet joy of being inexplicably over-whelmed by her. But when they got to the foot of the stairs:

"This fellow remembered you best," he blurted out, thrusting his left fist, with the index finger sticking out, into her face.

"Really?" Grabbing his finger, the woman kept hold of it as she climbed up the stairs, as if to lead him after her by the hand. When she released it in front of the *kotatsu*, she immediately blushed all the way down to her throat. To hide her confusion, she impetuously reached for his hand again.

14
こいつ BRUSQUE this fellow
一番よく 【いちばんよく】 best
君 【きみ】 FAMILIAR you
覚える 【おぼえる】 remember
人差指 【ひとさしゆび】 index finger
伸す 【のばす】 stretch out
左手 【ひだりて】 left hand
握り拳 【にぎりこぶし】 fist
いきなり suddenly
女 【おんな】 woman, she ⊛
〜の前に 【〜のまえに】 in front of
突きつける 【つきつける】 thrust out (in front of)

15
そう？ is that so?
指 【ゆび】 finger
握る 【にぎる】 grasp

そのまま having done so
離す 【はなす】 let go of ⊛
手 【て】 hand ⊛
引く 【ひく】 pull
上る 【あがる】 go up
〜て行く 【〜ていく】 indicates movement away from the narrator
火燵 【こたつ】 blanket-covered table with a heater beneath it
〜の前で 【〜のまえで】 in front of
さっと all of a sudden
首 【くび】 neck
赤い 【あかい】 red
ごまかす cover up, divert attention from
あわてて hastily, in a panic
また again
拾う 【ひろう】 pick up, grab

16▶　「これが覚えていてくれたの？」
17▶　「右じゃない、こっちだよ。」と、女の掌の間から右手を
　　抜いて、改めて左の握拳を出した。彼女はすました顔で、
18▶　「ええ、分ってるわ。」
19▶　　ふふと、含み笑いしながら、島村の掌を拡げて、その上
　　に顔を押しあてた。
20▶　「これが覚えていてくれたの？」
21▶　「ほう冷たい。こんな冷たい髪の毛初めてだ。」
22▶　「東京はまだ雪が降らないの？」

16

覚える 【おぼえる】 remember ❀

〜の particle indicating a question; spoken with rising intonation ❀

17

右 【みぎ】 right

女 【おんな】 woman

掌 【てのひら】 palm of the hand ❀

〜の間から 【〜のあいだから】 from between

右手 【みぎて】 right hand

抜く 【ぬく】 pull out

改めて 【あらためて】 again, anew

左 【ひだり】 left

握拳 【にぎりこぶし】 fist

出す 【だす】 hold out

彼女 【かのじょ】 she, the woman

すました demure

顔 【かお】 face, expression

18

ええ yes

分る 【わかる】 know, understand

〜わ FEMININE particle used to soften an assertion

19

ふふ（と）ONOMATOPOEIC describes the sound of quiet laughter

含み笑い 【ふくみわらい】 suppressed laugh

島村 【しまむら】 Shimamura

拡げる 【ひろげる】 spread out

その上に 【そのうえに】 on top of it, upon it

顔 【かお】 face

押しあてる 【おしあてる】 press against

"So this remembered me?"

"Not the right one. This one." He slid his right hand out of her hand and again thrust out his left fist. Her face was innocence itself.

"I know."

With a soft, half-stifled laugh, she spread open Shimamura's palm and pressed her face against it.

"So this remembered me?"

"How cold. I've never felt such cold hair."

"Has it snowed yet in Tokyo?"

21
ほう exclamation of surprise
冷たい【つめたい】cold ✵
こんな such, so
髪の毛【かみのけ】hair
初めて【はじめて】for the first time
22
東京【とうきょう】Tokyo
雪【ゆき】snow
降る【ふる】fall

23 ▶ 　島村は宿の玄関で若葉の匂いの強い裏山を見上げる
と、それに誘われるように荒っぽく登って行った。

24 ▶ 　なにがおかしいのか、一人で笑いが止まらなかった。

25 ▶ 　ほどよく疲れたところで、くるっと振り向きざま浴衣の
尻からげして、一散に駈け下りて来ると、足もとから黄蝶
が二羽飛び立った。

26 ▶ 　蝶はもつれ合いながら、やがて国境の山より高く、黄色
が白くなってゆくにつれて、遙かだった。

27 ▶ 「どうなさったの。」

28 ▶ 　女が杉林の陰に立っていた。

29 ▶ 「うれしそうに笑ってらっしゃるわよ。」

23

島村【しまむら】Shimamura

宿【やど】inn

玄関【げんかん】entrance, doorway

若葉【わかば】fresh greenery

匂い【におい】smell

強い【つよい】strong

裏山【うらやま】hill behind one's house

見上げる【みあげる】look up at

誘う【さそう】seduce

荒っぽく【あらっぽく】roughly

登る【のぼる】climb

〜て行く【〜ていく】indicates movement away from the narrator

24

おかしい funny

一人で【ひとりで】by oneself

笑い【わらい】laugh

止まる【とまる】stop

25

ほどよく suitably, properly

疲れる【つかれる】get tired

ところ point, moment

くるっと MIMETIC briskly (of turning motion)

振り向く【ふりむく】turn around

〜ざま the moment (one does something), just when

浴衣【ゆかた】light cotton kimono

尻からげする【しりからげする】tuck up one's skirts

一散に【いっさんに】at full speed

駈け下りる【かけおりる】run down (a slope)

〜て来る【〜てくる】indicates movement toward the narrator

At the doorway of the inn, Shimamura looked back at the mountainside with its strong smell of fresh young leaves. Unable to resist, he went scrambling madly up the slope.

He didn't know what was so funny. He couldn't stop laughing to himself.

When he felt good and tired, he spun around sharply, tucked the skirts of his *yukata* into his sash, and came charging back down at full tilt. Two yellow butterflies flew up from beneath his feet.

The butterflies flitter-fluttered away. Soon they were above the border range and so far away that their yellow hues had turned white.

"What is it?"

The woman was standing in the shade of a cedar grove.

"You're laughing and you look so happy."

足もとから 【あしもとから】 from around one's feet

黄蝶 【きちょう】 yellow butterfly

二羽 【にわ】 two (winged creatures)

飛び立つ 【とびたつ】 fly up

26

蝶 【ちょう】 butterfly

もつれ合う 【もつれあう】 get entangled

やがて in due course

国境 【こっきょう】 border (between prefectures)

山 【やま】 mountain

〜より more than 〜

高い 【たかい】 high

黄色 【きいろ】 yellow

白い 【しろい】 white

〜てゆく indicates an increase in tendency

〜につれて as

遙かな 【はるかな】 far away

27

なさる HONORIFIC do

〜の particle indicating a question; spoken with rising intonation

28

女 【おんな】 woman

杉林 【すぎばやし】 cedar grove

陰 【かげ】 shadow, shade

立つ 【たつ】 stand

29

うれしい happy

笑う 【わらう】 laugh

〜てらっしゃる＝〜ていらっしゃる HONORIFIC be ——ing

〜わよ FEMININE particle combination used to express a belief

30▶ 「止めたよ。」と、島村はわけのない笑いがこみ上げて来
て、

31▶ 「止めた。」

32▶ 「そう？」

33▶ 　女はふいとあちらを向くと、杉林のなかへゆっくり入っ
た。彼は黙ってついて行った。

34▶ 　神社であった。苔のついた狛犬の傍の平な岩に女は腰を
おろした。

35▶ 「ここが一等涼しいの。真夏でも冷たい風があります
わ。」

36▶ 「ここの芸者って、みなあんなのかね。」

30

止める【やめる】abandon, not do ⊛
　(NOTE: This refers to Shimamura hav-
　ing previously summoned another gei-
　sha to the inn in order to have sex with
　her—a plan he gave up when he found
　himself uninterested in the girl who
　came. This episode is mentioned in the
　full-length version of *Snow Country* but
　omitted here. What Shimamura "aban-
　doned" was sex with a geisha other than
　Komako.)

島村【しまむら】Shimamura

わけのない senseless

笑い【わらい】laughter

こみ上げる【こみあげる】well up

〜て来る【〜てくる】indicates a condi-
　tion coming into effect

32

そう？ is that so?

33

女【おんな】woman ⊛

ふいと suddenly

あちらを向く【あちらをむく】look away

杉林【すぎばやし】cedar grove

〜のなかへ into

ゆっくり slowly

入る【はいる】enter

彼【かれ】he

黙る【だまる】say nothing

ついて行く【ついていく】follow after

34

神社【じんじゃ】Shinto shrine

苔のついた【こけのついた】covered with
　moss

狛犬【こまいぬ】pair of carved guardian
　dogs

〜の傍の【〜のそばの】beside, near

"I didn't do it." Shimamura felt the meaningless laughter welling up inside him.

"I didn't do it."

"Oh?"

The woman turned abruptly away, then wandered slowly off into the cedar grove. He followed her, saying nothing.

There was a shrine. The woman sat down on a flat rock next to a pair of guardian dogs overgrown with moss.

"This is the coolest spot. Even in midsummer there's a cool breeze."

"Are all the geisha here like her?"

平な 【たいらな】 flat
岩 【いわ】 stone, rock
腰をおろす 【こしをおろす】 sit down

35
一等 【いっとう】 the most
涼しい 【すずしい】 cool
〜の FEMININE particle used with falling intonation to soften an assertion
真夏 【まなつ】 midsummer
冷たい 【つめたい】 cold, cool
風 【かぜ】 wind
〜わ FEMININE particle used to soften an assertion

36
芸者 【げいしゃ】 geisha
〜って as for
みな all
あんな like that

〜かね particle combination used to express doubt or suspicion

37▶ 「似たようなものでしょう。年増にはきれいな人がありますわ。」と、うつ向いて素気なく言った。その首に杉林の小暗い青が映るようだった。

38▶ 　島村は杉の梢を見上げた。

39▶ 「もういいよ。体の力がいっぺんに抜けちゃって、おかしいようだよ。」

40▶ 　その杉は岩にうしろ手を突いて胸まで反らないと目の届かぬ高さ、しかも実に一直線に幹が立ち並び、暗い葉が空をふさいでいるので、しいんと静けさが鳴っていた。

37

似た【にた】alike, similar

もの thing

年増【としま】middle-aged woman

きれいな beautiful

人【ひと】person

〜わ FEMININE particle used to soften an assertion

うつ向く【うつむく】look down

素気なく【そっけなく】brusquely

言う【いう】say

首【くび】neck

杉林【すぎばやし】cedar grove ✿

小暗い【こぐらい】somewhat dark

青【あお】green

映る【うつる】be reflected

38

島村【しまむら】Shimamura

杉【すぎ】cedar

梢【こずえ】treetop

見上げる【みあげる】look up at

39

いい enough

体【からだ】body

力【ちから】strength, power

いっぺんに all at once

抜ける【ぬける】go away

〜ちゃって＝〜てしまって completely

おかしい strange, funny

40

岩【いわ】rock

うしろ手を突く【うしろでをつく】stick out one's hands behind one's back

胸【むね】chest

反る【そる】lean back

目【め】eye

"They're all much the same. Some of the older ones are beautiful, you know," she said tersely, looking at the ground. The dark green of the cedar grove seemed to have cast its tinge on her neck.

Shimamura looked up toward the tops of the cedars.

"I'm not interested. My powers have deserted me all of a sudden. Strange."

The cedars were so tall you couldn't see their tops unless you rested your hands on the rock behind you and leaned your head all the way back. The tree trunks stood in a perfectly straight line, their dark leaves blocking out the sky, and there was a ringing silence.

届く 【とどく】 reach
高さ 【たかさ】 height
しかも moreover
実に 【じつに】 truly
一直線に 【いっちょくせんに】 in a straight line
幹 【みき】 trunk
立ち並ぶ 【たちならぶ】 stand in a line
暗い 【くらい】 dark
葉 【は】 leaf, foliage
空 【そら】 sky
ふさぐ block out, obstruct
しいんと ONOMATOPOEIC describes utter silence
静けさ 【しずけさ】 silence
鳴る 【なる】 make a sound, ring

島村が背を寄せている幹は、なかでも最も年古りたものだったが、どうしてか北側の枝だけが上まですっかり枯れて、その落ち残った根元は尖った杭を逆立ちに幹へ植え連ねたと見え、なにか恐ろしい神の武器のようであった。

41▶　西日に光る遠い川を女はじっと眺めていた。手持無沙汰になった。

42▶　「あら忘れてたわ。お煙草でしょう。」と、女はつとめて気軽に、

43▶　「さっきお部屋へ戻ってみたら、もういらっしゃらないんでしょう。どうなすったかしらと思うと、えらい勢いでおひとり山へ登ってらっしゃるんですもの。窓から見えたの。おかしかったわ。

島村【しまむら】Shimamura
背を寄せる【せをよせる】lean one's back (against)
幹【みき】tree trunk ❀
なかでも of all
最も【もっとも】the most
年古りた【としふりた】ARCHAIC old
もの thing
どうしてか for some reason
北側【きたがわ】north side
枝【えだ】branch
上まで【うえまで】up to the top
すっかり completely
枯れる【かれる】wither
落ち残る【おちのこる】be left behind after having the rest fall
根元【ねもと】part near the base, root
尖った【とがった】sharp

杭【くい】stake, post
逆立ちに【さかだちに】standing upside down
植え連ねる【うえつらねる】plant in a row
見える【みえる】appear, seem
なにか something or other, some kind of
恐ろしい【おそろしい】fearful
神【かみ】god
武器【ぶき】weapon

41
西日【にしび】afternoon, evening sun
光る【ひかる】shine
遠い【とおい】distant
川【かわ】river
女【おんな】woman, she ❀
じっと MIMETIC fixedly
眺める【ながめる】gaze at, look at

The tree Shimamura was leaning against was the oldest of them all. For some reason the boughs on its north side were all dead up to the top, and the stumps of the fallen branches looked like stakes that had been planted along the trunk with their points facing out. It was like some dreadful weapon of a god.

The woman gazed at the far-off river as it glowed under the evening sun. She felt awkward and uncomfortable.

"Silly me, I forgot these. Your cigarettes," said the woman with forced lightness.

"You weren't there when I popped back into your room just now. I was just wondering what had happened to you, and there you were charging like the clappers all alone up the mountain. I saw you out the window. You looked funny.

手持無沙汰【てもちぶさた】anxiety due to an abundance of time

42

あら FEMININE exclamation of mild frustration

忘れる【わすれる】forget

〜わ FEMININE particle used to soften an assertion ⊛

お煙草【おタバコ】HONORIFIC cigarettes

つとめて気軽に【つとめてきがるに】with forced lightness

43

さっき before

お部屋【おへや】HONORIFIC room

戻る【もどる】return

〜てみる to see what is going on

いらっしゃる HONORIFIC be present, be

どうなすったかしら = どうなさったかしら HONORIFIC, FEMININE what happened to you, I wonder

〜かしら FEMININE I wonder

思う【おもう】think

えらい extraordinary

勢い【いきおい】energy

おひとり HONORIFIC alone

山【やま】mountain

登る【のぼる】climb

〜てらっしゃる = 〜ていらっしゃる HONORIFIC be ——ing

〜もの FEMININE used in sentence-final position to softly put forth a reason; expresses the speaker's wheedling desire to be indulged

窓【まど】window

見える【みえる】be visible

〜の FEMININE particle used with falling intonation to soften an assertion

おかしい strange, funny

お煙草を忘れていらしたらしいから、持って来て上げたんですわ。」

44▶ そして彼の煙草を袂から出すとマッチをつけた。

45▶ 「あの子に気の毒したよ。」

46▶ 「そんなこと、お客さんの自由じゃないの。いつ帰そうと。」

47▶ 石の多い川の音が甘い円さで聞えて来るばかりだった。杉の間から向うの山襞の陰るのが見えた。

48▶ 「君とそう見劣りしない女でないと後で君と会った時、心外じゃないか。」

49▶ 「知らないわ。負け惜しみの強い方ね。」と、女はむっと嘲るように言ったけれども、芸者を呼ぶ前とは別の感情が通っていた。

お煙草【おタバコ】HONORIFIC cigarettes ⊛
忘れる【わすれる】forget
～ていらした＝～ていらっしゃった HONORIFIC had ～
～らしい apparently
持って来る【もってくる】bring (someone)
～て上げる【～てあげる】do as a favor for
～わ FEMININE particle used to soften an assertion

44
彼【かれ】he
袂【たもと】sleeve
出す【だす】pull out
マッチをつける light a match

45
子【こ】child, girl

気の毒する【きのどくする】feel sorry (for), feel pity (for)

46
そんなこと that kind of thing
お客さん【おきゃくさん】POLITE customer
自由【じゆう】freedom, discretion
じゃない be
～の FEMININE particle used with falling intonation to soften an assertion
帰す【かえす】[volitional form in text] send back

47
石【いし】stone, rock
多い【おおい】numerous
川【かわ】river
音【おと】sound, noise
甘い【あまい】sweet
円さ【まるさ】roundness

Anyway, I brought your cigarettes, since you seemed to have forgotten them."

Producing the cigarettes from her sleeve, she struck a match.

"I feel bad about that girl."

"Don't be silly. It's completely up to the client. When to send the woman back."

All they could hear was the sweetly rounded babble of the rock-strewn river. Through the cedars they could see the folds of the mountains off in the distance as they darkened.

"The girl should be no less beautiful than you are, otherwise when I saw you after the event, I'd just feel ashamed of myself."

"Don't give me that! Chock-full of excuses, you are," said the woman in a bitter, mocking tone—but the emotions flowing between them had changed since he had called in the geisha.

聞える 【きこえる】 be audible

〜て来る 【〜てくる】 indicates a situation or phenomenon emerging

〜ばかり only

杉 【すぎ】 cedar

〜の間 【〜のあいだ】 between

向う 【むこう】 beyond, over there

山襞 【やまひだ】 folds of a mountain

陰る 【かげる】 darken

見える 【みえる】 be visible, seem

48

君 【きみ】 FAMILIAR you ⊛

見劣りする 【みおとりする】 be inferior

女 【おんな】 woman ⊛

後で 【あとで】 afterward

会う 【あう】 meet

〜時 【〜とき】 when

心外な 【しんがいな】 mortifying

49

知らないわ 【しらないわ】 FEMININE what do I care? don't give me that!

負け惜しみ 【まけおしみ】 sour grapes

強い 【つよい】 strong, intense

方 【かた】 POLITE person

むっと MIMETIC with annoyance

嘲る 【あざける】 deride, sneer

言う 【いう】 say

芸者 【げいしゃ】 geisha

呼ぶ 【よぶ】 call, summon

〜前とは 【〜まえとは】 from/than before

別の 【べつの】 different, other

感情 【かんじょう】 emotion

通う 【かよう】 pass between, move to and from

50▶　はじめからただこの女がほしいだけだ、それを例によって遠回りしていたのだと、島村ははっきり知ると、自分が厭になる一方、女がよけい美しく見えて来た。杉林の蔭で彼を呼んでからの女は、なにかすっと抜けたように涼しい姿だった。

51▶　細く高い鼻が少しさびしいけれども、その下に小さくつぼんだ唇はまことに美しい蛭の輪のように伸び縮みがなめらかで、もし皺があったり色が悪かったりすると、不潔に見えるはずだが、そうでなく濡れ光っていた。目尻が上りもせず、わざと真直ぐに描いたような眼はどこか、おかしいようながら、短い毛の生えつまった下り気味の眉が、それをほどよくつつんでいた。

50

はじめから from the start
ただ just, only
女【おんな】woman ✽
ほしい want, desire
例によって【れいによって】as usual
遠回りする【とおまわりする】be round-about, go about things the long way
島村【しまむら】Shimamura
はっきり clearly
知る【しる】become aware
自分【じぶん】oneself, himself
厭になる【いやになる】become disgusted, get sick (of)
一方【いっぽう】on the one hand
よけい all the more
美しい【うつくしい】beautiful ✽
見える【みえる】seem, appear

〜て来る【〜てくる】indicates a situation or phenomenon emerging
杉林【すぎばやし】cedar grove
〜の蔭で【〜のかげで】from behind, within
彼【かれ】he
呼ぶ【よぶ】call
なにか something or other, some kind of
すっと quickly, suddenly
抜ける【ぬける】be released, leave
涼しい【すずしい】cool, nonchalant
姿【すがた】figure

51

細い【ほそい】thin
高い【たかい】high, prominent
鼻【はな】nose
少し【すこし】slightly
さびしい lonely, forlorn

When Shimamura realized that this woman was the only one he had wanted from the start, and that, as usual, he was taking the long way around, he felt disgusted with himself. Meanwhile, the woman appeared to him all the more beautiful. Moments after calling to him from the cedar grove, she now looked nonchalant and relaxed, as if she had quietly let something go.

Her high, thin nose had a certain melancholy, but beneath it the small budded lips, with their smooth transition from narrowness to fullness, were like a beautiful circle of leeches. Had they been cracked or discolored, they would have surely looked gross and impure, but they were moist and glistening. The corners of her eyes had no upward slant, and there was something a bit odd about her eyes, which looked as though they'd been deliberately arranged perfectly straight across her face. The downward curves of her trim, thick eyebrows, however, framed them beautifully.

その下に 【そのしたに】 beneath it
小さい 【ちいさい】 small
つぼんだ pursed, budding
唇 【くちびる】 lip
まことに truly
蛭の輪 【ひるのわ】 ring of leeches
伸び縮み 【のびちぢみ】 expansion and contraction
なめらかな smooth
もし if
皺 【しわ】 wrinkle, line
色が悪い 【いろがわるい】 be of poor color, be pallid
不潔な 【ふけつな】 impure, dirty
見える 【みえる】 seem, appear
〜はず ought to
濡れ光る 【ぬれひかる】 shine moistly
目尻 【めじり】 outer corner of the eye

上りもせず 【あがりもせず】 not turning up
わざと deliberately
真直ぐに 【まっすぐに】 straight
描く 【えがく】 draw
眼 【め】 eye
どこか somehow
おかしい funny, unusual
短い 【みじかい】 short
毛 【け】 hair
生えつまった 【はえつまった】 thick-growing
下り気味の 【さがりぎみの】 tending to slope downward
眉 【まゆ】 eyebrow
ほどよく just right
つつむ surround

少し中高の円顔は、まあ平凡な輪郭だが、白い陶磁器に薄紅を刷いたような皮膚で、首のつけ根もまだ肉づいていないから、美人というよりもなによりも、清潔だった。

52 ▶ 　お酌に出たことのある女にしては、こころもち鳩胸だった。

53 ▶ 「ほら、いつの間にかこんなに蚋が寄って来ましたわ。」と女は裾を払って立ち上った。

54 ▶ 　そしてその夜の十時頃だったろうか。女が廊下から大声に島村の名を呼んで、ばたりと投げ込まれたように彼の部屋へ入って来た。いきなり机に倒れかかると、その上のものを酔った手つきでつかみ散らして、ごくごく水を飲んだ。

少し【すこし】slightly
中高【なかだか】convex, not flat
円顔【まるがお】round face
まあ rather, I suppose
平凡な【へいぼんな】ordinary, average
輪郭【りんかく】profile
白い【しろい】white
陶磁器【とうじき】porcelain, pottery
薄紅【うすべに】pale red
刷く【はく】brush, paint on
皮膚【ひふ】skin
首【くび】neck
つけ根【つけね】base, root
肉づく【にくづく】be fleshy, be fat
美人【びじん】beautiful woman
〜というよりも even more than a so-called 〜
なによりも above all

清潔な【せいけつな】clean, pure

52
お酌に出る【おしゃくにでる】pour drinks for a living
ことのある＝ことがある has had the experience of
女【おんな】woman ✢
〜にしては for, considering
こころもち a little bit
鳩胸の【はとむねの】pigeon-breasted

53
ほら look!
いつの間にか【いつのまにか】before one notices
こんなに to this extent
蚋【ぶよ】sand fly
寄る【よる】come close
〜て来る【〜てくる】indicates movement toward the speaker ✢

The shape of her face—round and not too flat—was ordinary enough. With her skin that looked like porcelain brushed with pink and her throat that had not yet fleshed out, she was not so much beautiful as pure.

For a woman who made her living as an entertainer, she was a little pigeon-breasted.

"My, my. Look at all these sand flies," said the woman, getting to her feet and brushing down her skirts.

It was probably about ten o'clock that night. The woman shouted Shimamura's name from the corridor, then hurtled into his room as if she'd been pushed. She collapsed against the table, sending everything on it flying with flailing, drunken hands, then greedily gulped down some water.

〜わ FEMININE particle used to soften an assertion
裾を払う 【すそをはらう】 straighten out one's skirt
立ち上る 【たちあがる】 stand up
54
夜 【よる】 evening, night
十時頃 【じゅうじごろ】 around ten o'clock
〜だったろうか＝〜だっただろうか
廊下 【ろうか】 corridor
大声に 【おおごえに】 in a loud voice
島村 【しまむら】 Shimamura
名を呼ぶ 【なをよぶ】 call someone's name
ばたりと MIMETIC stumbling, lurching
投げ込む 【なげこむ】 [passive form in text] fling in
彼 【かれ】 he
部屋 【へや】 room

入る 【はいる】 come in
〜て来る 【〜てくる】 indicates movement toward the narrator ⊕
いきなり suddenly, unexpectedly
机 【つくえ】 table
倒れかかる 【たおれかかる】 fall over (onto)
その上の 【そのうえの】 on top of it
もの thing, object
酔った 【よった】 drunken
手つき 【てつき】 movement of the hands
つかみ散らす 【つかみちらす】 grab and fling about
ごくごく ONOMATOPOEIC in great gulps
水 【みず】 water
飲む 【のむ】 drink

55 ▶　　この冬スキー場でなじみになった男達が山を越えて来たのに出会い、誘われるまま宿屋に寄ると、芸者を呼んで大騒ぎとなって、飲まされてしまったとのことだった。

56 ▶　　頭をふらふらさせながら一人でとりとめなくしゃべり立ててから、

57 ▶　「悪いから行って来るわね。どうしたかと捜してるわ。後でまた来るわね。」と、よろけて出て行った。

58 ▶　　一時間ほどすると、また長い廊下をみだれた足音で、あちこちに突きあたったり倒れたりして来るらしく、

59 ▶　「島村さあん、島村さあん。」と、甲高く叫んだ。

Apparently she had run into some men whom she had got to know on the ski slopes that winter and who had dropped in from over the mountain. Having been invited, she'd gone over to their inn. There they'd proceeded to call in some geisha and have a rambunctious time. She had been made to drink, she said.

Her head lolling from side to side, she rambled on to herself.

"I really have to go. They'll be wondering where I've got to. I'll be back later." She stumbled out of the room.

After about an hour, once again he heard her coming unsteadily down the long corridor, bumping into things, losing her footing.

"Shimamura-saan! Shimamura-saan!" she shouted in a shrill voice.

行って来る【いってくる】go and come back

〜わね FEMININE particle combination used to softly express resolve concerning a matter previously mentioned ✪

どうしたかと wondering what happened

捜す【さがす】look for

〜してる = 〜している

〜わ FEMININE particle used to soften an assertion

後で【あとで】afterward

来る【くる】come

よろける stumble

出て行く【でていく】go out, leave

58

一時間【いちじかん】one hour

〜ほど about

すると having been

長い【ながい】long

廊下【ろうか】corridor

みだれた disorderly, uneven

足音【あしおと】footsteps

あちこち here and there

突きあたる【つきあたる】bump into things

倒れる【たおれる】fall over

〜て来る【〜てくる】indicates movement toward the narrator

〜らしく apparently

59

島村さあん【しまむらさあん】Mr. Shimamura (drawing out the last syllable) ✪

甲高く【かんだかく】in a shrill voice

叫ぶ【さけぶ】shout, cry ✪

60▶ 「ああ、見えない。島村さあん。」

61▶ 　それはもうまぎれもなく女の裸の心が自分の男を呼ぶ声であった。島村は思いがけなかった。しかし宿屋中に響き渡るにちがいない金切声だったから、当惑して立ち上ると、女は障子紙に指をつっこんで桟をつかみ、そのまま島村の体へぐらりと倒れた。

62▶ 「ああ、いたわね。」

63▶ 　女は彼ともつれて座って、もたれかかった。

64▶ 「酔ってやしないよ。ううん、酔ってるもんか。苦しい、苦しいだけなのよ。性根は確かだよ。ああっ、水飲みたい。ウイスキーとちゃんぽんに飲んだのがいけなかったの。

60
ああ oh! (exclamation of frustration) ⊛
見える【みえる】be visible
島村【しまむら】Shimamura ⊛

61
まぎれもなく unmistakably
女【おんな】woman ⊛
裸の心【はだかのこころ】naked heart
自分の男【じぶんのおとこ】one's man
呼ぶ【よぶ】call
声【こえ】voice
思いがけない【おもいがけない】be taken aback
しかし however
宿屋中【やどやじゅう】throughout the inn
響き渡る【ひびきわたる】resound through

〜にちがいない definitely be
金切声【かなきりごえ】shrill voice
当惑する【とうわくする】be embarrassed
立ち上る【たちあがる】stand up
障子紙【しょうじがみ】paper of a shoji screen
指をつっこむ【ゆびをつっこむ】poke one's fingers (into)
桟【さん】lattice frame (of a shoji)
つかむ grab hold of
そのまま in that state
体【からだ】body
ぐらりと MIMETIC heavily
倒れる【たおれる】fall over

62
〜わね FEMININE particle combination that functions as a tag question

"I can't see a thing. Shimamura-saan!"

It was quite clearly the voice of a woman, her heart laid bare, calling to her man. Shimamura was caught by surprise. Thinking that her screeching would be echoing throughout the inn, he got to his feet in a fluster, whereupon the woman stuck her fingers through the paper of the shoji, grabbed the doorframe and then collapsed against Shimamura.

"Ah, there you are."

Her limbs entangled with his, the woman sat down, resting against him.

"I'm not drunk. No, sir. It's just that I feel awful. Awful. I know what I'm doing though. Ah, I need a drink of water. I shouldn't have mixed whiskey with other drinks.

63

彼 【かれ】 he
もつれる get tangled up with
座る 【すわる】 sit down
もたれかかる lean on

64

酔う 【よう】 get drunk ✪
〜てやしない = 〜てはいない EMPHATIC not be
ううん uh-uh, no
〜てる = 〜ている
〜もんか = 〜ものか EMPHATIC it's hardly possible that 〜
苦しい 【くるしい】 feel bad ✪
〜のよ FEMININE particle combination used to soften an assertion
性根 【しょうね】 mind, reason
確かな 【たしかな】 sober, sane

ああっ oh my!
水 【みず】 water
飲む 【のむ】 drink ✪
ウイスキー whiskey
ちゃんぽんに drinking various alcoholic beverages in the course of a night
いけない be wrong
〜の FEMININE particle used with falling intonation to soften an assertion

あいつ頭へ来る、痛い。あの人達安壜を買って来たのよ。それ知らないで。」などと言って、掌でしきりに顔をこすっていた。

65 ▶ 　外の雨の音が俄に激しくなった。

66 ▶ 　少しでも腕をゆるめると、女はぐたりとした。女の髪が彼の頬で押しつぶされるほどに首をかかえているので、手は懐に入っていた。

67 ▶ 　彼がもとめる言葉には答えないで、女は両腕を閂のように組んでもとめられたものの上をおさえたが、酔いしびれて力が入らないのか、

68 ▶ 　「なんだ、こんなもの。畜生。畜生。だるいよ。こんなもの。」と、いきなり自分の肘にかぶりついた。

あいつ BRUSQUE that nasty stuff

頭へ来る【あたまへくる】go to one's head

痛い【いたい】ouch, it hurts

あの人達【あのひとたち】they, those people

安壜【やすびん】cheap bottle of liquor

買う【かう】buy, purchase

〜て来る【〜てくる】indicates the subject coming back to a previous location or condition, with emphasis on the completion of the action

〜のよ FEMININE particle combination used to soften an assertion

知る【しる】know

言う【いう】say

掌【てのひら】palm of the hand

しきりに constantly

顔【かお】face

こする rub

65

外【そと】outside

雨【あめ】rain

音【おと】sound

俄に【にわかに】suddenly

激しい【はげしい】intense, fierce

66

少しでも【すこしでも】even a little

腕【うで】arm

ゆるめる loosen

女【おんな】woman ⊛

ぐたりとする go limp

髪【かみ】hair, hairdo

彼【かれ】he ⊛

頬【ほお】cheek

押しつぶす【おしつぶす】[passive form in text] squash

〜ほど（に）to the extent that 〜

Goes straight to my head. It's killing me. They'd brought some cheap moonshine. How was I to know?" As she rambled on, she kept rubbing her face with her hands.

Outside, the sound of the rain suddenly grew stronger.

If he relaxed his grip at all, the woman would slump over. He was holding her head so tightly that her coiffure was crushed against his cheek, and his hand slipped into her bosom.

The woman did not respond to his pleading. She crossed her arms like a bar clamped over the objects of his desire, but possibly because she was so addled with drink, she had no strength.

"What's wrong with me? Damn you! Damn you! I'm all limp. These useful things." All of a sudden she bit her own arm.

首【くび】head, neck
かかえる hold in one's arms, embrace
手【て】hand
懐【ふところ】bosom, breast
入る【はいる】go into

67

もとめる seek, desire ⊛ (NOTE: Next usage is in the passive form.)
言葉【ことば】word, remark
答える【こたえる】respond
両腕【りょううで】both arms
閂【かんぬき】bar, bolt
組む【くむ】cross (limbs)
もの thing, object
〜の上【〜のうえ】the top of
おさえる cover, block
酔いしびれる【よいしびれる】be stupefied with drink

力が入る【ちからがはいる】focus one's strength

68

なんだ what the hell! (exclamation of disappointment or astonishment)
こんなもの this damn thing! ⊛
畜生【ちくしょう】damn, blast ⊛
だるい listless, enervated
いきなり suddenly, unexpectedly
自分の肘【じぶんのひじ】one's own elbow, one's outer arm
かぶりつく bite into

69▶　彼が驚いて離させると、深い歯形がついていた。

70▶　しかし、女はもう彼の掌（てのひら）にまかせて、そのまま落書をはじめた。好きな人の名を書いて見せると言って、芝居や映画の役者の名前を二三十も並べてから、今度は島村（しまむら）とばかり無数に書き続けた。

71▶　島村（しまむら）の掌（てのひら）のなかのありがたいふくらみはだんだん熱くなって来た。

72▶　「ああ、安心した。安心したよ。」と、彼はなごやかに言って、母のようなものさえ感じた。

73▶　女はまた急に苦しみ出して、身をもがいて立ち上ると、部屋の向うの隅に突っ伏した。

74▶　「いけない、いけない。帰る、帰る。」

69

彼【かれ】he ⊛

驚く【おどろく】be surprised

離す【はなす】[causative form in text] separate (two things), pull (two things) apart

深い【ふかい】deep

歯形【はがた】tooth mark

つく have, be attached to

70

しかし however

女【おんな】woman ⊛

掌【てのひら】palm of the hand ⊛

まかせる give oneself up (to)

そのまま in that way, as she was

落書【らくがき】doodling, scribbling

はじめる start

好きな【すきな】favorite

人【ひと】person

名【な】name

書いて見せる【かいてみせる】write down and show

言う【いう】say ⊛

芝居【しばい】stage play

映画【えいが】film

役者【やくしゃ】actor

名前【なまえ】name

二三十も【にさんじゅうも】as many as 20 or 30

並べる【ならべる】rank, list

今度は【こんどは】now, presently

島村【しまむら】Shimamura ⊛

〜ばかり only

無数に【むすうに】countless times

書き続ける【かきつづける】keep writing

71

〜のなかの inside

Shocked, he pulled her arm away. Deep tooth marks were imprinted on it.

Letting him have his way with her, the woman started doodling. She said she was going to write down the names of the men she liked, and after listing some twenty or thirty stage and movie actors' names, she wrote "Shimamura" over and over again.

The delectable swelling beneath Shimamura's hand grew gradually warmer.

"Ah, I'm glad that's all over. What a relief," he said gently. He even felt slightly maternal toward her.

The woman suddenly started feeling unwell again, and she squirmed her way to her feet before pitching forward into the far corner of the room.

"It isn't right. Not right. I'm going. Going home."

ありがたい welcome, pleasant
ふくらみ bulge, swelling
だんだん gradually
熱い【あつい】hot
〜て来る【〜てくる】indicates a situation or phenomenon emerging ✽

72
ああ phew (exclamation of relief)
安心する【あんしんする】be relieved ✽
なごやかに gently, amiably
母【はは】mother
もの thing, something
〜さえ even
感じる【かんじる】feel

73
急に【きゅうに】suddenly
苦しみ出す【くるしみだす】start to feel pain

身をもがく【みをもがく】writhe
立ち上る【たちあがる】stand up
部屋【へや】room
向うの【むこうの】opposite
隅【すみ】corner
突っ伏す【つっぷす】crash forward

74
いけない be wrong ✽
帰る【かえる】go home ✽

75 ▶ 「歩けるもんか。大雨だよ。」

76 ▶ 「跣足で帰る。這って帰る。」

77 ▶ 「危いよ。帰るなら送ってやるよ。」

78 ▶ 　宿は丘の上で、嶮しい坂がある。

79 ▶ 「帯をゆるめるか、少し横になって、醒ましたらいいだろう。」

80 ▶ 「そんなことだめ。こうすればいいの。慣れてる。」と、女はしゃんと座って胸を張ったが、息が苦しくなるばかりだった。窓をあけて吐こうとしても、出なかった。身をもんで転りたいのを嚙みこらえているありさまが続いて、時々意志を奮い起すように、帰る帰ると繰り返しながら、いつか午前二時を過ぎていた。

75

歩く【あるく】[potential form in text] walk

〜もんか＝〜ものか it's hardly possible that 〜

大雨【おおあめ】torrential rain

76

跣足【はだし】barefoot

帰る【かえる】go home ✽

這う【はう】crawl

77

危い【あぶない】dangerous

〜なら if

送る【おくる】see (someone) home

〜てやる do as a favor for (someone of lower social status than oneself) (NOTE: Expresses the speaker's eagerness but sounds condescending.)

78

宿【やど】inn

丘【おか】hill

上【うえ】top

嶮しい【けわしい】steep

坂【さか】slope

79

帯【おび】sash

ゆるめる loosen

少し【すこし】a little

横になる【よこになる】lie down

醒ます【さます】sober up

〜たらいい it would be good if

80

そんなこと that kind of thing

だめな no good

こうすればいい it would be fine if I did it this way

"You can hardly even walk. And it's bucketing down."

"I'll go barefoot. I'll crawl."

"It's not safe. If you want to leave, I'll go with you."

The inn was on the top of a hill and it was a steep slope.

"Why not loosen your sash a bit? Better to lie down a while and sober up."

"That's no good. This is the way to do it. I always do this," said the woman, sitting up straight and puffing out her chest. But she only found it hard to breathe. Opening the window she tried to vomit, but nothing came. As she fought down the urge to roll around on the floor, clutched at herself and just occasionally pulled herself together enough to repeat, "I've got to go, got to go," it was soon after two in the morning.

～の FEMININE particle used with falling intonation to soften an assertion

慣れる 【なれる】 get used to

～てる = ～ている

女 【おんな】 woman

しゃんと straight, upright

座る 【すわる】 sit

胸を張る 【むねをはる】 puff out one's chest

息 【いき】 breath, breathing

苦しい 【くるしい】 painful, difficult

～ばかり only, just

窓 【まど】 window

あける open

吐く 【はく】 [volitional form in text] vomit

～（こ）うとしても even though one tried to ～

出る 【でる】 come up, come out

身をもむ 【みをもむ】 clutch oneself

転る 【ころがる】 roll around

噛みこらえる 【かみこらえる】 suppress

ありさま state, spectacle

続く 【つづく】 continue

時々 【ときどき】 sometimes

意志 【いし】 will, willpower

奮い起す 【ふるいおこす】 rouse

繰り返す 【くりかえす】 repeat

いつか at some point

午前二時 【ごぜんにじ】 2 A.M.

過ぎる 【すぎる】 pass

81 ▶ 　やがて、顔をあちらに反向けこちらに隠していた女が、突然激しく唇を突き出した。しかしその後でも、寧ろ苦痛を訴える譫言のように、

82 ▶ 「いけない。いけないの。お友達でいるようって、あなたがおっしゃったじゃないの。」と、幾度繰り返したかしれなかった。

83 ▶ 　島村はその真剣な響きに打たれ、額に皺立て顔をしかめて懸命に自分を抑えている意志の強さには、味気なく白けるほどで、女との約束を守ろうかとも思った。

84 ▶ 「私はなんにも惜しいものはないのよ。決して惜しいんじゃないのよ。だけど、そういう女じゃない。私はそういう女じゃないの。きっと長続きしないって、あんた自分で言ったじゃないの。」酔いで半ば痺れていた。

81

やがて in due course
顔【かお】face
反向ける【そむける】turn away
隠す【かくす】hide
女【おんな】woman
突然【とつぜん】suddenly
激しく【はげしく】fiercely, aggressively
唇【くちびる】lip
突き出す【つきだす】stick out
しかし however
その後【そのご／そのあと】afterward
寧ろ【むしろ】rather
苦痛【くつう】pain, torment
訴える【うったえる】complain about
譫言【うわごと】nonsensical babble

82

いけない be wrong ⊛
〜の FEMININE particle used with falling intonation to soften an assertion ⊛
お友達【おともだち】POLITE friend
〜よう let's
〜って indicates reported speech ⊛
おっしゃる HONORIFIC say
じゃない be, it's a fact that 〜
幾度【いくど】many times
繰り返す【くりかえす】repeat
しれる be able to know

83

島村【しまむら】Shimamura
真剣な【しんけんな】serious, earnest
響き【ひびき】sound, ring
打つ【うつ】[passive form in text] strike

The woman had turned away to hide her face, but soon thrust her lips toward him, suddenly and fiercely. Then as if moaning in a delirium of pain:

"We shouldn't. We shouldn't. You were the one who said 'Let's just be friends,'" she repeated countless times.

Struck by the seriousness in her voice and the strength of will evident in her frowning determination to control herself, Shimamura felt rather bored, and his interest waned. It even occurred to him to maybe keep his promise to the woman.

"I have no regrets. None at all. It's just that I'm not that kind of woman. That's not the sort of woman I am. You were the one who said it could never last." She was half-numb with liquor.

額 【ひたい】 forehead
皺立てる 【しわたてる】 wrinkle
顔をしかめる 【かおをしかめる】 frown, grimace
懸命に 【けんめいに】 assiduously
自分 【じぶん】 herself, oneself
抑える 【おさえる】 restrain, hold back
意志 【いし】 will
強さ 【つよさ】 strength
味気ない 【あじけない】 irksome, dull
白ける 【しらける】 lose interest
〜ほど to the extent that 〜
女 【おんな】 woman ⊛
約束 【やくそく】 promise
守る 【まもる】 [volitional form in text] keep (a promise)
〜（ろ）うかとも even whether or not to 〜

思う 【おもう】 consider

私 【わたし】 I ⊛
なんにも 〜ものはない there is nothing 〜
惜しい 【おしい】 regrettable ⊛
〜のよ FEMININE particle combination used to soften an assertion ⊛
決して〜ない 【けっして〜ない／けして〜ない】 definitely . . . not
きっと certainly
長続きする 【ながつづきする】 continue
あんた FAMILIAR you
自分で 【じぶんで】 yourself
言う 【いう】 say, speak
酔い 【よい】 drunkenness
半ば 【なかば】 half
痺れる 【しびれる】 be numb

85▶ 「私が悪いんじゃないわよ、あんたが悪いのよ。あんたが負けたのよ。あんたが弱いのよ。私じゃないのよ。」などと口走りながら、よろこびにさからうためにそでをかんでいた。

86▶ しばらく気が抜けたみたいに静かだったが、ふと思い出して突き刺すように、

87▶ 「あんた笑っているわね。私を笑ってるわね。」

88▶ 「笑ってやしない。」

89▶ 「心の底で笑ってるでしょう。今笑ってなくっても、きっと後で笑うわ。」と、女はうつぶせになってむせび泣いた。

85

私【わたし】I

悪い【わるい】bad ✽

〜わよ FEMININE particle combination used to express a belief

あんた FAMILIAR you ✽

〜のよ FEMININE particle combination used to soften an assertion ✽

負ける【まける】lose

弱い【よわい】weak

口走る【くちばしる】babble, run on

よろこび joy

さからう resist, oppose

そで sleeve

かむ bite

86

しばらく for a while

気が抜ける【きがぬける】become dispirited, be let down

〜みたいに as though

静かな【しずかな】quiet

ふと suddenly, unexpectedly

思い出す【おもいだす】remember, recall

突き刺す【つきさす】stab

87

笑う【わらう】ridicule, laugh at ✽

〜わね FEMININE particle combination that functions as a tag question ✽

88

〜てやしない = 〜てはいない EMPHATIC not be ——ing

89

心の底で【こころのそこで】internally

〜てる = 〜ている

今【いま】now

"I'm not doing anything wrong. It's you. You lost. You're the weak one. Not me." She babbled on, biting her sleeve to muffle her delight.

For a while she was quiet, seemingly dazed, then, as if she had suddenly remembered something, she said sharply:

"You don't respect me, do you? You think I'm a joke."

"No, I do not."

"Deep inside, you don't take me seriously, do you? Even if you're not laughing at me now, I bet you will later." The woman rolled over onto her front and sobbed.

〜てなくっても = 〜ていなくても
きっと definitely
後で【あとで】afterward
〜わ FEMININE particle used to soften an
　assertion
女【おんな】woman
うつぶせになる lie face down
むせび泣く【むせびなく】weep

90 ▶　でも直ぐに泣き止むと、自分をあてがうように、柔かくして、人なつっこくこまごまと身の上などを話し出した。酔いの苦しさは忘れたように抜けたらしかった。今のことにはひとことも触れなかった。

91 ▶「あら、お話に夢中になっていて、ちっとも知らなかったわ。」と、今度はぼうっと微笑んだ。

92 ▶　夜のあけないうちに帰らねばならないと言って、

93 ▶「まだ暗いわね。この辺の人はそれは早起きなの。」と、幾度も立ち上って窓をあけてみた。

94 ▶「まだ人の顔は見えませんわね。今朝は雨だから、誰も田へ出ないから。」

90

直ぐに【すぐに】soon
泣き止む【なきやむ】stop crying
自分【じぶん】oneself, herself
あてがう pair oneself off, matchmake
柔かい【やわらかい】soft, tender
人なつっこく【ひとなつっこく】amiably
こまごまと in great detail
身の上【みのうえ】personal affairs
話し出す【はなしだす】start to talk
酔い【よい】drunkenness
苦しさ【くるしさ】discomfort, pain
忘れる【わすれる】forget
抜ける【ぬける】disappear, leave one
今のこと【いまのこと】events of the
　moment
ひとことも～ない not a single word
触れる【ふれる】mention

91

あら FEMININE oh my! (exclamation of
　concern)
お話【おはなし】POLITE talk
夢中になる【むちゅうになる】become
　engrossed
ちっとも～ない not in the slightest
知る【しる】know
～わ FEMININE particle used to soften an
　assertion
今度は【こんどは】now, presently
ぼうっと MIMETIC dazedly, dreamily
微笑む【ほほえむ】smile

92

夜【よ】night
あける break (of night)
～うちに [preceded by a negative] before

But she soon stopped crying and started to talk all about herself in a relaxed, friendly manner, as if providing a personal profile to a suitor. Her drunken discomfort was apparently gone and forgotten. She did not say a word about what had just happened.

"Look at that! I was so busy talking, I lost track of the time." She smiled dreamily.

She had to get home before daybreak, she said.

"It's still dark. But the people around here are early risers," she said, getting to her feet again and again to open the window and peek outside.

"I still can't see anyone around. It's raining this morning, so no one will be going out to the fields."

帰る 【かえる】 return home
〜ねばならない ought to
言う 【いう】 say

93

暗い 【くらい】 dark
〜わね FEMININE particle combination that functions as a tag question ⊛
辺 【あたり】 vicinity, neighborhood
人 【ひと】 person ⊛
早起き 【はやおき】 getting up early
〜の FEMININE particle used with falling intonation to soften an assertion
幾度も 【いくども】 repeatedly
立ち上る 【たちあがる】 get up
窓 【まど】 window
あける open
〜てみる to see what it is like

94

顔 【かお】 face
見える 【みえる】 be visible
今朝 【けさ】 this morning
雨 【あめ】 rain
誰も〜ない 【だれも〜ない】 nobody
田 【た】 field, rice paddy
出る 【でる】 go out to

95 ▶
　　雨のなかに向うの山や麓の屋根の姿が浮び出してからも、女は立ち去りにくそうにしていたが、宿の人の起きる前に髪を直すと、島村が玄関まで送ろうとするのも人目を恐れて、あわただしく逃げるように一人で抜け出して行った。

96 ▶
　　女がふっと顔を上げると、島村の掌に押しあてていた瞼から鼻の両側へかけて赤らんでいるのが、濃い白粉を透して見えた。それはこの雪国の夜の冷たさを思わせながら、髪の色の黒が強いために、温いものに感じられた。

95

雨【あめ】rain

〜のなかに in

向う【むこう】opposite, over there

山【やま】mountain

麓【ふもと】foot (of a mountain)

屋根【やね】roof

姿【すがた】shape, appearance

浮び出す【うかびだす】come into view, start to show themselves

女【おんな】woman ⊛

立ち去りにくい【たちさりにくい】hard to get up and go away

宿【やど】inn

人【ひと】person

起きる【おきる】get up

前【まえ】before

髪【かみ】hair ⊛

直す【なおす】tidy up

島村【しまむら】Shimamura ⊛

玄関【げんかん】entrance, doorway

送る【おくる】[volitional form in text] see off

〜（ろ）うとする be about to 〜

のも although

人目【ひとめ】public attention

恐れる【おそれる】fear

あわただしく hastily

逃げる【にげる】run away

一人で【ひとりで】alone, by oneself

抜け出す【ぬけだす】sneak away

〜て行く【〜ていく】indicates movement away from the speaker

96

ふっと suddenly

顔【かお】face

上げる【あげる】lift up

66　雪国抄

Even after the mountains opposite and the roofs of the houses at their foot became visible through the rain, the woman still seemed reluctant to leave. She fixed her hair before the inn staff got up, and though Shimamura offered to take her down to the hallway, the thought of being seen terrified her, so she slipped off by herself in a panicky escape.

When the woman abruptly raised her head, Shimamura could see through the thick white make-up that her face was red from her eyelids down along the sides of her nose, where it had been pressing against his hand. The mark evoked the cold of the nights in the snow country, but somehow it felt warm too because of the sheer blackness of her hair.

掌 【てのひら】 palm of the hand
押しあてる 【おしあてる】 press against
瞼 【まぶた】 eyelid
〜から〜へかけて extending from ~ to ~
鼻 【はな】 nose
両側 【りょうがわ】 both sides
赤らむ 【あからむ】 turn red
濃い 【こい】 thick
白粉 【おしろい】 make-up
〜を透して 【〜をすかして】 through
見える 【みえる】 be visible
雪国 【ゆきぐに】 snow country
夜 【よる】 night
冷たさ 【つめたさ】 coldness
思う 【おもう】 [causative form in text] think about
色 【いろ】 color

黒 【くろ】 black
強い 【つよい】 strong
温い 【あたたかい】 warm
もの thing, something
感じる 【かんじる】 [spontaneous form in text] feel

その顔は眩しげに含み笑いを浮べていたが、そうするうちにも「あの時」を思い出すのか、まるで島村の言葉が彼女の体をだんだん染めてゆくかのようだった。女はむっとしてうなだれると、襟をすかしているから、背なかの赤くなっているのまで見え、なまなましく濡れた裸を剥き出したようであった。髪の色との配合のために、尚そう思われるのかもしれない。前髪が細かく生えつまっているというのではないけれども、毛筋が男みたいに太くて、後れ毛一つなく、なにか黒い鉱物の重ったいような光だった。

顔【かお】face

眩しげに【まぶしげに】dazzlingly

含み笑い【ふくみわらい】suppressed laugh

浮べる【うかべる】wear (an expression)

〜うちに while, as

時【とき】time, occasion

思い出す【おもいだす】remember, recall

まるで〜のよう seem literally as if

島村【しまむら】Shimamura

言葉【ことば】word, remark

彼女【かのじょ】she

体【からだ】body

だんだん gradually

染める【そめる】dye, imbue

〜てゆく indicates an increase in tendency

女【おんな】woman, she

むっとする MIMETIC be sullen, be indignant

うなだれる hang one's head

襟【えり】collar

すかす leave open

背なか【せなか】back

赤い【あかい】red

見える【みえる】be visible

なまなましく vividly, freshly

濡れた【ぬれた】wet, moist

裸【はだか】nakedness

剥き出す【むきだす】expose

髪【かみ】hair

色【いろ】color

配合【はいごう】harmony, combination

〜のために because of

尚【なお】more, further

There were the radiant beginnings of a smile on her face. As she smiled, it could be she was recalling "that time," for Shimamura's words seemed literally to be seeping into her body like dye. Her collar was pulled back at the nape, so when she hung her head in a fit of pique he saw that she had flushed red all the way down to her back. It was as if she had exposed her nakedness in all its moist freshness. Maybe the contrast with the color of her hair made the impression even stronger. It was not that the hair pulled back from her forehead was fine or luxuriant; the individual strands were thick like a man's, not a single lock was out of place, and it had a heavy sheen like some black mineral.

思う 【おもう】 [spontaneous form in text]
　　think, feel
〜かもしれない maybe
前髪 【まえがみ】 hair at the front of the
　　head
細かく 【こまかく】 finely
生えつまる 【はえつまる】 grow thick
〜というのではない it is not that 〜
毛筋 【けすじ】 hair
男 【おとこ】 man
〜みたいに like
太い 【ふとい】 thick
後れ毛 【おくれげ】 stray hair
一つない 【ひとつない】 not a single one
なにか some, some kind of
黒い 【くろい】 black
鉱物 【こうぶつ】 mineral
重ったい 【おもったい】 heavy

光 【ひかり】 sheen

98▸　今さっき手に触れてこんな冷たい髪は初めてだとびっくりしたのは、寒気のせいではなく、こういう髪そのもののせいであったかと思えて、島村が眺め直していると、女は火燵板の上で指を折りはじめた。それがなかなか終らない。

99▸　「なにを勘定しているんだ。」と聞いても、黙ってしばらく指折り数えていた。

100▸　「五月の二十三日ね。」

101▸　「そうか。日数を数えてたのか。七月と八月の大が続くんだよ。」

102▸　「ね、百九十九日目だわ。ちょうど百九十九日だわ。」

103▸　「零時の上りだわ。」と、ちょうどその時聞えた汽笛に

98

今さっき【いまさっき】just a little while ago

手【て】hand

触れる【ふれる】touch

冷たい【つめたい】cold

髪【かみ】hair ✽

初めて【はじめて】for the first time

びっくりする be surprised

寒気【かんき】chill

〜のせい due to, the fault of ✽

〜そのもの the thing itself

思える【おもえる】feel

島村【しまむら】Shimamura

眺め直す【ながめなおす】look again at

女【おんな】woman

火燵板【こたついた】tabletop of a *kotatsu*

〜の上で【〜のうえで】atop, on top of

指を折りはじめる【ゆびをおりはじめる】start to count on one's fingers

なかなか〜ない not readily

終る【おわる】finish

99

勘定する【かんじょうする】count, calculate

聞く【きく】ask

黙る【だまる】say nothing

しばらく for a while

指折り数える【ゆびおりかぞえる】count on one's fingers

100

五月【ごがつ】May

二十三日【にじゅうさんにち】the 23rd

101

そうか is that right?

Realizing that the surprise he'd felt when he touched such cold hair for the first time was not due to its coldness but to the nature of the hair itself, Shimamura scrutinized it afresh. The woman then started to count her fingers on top of the kotatsu. It went on and on.

"What are you counting?" he asked, but she said nothing and just kept on counting in silence.

"It was the twenty-third of May."

"Ah, I see. So you were counting the number of days. July and August are two long months in a row."

"This is the one-hundred and ninety-ninth day, you know. Today's exactly the hundred and ninety-ninth day."

"It's the midnight train for Tokyo." At the sound of the train's whistle

---

日数【にっすう】number of days
数える【かぞえる】count
〜てた＝〜ていた
七月【しちがつ】July
八月【はちがつ】August
大【だい】largeness (of long months with 31 days)
続く【つづく】come in succession

102

百九十九日目【ひゃくきゅうじゅうきゅうにちめ】the 199th day ✱

〜わ FEMININE particle used to soften an assertion ✱

103

零時【れいじ】midnight
上り【のぼり】going "up" to Tokyo
時【とき】time, moment

聞える【きこえる】be audible
汽笛【きてき】steam whistle

立ち上って、思い切り乱暴に紙障子とガラス戸とをあけ、手摺へ体を投げつけざま窓に腰かけた。

104 ▶　冷気が部屋へいちどきに流れ込んだ。汽車の響きは遠ざかるにつれて、夜風のように聞えた。

105 ▶「おい、寒いじゃないか。馬鹿」と、島村も立ち上って行くと風はなかった。

106 ▶　一面の雪が凍りつく音が地の底深く鳴っているような、厳しい夜景であった。月はなかった。嘘のように多い星は、見上げていると、虚しい早さで落ちつつあると思われるほど、あざやかに浮き出ていた。星の群が目へ近づいて来るにつれて、空はいよいよ遠く夜の色を深めた。

立ち上る【たちあがる】stand up
思い切り【おもいきり】without restraint
乱暴に【らんぼうに】roughly
紙障子【かみしょうじ】shoji, paper screen
ガラス戸【ガラスど】sliding glass door
あける open
手摺【てすり】railing
体【からだ】body
投げつける【なげつける】throw against
～ざま the moment (one does something), just when
窓【まど】window
腰かける【こしかける】sit down

104
冷気【れいき】cold air
部屋【へや】room
いちどきに in one go, at a time
流れ込む【ながれこむ】flow in

汽車【きしゃ】steam locomotive
響き【ひびき】sound
遠ざかる【とおざかる】become distant
～につれて as ⊛
夜風【よかぜ】night wind
聞える【きこえる】be audible, sound

105
おい MASCULINE hey!
寒い【さむい】cold
～じゃないか it's ~, don't you know it's ~
馬鹿【ばか】idiot
島村【しまむら】Shimamura
立ち上る【たちあがる】stand up
～て行く【～ていく】indicates movement away from the narrator
風【かぜ】wind

she sprang to her feet, tore open the shoji and window, flung herself against the railings and sat down on the window sill.

Cold air surged into the room immediately. The train sounded like the night wind as it faded into the distance.

"Hey, you idiot, it's freezing." Shimamura got up and went over to the window, but there was no wind.

The austere nighttime landscape was ringing to its depths, it seemed, with the sound of the great expanse of snow freezing. There was no moon. The number of stars was incredible. Looking at them, they shone so brightly that they seemed to be falling earthward at a hopeless speed. As the clusters of stars became clearer, the sky took on the color of night to ever-greater distances.

106

一面【いちめん】surface, sheet
雪【ゆき】snow
凍りつく【こおりつく】freeze hard
音【おと】sound
地【ち】earth, ground
底深く【そこふかく】deep
鳴る【なる】ring
厳しい【きびしい】severe
夜景【やけい】night view
月【つき】the moon
嘘のように【うそのように】unbelievably
多い【おおい】numerous
星【ほし】stars ⊛
見上げる【みあげる】look up at
虚しい【むなしい】futile, vain
早さ【はやさ】speed

落ちつつある【おちつつある】fall continuously
思う【おもう】[spontaneous form in text] think, feel
〜ほど to the extent that 〜
あざやかに vividly, brightly
浮き出る【うきでる】appear (in the sky)
群【むれ】cluster
目【め】eye
近づく【ちかづく】come close
〜て来る【〜てくる】indicates movement toward the narrator
空【そら】sky
いよいよ more and more
遠く【とおく】far away
夜【よる】night
色【いろ】color
深める【ふかめる】deepen

国境の山山はもう重なりも見分けられず、そのかわりそれ
だけの重みを垂れていた。すべて冴え静まった調和であっ
た。

107 ▶　島村が近づくのを知ると、女は手摺に胸を突っ伏せた。
それは弱々しさではなく、こういう夜を背景にして、これ
より頑固なものはないという姿であった。島村はまたかと
思った。

108 ▶　しかし、山山の色は黒いにかかわらず、どうしたはずみ
かそれがまざまざと白雪の色に見えた。そうすると山山が
透明で寂しいものであるかのように感じられて来た。空と
山とは調和などしていない。

109 ▶　「窓をしめてくれ。」

国境【こっきょう】border (between pre-
　fectures)
山山【やまやま】mountains ❀
重なり【かさなり】overlapping, layering
見分けられず【みわけられず】be unable
　to distinguish
そのかわり instead
それだけ that much
重み【おもみ】weight
垂れる【たれる】hang down
すべて all
冴え静まった【さえしずまった】clear
　and calm
調和【ちょうわ】harmony

107
島村【しまむら】Shimamura ❀
近づく【ちかづく】get closer
知る【しる】notice, realize

女【おんな】woman
手摺【てすり】rail
胸【むね】chest
突っ伏せる【つっぷせる】press flat
　against
弱々しさ【よわよわしさ】weakness
こういう this kind of
夜【よる】evening, night
背景【はいけい】background
これより more than this
頑固な【がんこな】stubborn
もの thing, something ❀
姿【すがた】form, figure
またか again?
思う【おもう】think

108
しかし however
色【いろ】color ❀

You could no longer make out the vistas of mountain upon mountain in the border range; instead they looked like one heavy, sagging mass. Everything was clear, calm and harmonious.

When the woman realized that Shimamura was coming over, she hung forward over the rail from her chest. It was not a sign of weakness. Set against a night like this, it was a pose of invincible obstinacy. Here we go again, thought Shimamura to himself.

Black though the mountain ranges were, for some strange reason they looked as brilliant and as white as snow. He had a sense that the mountains were diaphanous and melancholy things. The sky and the mountains were not in harmony after all.

"Close the window."

黒い【くろい】black
〜にかかわらず despite 〜
どうしたはずみか for some strange reason
まざまざと vividly
白雪【しらゆき】white snow
見える【みえる】appear
そうすると whereupon
透明な【とうめいな】transparent
寂しい【さびしい】lonely, forlorn
感じる【かんじる】[spontaneous form in text] feel
〜て来る【〜てくる】indicates a condition coming into effect
空【そら】sky
山【やま】mountain
調和する【ちょうわする】harmonize

窓【まど】window
しめる shut
〜てくれ [imperative form] BLUNT, MASCULINE please

110▶ 「もうしばらくこうさしといて。」

111▶　村は鎮守の杉林の陰に半ば隠れているが、自動車で十分足らずの灯火は、寒さのためぴいんと音を立てて毀れそうに瞬いていた。

112▶　女の顔も窓のガラスも、自分のどてらの袖も、手に触れるものは皆、島村にはこんな冷たさは初めてだと思われた。

113▶　足の下の畳までが冷えて来るので、一人で湯に行こうとすると、

114▶　「待って下さい。私も行きます。」と、今度は女が素直について来た。

115▶　彼が脱ぎ散らすものを女が乱れ箱へ揃えているところ

110

もうしばらく for a little longer

こうさしといて = こうさせておいて
HUMBLE, FEMININE allow me to do this

111

村【むら】village

鎮守【ちんじゅ】Shinto deity, tutelary god

杉林【すぎばやし】cedar grove

陰【かげ】shadow, behind

半ば【なかば】half

隠れる【かくれる】conceal

自動車【じどうしゃ】car

十分足らず【じゅっぷんたらず】taking under ten minutes

灯火【とうか】light

寒さ【さむさ】coldness

〜のため due to

ぴいんと ONOMATOPOEIC describes a high-pitched sound

音を立てる【おとをたてる】make a sound

毀れる【やぶれる】crack, fail

瞬く【またたく】emit light

112

女【おんな】woman ⊗

顔【かお】face

窓【まど】window

ガラス glass

自分【じぶん】oneself, himself

どてら padded dressing gown

袖【そで】sleeve

手【て】hand

触れる【ふれる】touch

もの thing, something

皆【みな】everything

"Let me stay here a little longer."

The village was half-hidden by the black bulk of the cedar grove of the shrine. Not ten minutes away by car, its lights seemed to emit a high-pitched hum as they blinked weakly in the cold.

The woman's face; the glass of the window; the sleeves of his padded kimono—whatever he touched, it seemed to Shimamura that he had never experienced such cold before.

The tatami began to get cold beneath his feet, so he made as if to go to the bath alone.

"Wait a minute. I'll come too." The woman followed him tamely this time.

Just as the woman was putting his cast-off clothes into a basket,

---

島村【しまむら】Shimamura
冷たさ【つめたさ】coldness
初めて【はじめて】the first time
思う【おもう】[spontaneous form in text] think, feel
113
足【あし】feet
〜の下の【〜のしたの】beneath
畳【たたみ】tatami mat
冷える【ひえる】grow cold
〜て来る【〜てくる】indicates a situation or phenomenon emerging
一人で【ひとりで】by oneself, alone
湯【ゆ】hot bath
行く【いく】[volitional form in text] go
〜(こ)うとする be about to 〜
114
待つ【まつ】wait

〜て下さい【〜てください】please
私【わたし】I
行く【いく】go
今度は【こんどは】this time
素直に【すなおに】mildly, obediently
ついて来る【ついてくる】follow, accompany
115
彼【かれ】he
脱ぎ散らす【ぬぎちらす】fling off (clothing)
もの thing
乱れ箱【みだればこ】clothes basket
揃える【そろえる】arrange
ところ moment

へ、男の泊り客が入って来たが、島村の胸の前へすくんで
顔を隠した女に気がつくと、

116▶ 「あっ、失礼しました。」

117▶ 「いいえ、どうぞ。あっちの湯へ入りますから。」と、島
村はとっさに言って、裸のまま乱れ箱を抱えて隣りの女湯
の方へ行った。女は無論夫婦面でついて来た。島村は黙っ
て後も見ずに温泉に飛びこんだ。安心して高笑いがこみ上
げて来るので、湯口に口をあてて荒っぽく嗽いをした。

118▶ 　部屋に戻ってから、女は横にした首を軽く浮かして鬢を
小指で持ち上げながら、

119▶ 「悲しいわ。」と、ただひとこと言っただけであった。

男【おとこ】man
泊り客【とまりきゃく】overnight guest
入る【はいる】enter
〜て来る【〜てくる】indicates movement
　toward the narrator
島村【しまむら】Shimamura ⊛
胸【むね】chest
〜の前【〜のまえ】before, in front of
すくむ quail, cringe
顔【かお】face
隠す【かくす】hide
女【おんな】woman ⊛
気がつく【きがつく】notice

あっ oh
失礼します【しつれいします】excuse me

あっち over there
湯【ゆ】hot bath
入る【はいる】get into
とっさに immediately, at once
言う【いう】say ⊛
裸のまま【はだかのまま】naked as he was
乱れ箱【みだればこ】clothes basket
抱える【かかえる】hold
隣り【となり】next door
女湯【おんなゆ】women's bath
〜の方へ【〜のほうへ】in the direction of
行く【いく】go
無論【むろん】naturally, of course
夫婦面【ふうふづら】looking like a mar-
　ried couple
ついて来る【ついてくる】follow, accom-
　pany

another man staying at the inn came in. But when he noticed the woman cowering up against Shimamura's chest and hiding her face, he said:

"Oh, I do beg your pardon."

"Not at all. Come on in. We'll go to the other bath," replied Shimamura briskly, and, still naked, picked up the basket and went into the women's bath next door. The woman followed, looking every inch his wife. Shimamura said nothing and leaped into the bath without so much as a glance at her. In his contentment, he felt a loud laugh welling up in his throat, so he put his mouth to the tap and gargled coarsely.

Once they were back in the room, the woman, who had lain down, raised her head slightly and tugged at the hair on the side of her head with her little finger.

"I feel miserable" was all she said.

黙る【だまる】say nothing
後も見ずに【あともみずに】without looking around
温泉【おんせん】hot spring
飛びこむ【とびこむ】leap into
安心する【あんしんする】be relieved, feel at ease
高笑い【たかわらい】loud laugh
こみ上げる【こみあげる】well up
〜て来る【〜てくる】indicates a condition coming into effect
湯口【ゆぐち】tap, faucet
口【くち】mouth
あてる place against
荒っぽく【あらっぽく】roughly
嗽いをする【うがいをする】gargle

部屋【へや】room

戻る【もどる】return to
横にする【よこにする】lay down
首【くび】head
軽く【かるく】lightly
浮かす【うかす】lift up
鬢【びん】locks of hair on side of the face
小指【こゆび】little finger
持ち上げる【もちあげる】pick up

悲しい【かなしい】sad
〜わ FEMININE particle used to soften an assertion
ただ just
ひとこと a single word

120▶　女が黒い眼を半ば開いているのかと、近々のぞきこんでみると、それは睫毛であった。

121▶　神経質な女は一睡もしなかった。

122▶　固い女帯をしごく音で島村は目が覚めたらしかった。

123▶　帯を結び終ってからも、女は立ったり座ったり、そうしてまた窓の方ばかり見て歩き回った。それは夜行動物が朝を恐れて、いらいら歩き回るような落ちつきのなさだった。妖しい野生がたかぶって来るさまであった。

124▶　そうするうちに部屋のなかまで明るんで来たか、女の赤い頬が目立って来た。島村は驚くばかりあざやかな赤い色に見とれて、

120

女【おんな】woman ✻
黒い【くろい】black
眼【め】eye
半ば【なかば】half
開く【ひらく】open
近々【ちかぢか】close up
のぞきこむ scrutinize
〜てみる to see what it is like
睫毛【まつげ】eyelash

121

神経質な【しんけいしつな】nervous, high-strung
一睡もしない【いっすいもしない】not sleep a wink

122

固い【かたい】stiff
女帯【おんなおび】woman's sash

しごく pull tight
音【おと】sound
島村【しまむら】Shimamura ✻
目が覚める【めがさめる】wake up

123

帯【おび】sash
結び終る【むすびおわる】finish tying
立つ【たつ】stand up
座る【すわる】sit down
そうして and then
窓【まど】window
〜の方【〜のほう】the direction of
〜ばかり only
見る【みる】look
歩き回る【あるきまわる】walk around ✻
夜行動物【やこうどうぶつ】nocturnal animal
朝【あさ】morning

It looked as though the woman's black eyes were half-open, but when he took a closer look, he realized it was only the effect of her eyelashes.

The woman was too nervous to sleep a wink.

It was probably the sound of her stiff sash being pulled tight that woke Shimamura.

Even after tying on the sash, the woman kept getting up and sitting down again, and walking around always looking toward the window. It was the restlessness of a nocturnal animal pacing about in agitation, fearing the onset of the morning. There seemed to be a strange wildness building inside her.

Perhaps the room had grown brighter, for as she paced to and fro, he was able to make out the red of her cheeks. Shimamura found himself mesmerized by the astoundingly fresh red color.

恐れる【おそれる】fear

いらいら in a state of irritation

落ちつきのなさ【おちつきのなさ】lack of calm

妖しい【あやしい】strange, bewitching

野生【やせい】wildness

たかぶる build up, increase in intensity

〜て来る【〜てくる】indicates a condition coming into effect ⊛

さま state, appearance

124

〜うちに while, as

部屋【へや】room

〜のなかまで to the middle of

明るむ【あかるむ】grow bright

赤い【あかい】red ⊛

頬【ほお】cheek

目立つ【めだつ】stand out

驚く【おどろく】be surprised

〜ばかり keep on (doing)

あざやかな vivid, fresh

色【いろ】color

見とれる【みとれる】stare in wonder

125▶　「頬ぺたが真赤じゃないか。寒くて。」

126▶　「寒いんじゃないわ。白粉を落したからよ。私は寝床に入ると直ぐ、足の先までぽっぽして来るの。」と枕もとの鏡台に向って、

127▶　「とうとう明るくなってしまったわ。帰りますわ。」

128▶　島村はその方を見て、ひょっと首を縮めた。鏡の奥が真白に光っているのは雪である。その雪のなかに女の真赤な頬が浮んでいる。なんとも言えぬ清潔な美しさであった。

129▶　もう日が昇るのか、鏡の雪は冷めたく燃えるような輝きを増して来た。それにつれて雪に浮ぶ女の髪もあざやかな紫光りの黒を強めた。

125

頬ぺた【ほっぺた】cheek
真赤【まっかな／まあかな】bright-red ⊛
じゃないか be
寒い【さむい】cold ⊛

126

〜わ FEMININE particle used to soften an assertion ⊛
白粉【おしろい】make-up
落す【おとす】remove
私【わたし】I
寝床に入る【ねどこにはいる】go to bed
直ぐ【すぐ】immediately, instantly
足の先【あしのさき】tips of one's toes
ぽっぽする MIMETIC turn warm
〜て来る【〜てくる】indicates a condition coming into effect
〜の FEMININE particle used with falling

intonation to soften an assertion
枕もと【まくらもと】bedside
鏡台【きょうだい】mirror stand
向う【むかう】face

127

とうとう at last
明るい【あかるい】bright
〜てしまう expresses with regret the completion of process
帰る【かえる】go home

128

島村【しまむら】Shimamura
その方【そのほう】that way
見る【みる】look
ひょっと suddenly
首を縮める【くびをちぢめる】shrug one's shoulders
鏡【かがみ】mirror ⊛

"Your cheeks are bright red. Must be the cold."

"I'm not cold. It's because I took off my make-up. As soon as I get into bed, I get warm right down to the tips of my toes." She settled herself in front of the mirror-stand by the pillow.

"Well, it's daylight now. I've got to go home."

Shimamura looked over toward her, then shrugged his shoulders. The immaculate white glowing in the depths of the mirror was snow. And floating in the midst of that snow were the bright red cheeks of the woman. There was something indescribably pure about the beauty of it.

Perhaps because the sun was rising, the snow in the mirror was glowing more fiercely, as though it were burning coldly. At the same time, the woman's brilliant black hair with its purple gleam grew brighter against the snow.

奥【おく】depth
真白【まっしろ／ましろ】perfect white
光る【ひかる】shine
雪【ゆき】snow ⊛
女【おんな】woman ⊛
頬【ほお】cheek
浮ぶ【うかぶ】appear, float ⊛
なんとも言えぬ【なんともいえぬ】inexpressible
清潔な【せいけつな】pure, clean
美しさ【うつくしさ】beauty

129

日【ひ】the sun
昇る【のぼる】rise
冷めたく【つめたく】coldly
燃える【もえる】burn
輝き【かがやき】glow
増す【ます】increase

～て来る【～てくる】indicates a situation or phenomenon emerging
～につれて as, together with
髪【かみ】hair
あざやかな fresh, vivid
紫光り【むらさきびかり】purple sheen
黒【くろ】black
強める【つよめる】strengthen

三島由紀夫

YUKIO MISHIMA
(1925–1970)

Oscar Wilde famously claimed to have put his genius into his life rather than his art. Yukio Mishima seems to have successfully put his genius into both. In the course of his short life, he produced forty novels, twenty volumes of short stories and eighteen plays, while also finding the time to act in films, direct plays, travel the world, and practice kendo, boxing and bodybuilding. This multifaceted hyper-activity certainly makes Mishima into the most fascinating literary personality of twentieth-century Japan, if not its greatest writer. After all, how else can one account for him being the subject of multiple English-language biographies, a feature-length movie (Paul Schrader's *Mishima*) and a punk rock song (The Stranglers' "Death & Night & Blood")?

Kimitake Hiraoka—Yukio Mishima was a pen name the young writer assumed for the serialization of his first major work at age sixteen—was born in Tokyo in 1925. Taken from his mother when only a few weeks old, the infant Mishima was brought up in a shuttered room by his sickly and mentally unstable grandmother, Natsu, for the first twelve years of his life. When worsening health forced her to relinquish the boy to her daughter-in-law, mother and son compensated for years of enforced separation by becoming almost unnaturally close. The strain of morbidity that runs throughout Mishima's work probably has its origins in the unwholesome emotional hothouse that was his childhood.

At the aristocratic Peers' School, Mishima started contributing to the student magazine from the age of twelve, and his first book was published in 1944, when he was nineteen and war was still raging. Despite these signs of literary promise, the young Mishima bowed to the wishes of his civil-servant father and enrolled in the law faculty of Tokyo Imperial University. Upon graduating in 1947, he again went along with his father by taking the exam for the elite Ministry of Finance, working there for nine months before resigning to become a full-time writer. The result was *Confessions of a Mask*, an autobiographical novel in which he dissected himself, revealing his homosexuality and his preoccupation with violent death. The book, published in July 1949, turned Mishima into a celebrity overnight. The pattern of his life was now set and he began to churn out novels, plays and essays, working from midnight to dawn with the iron self-discipline of the bureaucrat he had so nearly become.

A 1952 journey to Greece was a conscious effort on Mishima's part to break away from the obsession with death and darkness found in early works like *Thirst for Love* and *Forbidden Colors*. The trip resulted in *The Sound of Waves*, a reworking of the Daphnis and Chloë myth that John Nathan (1974, 121) describes as "the only love story Mishima ever wrote that was neither perverted nor sardonic." The year 1956 witnessed the publication of *The Temple of the Golden Pavilion*, often regarded as his finest novel.

In 1958, Mishima married Yōko Sugiyama, with Yasunari Kawabata acting as best man. *Kyōko's House*, published the next year, was his first critical failure. The characters—a businessman who looks back with nostalgia to the omnipresence of death during the war, a failed boxer who joins a group of right-wing extremists, and an actor fixated on suicide—are seen as prefiguring the direction Mishima's life was about to take.

Mishima did much of his best work as a playwright in the 1960s, when his fiction began to lose out in the face of competition from new authors like Kōbō Abe and Kenzaburō Ōe. Wracked with student riots, Japan veered off to the left, but Mishima went in quite the opposite direction, whether in short stories like the militaristic "Patriotism" or in essays like "The Voice of the Hero Spirits," where the ghosts of kamikaze pilots reprove the emperor for having forsworn his divinity.

On November 25, 1970, after leaving the final installment of *The Sea of Fertility* tetralogy for his publisher at the entrance to his house, Mishima set out for the Eastern Army HQ in Ichigaya, Tokyo, with four companions from the Shield Society, the private army he had set up two years earlier. First taking a general hostage, Mishima went out onto the balcony overlooking the parade ground to urge the Self-Defense Forces to rise up, march on the Diet and force a revision of Japan's pacifist constitution. His proposals, barely audible above the buzzing of the media helicopters, were met with jeers. Mishima then retreated indoors and killed himself by slicing open his stomach in an act of ritual suicide. "The Romantic showman chose to die as he had lived," remarked Gore Vidal acidly, "in a blaze of publicity" (Vidal 1971).

Why Mishima chose to die remains something of a mystery. Did he want to express his rejection of postwar prosperity and a yearning for Japan's heroic imperial past? Was he simply peeved at not having been awarded the Nobel Prize for which he had been thrice nominated? Did he have the sense that he had written himself dry? Or was dying with extreme violence surrounded by younger men simply a sadomasochistic fantasy that he was eager to act out on the public stage?

Even in death Mishima remains a controversial figure, with some critics dismissing him as a "B-list author with one topic, himself" (quoted in Ross 2006, 24), while others praise him as "one of the most important writers of the post-war era" (Washburn 2001, 213). Nonetheless, the international book-buying public continues to respond to the compelling intensity of his storytelling and the famously rich beauty of his prose style.

Patriotism

Chronicle of a Death Foretold

On November 25, 1970, Mishima committed hara-kiri after his impassioned appeal to the Self-Defense Forces to march on the Diet and restore the imperial system was met with derision. Ten years earlier, he had written this story: based on a real incident in February 1936, it describes the ritual suicide of an army lieutenant whose officer comrades stage a mutiny in the emperor's name only to find themselves repudiated by him. "Patriotism" is thus not only the most exquisite and excruciating expression of Mishima's own lifelong death wish, it also served as the template for his own suicide. Mishima directed and starred in a twenty-eight-minute film version of "Patriotism" in 1965, and—if Ryūtarō, a self-professed former male lover of his, is to be believed (Ross 2006)—playing at pretend hara-kiri, with a bunch of red ribbons standing in for blood and guts, was among his favorite erotic games. With its long, imagery-laden sentences and its sustained loftiness of tone, "Patriotism" is much closer to an extended prose poem—part epithalamium, part elegy—than to a conventional short story.

Go to www.speaking-japanese.com to join an online discussion about this story and share your questions, translations and insights with other readers.

壱 (いち)

1▶ 　昭和十一年二月二十八日、（すなわち二・二六事件突発第三日目）、近衛歩兵一聯隊勤務武山信二中尉は、事件発生以来親友が叛乱軍に加入せることに対し懊悩を重ね、皇軍相撃の事態必至となりたる情勢に痛憤して、四谷区青葉町六の自宅八畳の間に於て、軍刀を以て割腹自殺を遂げ、麗子夫人も亦夫君に殉じて自刃を遂げたり。

壱【いち】one

1

昭和【しょうわ】Shōwa era (1926–1989)

十一年【じゅういちねん】11th year (1936)

二月【にがつ】February

二十八日【にじゅうはちにち】28th

すなわち namely, that is, in other words

二・二六事件【に・にろくじけん】February 26th Incident

突発【とっぱつ】outbreak

第三日目【だいさんにちめ】the third day

近衛歩兵【このえほへい】Imperial Guard (lit., "Konoe Infantry")

一聯隊【いちれんたい】First Regiment

勤務【きんむ】work, service

武山信二【たけやましんじ】Takeyama Shinji (man's name)

中尉【ちゅうい】lieutenant

事件【じけん】incident

発生【はっせい】start, outbreak

〜以来【〜いらい】since

親友【しんゆう】close friends

叛乱軍【はんらんぐん】mutinous army

加入せる【かにゅうせる】ARCHAIC join

〜に対し【〜にたいし】regarding, in respect of

懊悩【おうのう】anguish

重ねる【かさねる】go through time and again

皇軍【こうぐん】Imperial Army

相撃【あいうち】internecine strife

事態【じたい】situation

必至となりたる【ひっしとなりたる】ARCHAIC had become inevitable

情勢【じょうせい】circumstances

痛憤する【つうふんする】be indignant

1

On the twenty-eighth of February, 1936 (the third day, in other words, of the February 26 Incident), Lieutenant Takeyama Shinji of the First Regiment of the Imperial Guard—whose anxiety about his close friends being part of the mutinous force had been growing from the start of the affair, and who was indignant at the inevitability of the Imperial Army having to turn its fire upon its own kind—used his army sword to commit suicide by disembowelment in the eight-mat room of his house in block six of Aoba-chō in Yotsuya. His wife, Reiko, followed her husband, stabbing herself to death.

四谷区【よつやく】Yotsuya Ward (in Tokyo)

青葉町六【あおばちょうろく】block six of Aoba-chō

自宅【じたく】private home

八畳の間【はちじょうのま】eight-tatami-mat room

〜に於て【〜において】in

軍刀【ぐんとう】military sword

〜を以て【〜をもって】by means of, with

割腹自殺【かっぷくじさつ】suicide by disembowelment

遂げる【とげる】go through with

麗子【れいこ】Reiko (woman's given name)

夫人【ふじん】wife, married lady

亦【また】also, and

夫君【ふくん】HONORIFIC husband

〜に殉じる【〜にじゅんじる】follow (to the grave)

自刃【じじん】stabbing oneself

遂げたり【とげたり】ARCHAIC went through with

中尉の遺書は只一句のみ「皇軍の万歳を祈る」とあり、夫人の遺書は両親に先立つ不孝を詫び、「軍人の妻として来るべき日が参りました」云々と記せり。烈夫烈婦の最期、洵に鬼神をして哭かしむの概あり。因みに中尉は享年三十歳、夫人は二十三歳、華燭の典を挙げしより半歳に充たざりき。

The lieutenant's final note consisted of only a single phrase: "May the Imperial Army last forever." Apologizing to her parents for her want of piety in preceding them to the grave, his wife's note stated in short: "The day that inevitably comes for a soldier's wife has come." The last moments of this virtuous couple were truly enough to make even the gods weep. Incidentally, when they died, the lieutenant was thirty and his wife twenty-three, and not yet half a year had passed since they had celebrated their marriage.

享年【きょうねん】person's age at death

三十歳【さんじゅっさい】30 years old

二十三歳【にじゅうさんさい】23 years old

華燭の典【かしょくのてん】marriage ceremony

挙げし【あげし】ARCHAIC had celebrated, had had

〜より since

半歳【はんとし】half a year

充たざりき【みたざりき】ARCHAIC had not yet been filled

弐（に）

2▶　　武山中尉の結婚式に参列した人はもちろん、新郎新婦の記念写真を見せてもらっただけの人も、この二人の美男美女ぶりに改めて感嘆の声を洩らした。軍服姿の中尉は軍刀を左手に突き右手に脱いだ軍帽を提げて、雄々しく新妻を庇って立っていた。まことに凛々しい顔立ちで、濃い眉も大きくみひらかれた瞳も、青年の潔らかさといさぎよさをよく表わしていた。新婦の白い裲襠姿の美しさは、例えん方もなかった。やさしい眉の下のつぶらな目にも、ほっそりした形のよい鼻にも、ふくよかな唇にも、艶やかさと高貴とが相映じている。

弐【に】two

2

武山【たけやま】Takeyama
中尉【ちゅうい】lieutenant ✺
結婚式【けっこんしき】wedding ceremony
参列する【さんれつする】attend
人【ひと】person ✺
もちろん of course
新郎新婦【しんろうしんぷ】newly wed couple
記念写真【きねんしゃしん】commemorative photograph
見せる【みせる】show
この二人【このふたり】these two people
美男美女【びなんびじょ】beautiful couple
〜ぶり with the style of 〜
改めて【あらためて】again, anew

感嘆の声【かんたんのこえ】exclamation of wonder
洩らす【もらす】utter
軍服姿【ぐんぷくすがた】appearance in military uniform
軍刀【ぐんとう】military sword
左手【ひだりて】left hand
突く【つく】touch
右手【みぎて】right hand
脱ぐ【ぬぐ】take off
軍帽【ぐんぼう】military cap
提げる【さげる】carry
雄々しく【おおしく】heroically, bravely
新妻【にいづま】bride
庇う【かばう】defend, shield
立つ【たつ】stand
まことに truly, indeed
凛々しい【りりしい】imposing, manly

2

It was not just those who had attended Lieutenant Takeyama's wedding ceremony, but even people who were simply shown the commemorative photograph of the bride and bridegroom: everyone invariably let out a gasp of astonishment at their beauty. Dressed in his military uniform, his left hand resting on his sword and his doffed cap clasped in his right, the lieutenant stood valiant and protective of his bride. His commanding features, thick eyebrows, and wide-open eyes expressed all the purity and bravery of youth. The beauty of the bride, attired in a long, white outer robe, was beyond compare. Both sensuality and nobility were evident in her eyes, round under gentle brows, in her delicate, shapely nose and in her full lips.

顔立ち 【かおだち】 features (of the face)

濃い 【こい】 thick, dense

眉 【まゆ】 eyebrow ⊛

大きく 【おおきく】 widely

みひらく [passive form in text] open (one's eyes) wide

瞳 【ひとみ】 pupil, eye

青年 【せいねん】 young man

潔らかさ 【きよらかさ】 purity, clarity

いさぎよさ bravery, righteousness

よく well

表わす 【あらわす】 show, express

新婦 【しんぷ】 bride

白い 【しろい】 white

補襠姿 【うちかけすがた】 appearance when dressed in an outer robe

美しさ 【うつくしさ】 beauty

例えん方もない 【たとえんかたもない】 ARCHAIC beyond comparison

やさしい gentle

〜の下の 【〜のしたの】 beneath

つぶらな round

目 【め】 eye

ほっそりした slender, fine

形のよい 【かたちのよい】 shapely

鼻 【はな】 nose

ふくよかな rich, plump

唇 【くちびる】 lip

艶やかさ 【あでやかさ】 sensual beauty

高貴 【こうき】 nobility

相映じる 【あいえいじる】 be apparent (of two things)

忍びやかに裲襠の袖からあらわれて扇を握っている指先は、繊細に揃えて置かれたのが、夕顔の蕾のように見えた。

3▶ 　二人の自刃のあと、人々はよくこの写真をとりだして眺めては、こうした申し分のない美しい男女の結びつきは不吉なものを含んでいがちなことを嘆いた。事件のあとで見ると、心なしか、金屛風の前の新郎新婦は、そのいずれ劣らぬ澄んだ瞳で、すぐ目近の死を透かし見ているように思われるのであった。

4▶ 　二人は仲人の尾関中将の世話で、四谷青葉町に新居を構えた。新居と云っても、小さな庭を控えた三間の古い借家で、階下の六畳も四畳半も日当りがわるいので、

忍びやかに【しのびやかに】discreetly
裲襠【うちかけ】outer robe
袖【そで】sleeve
あらわれる appear
扇【おうぎ】folding fan
握る【にぎる】grip, hold
指先【ゆびさき】fingertip
繊細に【せんさいに】delicately
揃える【そろえる】arrange, lay out
〜て置く【〜ておく】and leave as is
夕顔【ゆうがお】moonflower
蕾【つぼみ】bud
見える【みえる】appear, look

3
二人【ふたり】the two of them, they ✻
自刃【じじん】stabbing oneself
人々【ひとびと】people
写真【しゃしん】photograph

とりだす pick up
眺める【ながめる】gaze at
こうした this sort of
申し分のない【もうしぶんのない】fault-less, flawless
美しい【うつくしい】beautiful
男女【だんじょ】man and woman
結びつき【むすびつき】union
不吉な【ふきつな】inauspicious
もの thing, something
含んでいがちな【ふくんでいがちな】tending to include
こと state of affairs
嘆く【なげく】lament
事件【じけん】affair
見る【みる】see, look ✻
心なしか【こころなしか】maybe it is just imagination

Her fingertips, peeping out from the sleeve of her robe, clasped a fan; exquisitely positioned, they resembled the bud of a moon-flower.

After their suicide, people would often bring out this photograph, gaze at it and lament that the unions of such impeccably beautiful men and women were often doomed. Maybe it was only imagination, but looking at it after the event, the bride and groom in front of the gilded screen appeared to be staring, each as clear-eyed as the other, at their own imminent deaths.

Thanks to the kindness of their matchmaker, Lieutenant General Ozeki, they had been able to establish a new home in Aoba-chō in Yotsuya. Despite the term "new home," it was, in fact, an old three-room rented house with a small garden; since the six- and four-and-a-half-mat rooms downstairs did not get much sun,

---

金屏風【きんびょうぶ】gilded screen

〜の前の【〜のまえの】in front of

新郎新婦【しんろうしんぷ】bridegroom and bride

いずれ劣らぬ【いずれおとらぬ】second to none, flawless

澄んだ【すんだ】clear

瞳【ひとみ】pupil, eye

すぐ close

目近の【まぢかの】close, nearby

死【し】death

透かし見る【すかしみる】see through to

思う【おもう】[spontaneous form in text] think, feel

4

仲人【なこうど】go-between, matchmaker

尾関中将【おぜきちゅうじょう】Lieutenant General Ozeki

世話【せわ】kind attentions

四谷青葉町【よつやあおばちょう】Aoba-chō in Yotsuya Ward

新居を構える【しんきょをかまえる】settle into a new house

新居【しんきょ】new house

〜と云っても【〜といっても】despite calling it 〜

小さな【ちいさな】small

庭【にわ】garden

控える【ひかえる】have close by

三間【みま】three rooms

古い【ふるい】old

借家【しゃくや】rented house

階下【かいか】downstairs

六畳【ろくじょう】six-mat room

四畳半【よじょうはん】four-and-a-half-mat room

日当りがわるい【ひあたりがわるい】get little sunlight

二階の八畳の寝室を客間に兼ね、女中も置かずに、麗子が一人で留守を守った。

5▶　新婚旅行は非常時だというので遠慮をした。二人が第一夜を過したのはこの家であった。床に入る前に、信二は軍刀を膝の前に置き、軍人らしい訓誡を垂れた。軍人の妻たる者は、いつなんどきでも良人の死を覚悟していなければならない。それが明日来るかもしれぬ。あさって来るかもしれぬ。いつ来てもうろたえぬ覚悟があるかと訊いたのである。麗子は立って簞笥の抽斗をあけ、もっとも大切な嫁入道具として母からいただいた懐剣を、良人と同じように、黙って自分の膝の前に置いた。

二階【にかい】second floor
八畳の寝室【はちじょうのしんしつ】eight-mat bedroom
客間【きゃくま】parlor, sitting room
兼ねる【かねる】use for a double purpose
女中【じょちゅう】maid
置かずに【おかずに】without installing
麗子【れいこ】Reiko ✻
一人で【ひとりで】alone, by oneself
留守を守る【るすをまもる】look after an empty house, hold the fort

5
新婚旅行【しんこんりょこう】honeymoon
非常時【ひじょうじ】crisis, emergency
遠慮をする【えんりょをする】refrain from doing
二人【ふたり】the two of them, they
第一夜【だいいちや】the first night

過す【すごす】spend
家【いえ】house
床に入る【とこにはいる】go to bed
〜前に【〜まえに】before
信二【しんじ】Shinji
軍刀【ぐんとう】military sword
膝【ひざ】knee ✻
〜の前に【〜のまえに】in front of ✻
置く【おく】put, place ✻
軍人【ぐんじん】soldier ✻
訓誡【くんかい】admonition
垂れる【たれる】give
妻たる者【つまたるもの】ARCHAIC person who is a wife
いつなんどきでも ARCHAIC anytime whatsoever
良人【おっと】husband
死【し】death

they used the eight-mat bedroom on the second floor as a room to receive guests and as a bedroom. They had no maid, so Reiko looked after the house by herself when her husband was away.

They did without a honeymoon, as it was a time of national emergency. This house was where they had spent the first night of their marriage. Before going to bed, Shinji had placed his sword before his knees and imparted a soldierly lecture. A soldier's wife had to be ready for the death of her husband at any time. It might come tomorrow. It might come the day after tomorrow. Did she have the resolve to remain calm, no matter when it might come? he asked. Reiko stood up, opened a drawer in the chest and, just like her husband, silently placed the dagger—which she had received from her mother and was the most important article in her trousseau—in front of her knees.

覚悟する【かくごする】show resolve,
   make up one's mind
明日【あした】tomorrow
来る【くる】come ⊛
〜かもしれぬ＝〜かもしれない ⊛
うろたえぬ not lose one's head
覚悟【かくご】resolve
訊く【きく】ask
立つ【たつ】stand up
簞笥【たんす】chest of drawers
抽斗【ひきだし】drawer
あける open
もっとも most
大切な【たいせつな】precious
嫁入道具【よめいりどうぐ】trousseau
〜として as
母【はは】mother
いただく HUMBLE receive

懐剣【かいけん】dagger
〜と同じように【〜とおなじように】in
   the same way as
黙る【だまる】keep quiet
自分【じぶん】oneself, herself

これでみごとな黙契が成立ち、中尉は二度と妻の覚悟をためしたりすることがなかった。

6▶　結婚して幾月かたつと、麗子の美しさはいよいよ磨かれて、雨後の月のようにあきらかになった。

7▶　二人とも実に健康な若い肉体を持っていたから、その交情ははげしく、夜ばかりか、演習のかえりの埃だらけの軍服を脱ぐ間ももどかしく、帰宅するなり中尉は新妻をその場に押し倒すことも一再でなかった。麗子もよくこれに応えた。最初の夜から一ト月をすぎるかすぎぬに、麗子は喜びを知り、中尉もそれを知って喜んだ。

みごとな amazing
黙契【もっけい】unspoken understanding
成立つ【なりたつ】be achieved
中尉【ちゅうい】lieutenant ✵
二度と〜ない【にどと〜ない】never again
妻【つま】wife
覚悟【かくご】resolve
ためす test

6
結婚する【けっこんする】get married
幾月【いくつき】several months
たつ pass (of time)
麗子【れいこ】Reiko ✵
美しさ【うつくしさ】beauty
いよいよ more and more
磨く【みがく】[spontaneous form in text] polish, improve
雨後【うご】after the rain

月【つき】the moon
あきらかな bright, clear

7
二人とも【ふたりとも】both of them
実に【じつに】really
健康な【けんこうな】healthy
若い【わかい】young
肉体【にくたい】body
持つ【もつ】possess
交情【こうじょう】sexual relations
はげしい intense, strong
夜【よる】night
〜ばかりか not only 〜 (but also . . .)
演習【えんしゅう】training
かえり return
埃だらけの【ほこりだらけの】dust-covered
軍服【ぐんぷく】military uniform

In this way, a profound unspoken understanding sprang up between them, and the lieutenant never again sought to test his wife's strength of will.

As the months passed after their marriage, Reiko's beauty only increased, and she became radiant like the moon after rain.

Since they both possessed truly healthy young bodies, their lovemaking was fierce and took place not just at night: more than once, immediately upon getting home from maneuvers and begrudging even the time it would take to remove his dusty uniform, the lieutenant had pushed his wife to the floor right then and there. Reiko had responded in kind. From the first night of their marriage and around a month thereafter, Reiko knew happiness, and the lieutenant, recognizing that, was happy too.

脱ぐ【ぬぐ】take off
間【ま】interval of time
もどかしい impatient
帰宅する【きたくする】return home
〜なり as soon as 〜
新妻【にいづま】new wife, bride
その場に【そのばに】on the spot
押し倒す【おしたおす】push down
こと act, action
一再でない【いっさいでない】happen
  more than once
よく well, properly
応える【こたえる】respond
最初【さいしょ】the first
夜【よる】night
一ト月【ひとつき】one month
すぎるかすぎぬに before or just after (a
  period of time) had passed

喜び【よろこび】joy
知る【しる】know, experience ⊛
喜ぶ【よろこぶ】be happy

8 ▶ 麗子の体は白く厳そかで、盛り上った乳房は、いかにも力強い拒否の潔らかさを示しながら、一旦受け容れたあとでは、それが塒の温かさを湛えた。かれらは床の中でも怖ろしいほど、厳粛なほどまじめだった。おいおい烈しくなる狂態のさなかでもまじめだった。

9 ▶ 昼間、中尉は訓練の小休止のあいだにも妻を想い、麗子はひねもす良人の面影を追っていた。しかし一人でいるときも、式のときの写真をながめると幸福が確かめられた。麗子はほんの数ヶ月前まで路傍の人にすぎなかった男が、彼女の全世界の太陽になったことに、もはや何のふしぎも感じなかった。

8

麗子【れいこ】Reiko ✹
体【からだ】body
白い【しろい】white
厳そかな【おごそかな】severe
盛り上る【もりあがる】swell
乳房【ちぶさ】breasts
いかにも truly
力強い【ちからづよい】powerful
拒否【きょひ】denial
潔らかさ【きよらかさ】purity
示す【しめす】show
一旦【いったん】once
受け容れる【うけいれる】assent, accept
塒【ねぐら】nest, roost
温かさ【あたたかさ】warmth
湛える【たたえる】fill
かれら they

床の中【とこのなか】in bed
怖ろしい【おそろしい】fearful
〜ほど to the extent that 〜 ✹
厳粛な【げんしゅくな】solemn
まじめな serious ✹
おいおい gradually
烈しい【はげしい】intense
狂態【きょうたい】mad behavior
〜のさなかでも even in the midst of

9

昼間【ひるま】daytime
中尉【ちゅうい】lieutenant
訓練【くんれん】training
小休止【しょうきゅうし】brief rest
〜のあいだに during an interval of
妻【つま】wife
想う【おもう】think about
ひねもす from dawn to dusk

Reiko's body was pale and dignified, and her firm breasts, which expressed the purity of emphatic refusal, would overflow with welcoming warmth once she had consented. Even in bed the couple were frighteningly stern in their seriousness. They were serious even in the midst of their ever-intensifying frenzy.

In the daytime, the lieutenant would think of his wife during the short rests in his training, while Reiko would picture her husband's countenance all the time. Even when she was by herself, she needed only to look at the photograph of their wedding ceremony for her happiness to be confirmed. Reiko no longer felt any wonder at the fact that a man who only a few short months ago was no more than a stranger to her should have become the sun of her whole universe.

良人【おっと】husband
面影【おもかげ】figure, face
追う【おう】pursue
しかし however
一人【ひとり】alone
式【しき】ceremony
写真【しゃしん】photograph
ながめる gaze at
幸福【こうふく】happiness
確かめる【たしかめる】[passive form in text] make sure of
ほんの just, merely
数ヶ月【すうかげつ】a few months
〜前【〜まえ】before
路傍の人【ろほうのひと】stranger in the street
〜にすぎない be no more than 〜
男【おとこ】man

彼女【かのじょ】she
全世界【ぜんせかい】whole world
太陽【たいよう】the sun
こと fact
もはや no longer
何の〜も〜ない【なんの〜も〜ない】 none whatsoever
ふしぎ marvel, miracle
感じる【かんじる】feel

10▶　これらのことはすべて道徳的であり、教育勅語の「夫婦相和シ」の訓えにも叶っていた。麗子は一度だって口ごたえはせず、中尉も妻を叱るべき理由を何も見出さなかった。階下の神棚には皇太神宮の御札と共に、天皇皇后両陛下の御真影が飾られ、朝毎に、出勤前の中尉は妻と共に、神棚の下で深く頭を垂れた。捧げる水は毎朝汲み直され、榊はいつもつややかに新らしかった。この世はすべて厳粛な神威に守られ、しかもすみずみまで身も慄えるような快楽に溢れていた。

10

これら these
こと thing, deed
すべて all ✹
道徳的な【どうとくてきな】moral
教育勅語【きょういくちょくご】Imperial Rescript on Education
夫婦【ふうふ】husband and wife
相和シ【あいわシ】ARCHAIC mutual harmony
訓え【おしえ】precept
叶う【かなう】be in agreement, accord
麗子【れいこ】Reiko
一度【いちど】once
〜だって even
口ごたえ【くちごたえ】answering back
せず not do
中尉【ちゅうい】lieutenant ✹

妻【つま】wife ✹
叱る【しかる】tell off
〜べき should, ought to
理由【りゆう】reason
何も〜ない【なにも〜ない】none whatsoever
見出す【みいだす】find
階下【かいか】downstairs
神棚【かみだな】household altar ✹
皇太神宮【こうたいじんぐう】Inner Shrine of Ise Shrine
御札【おふだ】amulet, talisman
〜と共に【〜とともに】together with ✹
天皇皇后両陛下【てんのうこうごうりょうへいか】their Highnesses, the Emperor and Empress
御真影【ごしんえい】HONORIFIC portrait, photograph

These things were all moral and consistent with the tenet of the Imperial Rescript on Education that "a husband and wife should be in mutual harmony." Reiko had never once answered back, and the lieutenant never found any reason to scold his wife. On the household altar downstairs, portraits of their Imperial Highnesses were displayed together with a talisman from the Ise Shrine, and every morning before going to work, the lieutenant would bow his head deeply beneath the altar together with his wife. The offertory water would be replaced every morning, and the sakaki was always fresh and alive. Every aspect of their lives here in this world was protected by the solemn power of the gods and overflowed with a pleasure that set every part of their bodies aquiver.

飾る【かざる】[passive form in text] decorate, display

朝毎【あさごと】every morning

出勤前【しゅっきんまえ】before going to work

〜の下で【〜のしたで】beneath

深く【ふかく】deeply

頭を垂れる【こうべをたれる】bow one's head

捧げる【ささげる】offer up

水【みず】water

毎朝【まいあさ】every morning

汲み直す【くみなおす】[passive form in text] ladle out again

榊【さかき】sakaki plant

いつも always

つややかに lustrously

新らしい【あたらしい】fresh

この世【このよ】this present life

厳粛な【げんしゅくな】solemn

神威【しんい】power of the gods

守る【まもる】[passive form in text] protect

しかも moreover

すみずみまで to every nook and cranny

身【み】body

慄える【ふるえる】shudder, tremble

快楽【かいらく】sensual pleasure

溢れる【あふれる】abound, brim

11▶　斎藤内府の邸は近くであったのに、二月二十六日の朝、二人は銃声も聞かなかった。ただ、十分間の惨劇がおわって、雪の暁闇に吹き鳴らされた集合喇叭が中尉の眠りを破った。中尉は跳ね起きて無言で軍服を着、妻のさし出す軍刀を佩して、明けやらぬ雪の朝の道へ駆け出した。そして二十八日の夕刻まで帰らなかったのである。

12▶　麗子はやがてラジオのニュースでこの突発事件の全貌を知った。それからの二日間の麗子の一人きりの生活は、まことに静かで、門戸を閉ざして過された。

参【さん】three

11

斎藤内府【さいとうないふ】Saitō Makoto, Lord Keeper of the Privy Seal (along with the finance minister and the inspector general of military education, Saitō was one of the key statesmen successfully assassinated by the army radicals in the February 26th Incident)

邸【やしき】mansion

近く【ちかく】vicinity

〜のに although

二月二十六日【にがつにじゅうろくにち】February 26th

朝【あさ】morning ❀

二人【ふたり】the two of them, they

銃声【じゅうせい】sound of gunfire

聞く【きく】hear

ただ just, only

十分間【じゅっぷんかん】period of ten minutes

惨劇【さんげき】tragedy

おわる end, conclude

雪【ゆき】snow ❀

暁闇【ぎょうあん】darkness of dawn

吹き鳴らす【ふきならす】[passive form in text] blow, sound

集合喇叭【しゅうごうラッパ】bugle for muster

中尉【ちゅうい】lieutenant ❀

眠り【ねむり】sleep

破る【やぶる】destroy, disrupt

跳ね起きる【はねおきる】spring up, start up

無言で【むごんで】in silence, silently

軍服【ぐんぷく】military uniform

着る【きる】put on

妻【つま】wife

3

Although the mansion of Lord Saitō, Keeper of the Privy Seal, was nearby, they did not hear the shots on the morning of February 26. It was only after the ten-minute-long tragedy was over that the sound of a bugle calling muster in the snowy darkness of the dawn disturbed the lieutenant's sleep. The lieutenant sprang up, and without a word put on his uniform, strapped on the sword that his wife held out, and rushed out into the snowy morning streets under the predawn sky. He did not return until the evening of the twenty-eighth.

In due course Reiko heard all about the dramatic event from the news on the radio. Over the next two days, her solitary life was extremely quiet, and spent behind locked doors.

さし出す 【さしだす】 hold (something) out (for someone)

軍刀 【ぐんとう】 military sword

佩す 【はいす】 strap on, put on

明けやらぬ 【あけやらぬ】 not yet fully lit, not yet broken (of dawn)

道 【みち】 road, street

駈け出す 【かけだす】 dash out

二十八日 【にじゅうはちにち】 the 28th

夕刻 【ゆうこく】 evening

帰る 【かえる】 return home

12

麗子 【れいこ】 Reiko ⊛

やがて in due course

ラジオ radio

ニュース news program, the news

突発事件 【とっぱつじけん】 sudden/unexpected event

全貌 【ぜんぼう】 full picture

知る 【しる】 know

それからの the following

二日間 【ふつかかん】 period of two days

一人きり 【ひとりきり】 all alone

生活 【せいかつ】 life

まことに truly

静かな 【しずかな】 calm

門戸を閉ざす 【もんこをとざす】 keep one's doors shut

過す 【すごす】 [passive form in text] spend (time)

13▶

麗子は雪の朝ものも言わずに駈け出して行った中尉の顔に、すでに死の決意を読んだのである。良人がこのまま生きて帰らなかった場合は、跡を追う覚悟ができている。彼女はひっそりと身のまわりのものを片づけた。数着の訪問着は学校時代の友達への形見として、それぞれの畳紙の上に宛名を書いた。常日頃、明日を思ってはならぬ、と良人に言われていたので、日記もつけていなかった麗子は、ここ数ヶ月の倖せの記述を丹念に読み返して火に投ずることのたのしみを失った。ラジオの横には小さな陶器の犬や兎や栗鼠や熊や狐がいた。さらに小さな壺や水瓶があった。

13

麗子【れいこ】Reiko ⊛

雪【ゆき】snow

朝【あさ】morning

ものも言わずに【ものもいわずに】without saying a word

駈け出す【かけだす】rush out

〜て行く【〜ていく】indicates movement away from narrator

中尉【ちゅうい】lieutenant

顔【かお】face

すでに already

死の決意【しのけつい】determination to die

読む【よむ】read, see

良人【おっと】husband ⊛

このまま as he was

生きて帰る【いきてかえる】come back home alive

場合【ばあい】event, case

跡を追う【あとをおう】follow after, follow suit

覚悟【かくご】resolve

彼女【かのじょ】she

ひっそりと quietly, discreetly

身のまわりのもの【みのまわりのもの】personal effects

片づける【かたづける】put in order

数着【すうちゃく】several (of clothes)

訪問着【ほうもんぎ】formal kimono for visiting

学校時代【がっこうじだい】schooldays

友達【ともだち】friends

形見【かたみ】keepsake

それぞれの each, respective

畳紙【たとう】folding paper case

〜の上に【〜のうえに】on top of

Reiko had already recognized the resolve to die in the face of the lieutenant as he rushed out without saying a word on that snowy morning. She had made up her mind to follow after her husband if he did not come back to her alive. She quietly tidied up her personal belongings. She wrote the names and addresses of old school friends on the paper wrappings of her formal kimonos, which were to serve as keepsakes. Since Reiko was always being instructed by her husband not to think of the morrow, she did not keep a diary, meaning that she was deprived of the pleasure of poring over her account of the happiness of the last few months before consigning it to the flames. By the side of the radio set stood a little dog, a rabbit, a squirrel, a bear and a fox, all made of china. There were also a small pot and a water jug.

宛名【あてな】name and address
書く【かく】write
常日頃【つねひごろ】always
明日【あす】tomorrow
思う【おもう】think about
〜てはならぬ = 〜てはならない must not 〜
言う【いう】[passive form in text] tell, say
日記【にっき】diary
つける keep (a diary)
ここ数ヶ月【ここすうかげつ】these several months
倖せ【しあわせ】happiness
記述【きじゅつ】description
丹念に【たんねんに】carefully
読み返す【よみかえす】reread
火に投ずる【ひにとうずる】throw in the fire

こと act, action
たのしみ pleasure
失う【うしなう】lose
ラジオ radio
〜の横に【〜のよこに】next to
小さな【ちいさな】small ❀
陶器【とうき】china, ceramics
犬【いぬ】dog
兎【うさぎ】rabbit
栗鼠【りす】squirrel
熊【くま】bear
狐【きつね】fox
さらに moreover
壺【つぼ】pot
水瓶【みずがめ】water jug

これが麗子の唯一のコレクションだったが、こんなものを形見に上げてもはじまらない。しかもわざわざ棺に納めてもらうにも当らない。するとそれらの小さな陶器の動物たちは、一そうあてどのない、よるべのない表情を湛えはじめた。

14▶　麗子はその一つの栗鼠を手にとってみて、こんな自分の子供らしい愛着のはるか彼方に、良人が体現している太陽のような大義を仰ぎ見た。自分は喜んで、そのかがやく太陽の車に拉し去られて死ぬ身であるが、今の数刻には、ひとりでこの無邪気な愛着にも浸っていられる。しかし自分が本当にこれらを愛したのは昔である。

麗子【れいこ】Reiko ⊛
唯一【ゆいいつ】only
コレクション collection
こんなもの these kinds of things
形見【かたみ】keepsake
上げる【あげる】elevate to the status of
〜てもはじまらない would be no good
　to 〜
しかも moreover
わざわざ expressly, specially
棺【ひつぎ】coffin
納める【おさめる】put in, store
〜にも当らない【〜にもあたらない】not
　be necessary to 〜
すると thinking such thoughts
それらの those
小さな【ちいさな】small
陶器【とうき】china, ceramics

動物たち【どうぶつたち】animals
一そう【いっそう】still more
あてどのない aimless, lost
よるべのない friendless, forlorn
表情【ひょうじょう】expression
湛えはじめる【たたえはじめる】start to
　wear (an expression)

14
一つ【ひとつ】one
栗鼠【りす】squirrel
手にとる【てにとる】pick up
〜てみる to see what it is like
こんな this kind of
自分【じぶん】oneself, herself, she ⊛
子供らしい【こどもらしい】childlike
愛着【あいちゃく】affection ⊛
はるか彼方に【はるかかなたに】in the far
　distance

This was Reiko's only collection. Such objects, she knew, could hardly be regarded as proper keepsakes, and they were not worthy of special placement in her coffin, either. As these thoughts went through her mind, the expressions of the little china animals began to look even more bewildered and hopeless.

Reiko picked one of them up—the squirrel—but she was looking up, far beyond this childish attachment of hers, to the sunlike aura of Noble Duty as personified in her husband. She would be willingly dragged off to her death in the brilliant chariot of that sun, but for just a few moments she was free to wallow alone in those feelings of innocent affection. It was a long time ago, however, that she had really loved these things.

良人【おっと】husband
体現する【たいげんする】embody
太陽【たいよう】the sun ✹
大義【たいぎ】great duty, noble cause
仰ぎ見る【あおぎみる】look up at
喜んで【よろんで】happily, willingly
かがやく shine
車【くるま】wheeled vehicle
拉し去る【らっしさる】drag off
死ぬ身【しぬみ】one prepared to die
今【いま】now
数刻【すうこく】a few moments
ひとりで alone
無邪気な【むじゃきな】innocent, guile-
　less
浸る【ひたる】soak in, indulge in
〜ていられる be able to be
しかし however

本当に【ほんとうに】really
愛する【あいする】love
昔【むかし】long ago

今は愛した思い出を愛しているにすぎないので、心はもっと烈しいもの、もっと狂おしい幸福に充たされている。……しかも麗子は、思うだにときめいて来る日夜の肉の悦びを、快楽などという名で呼んだことは一度もなかった。美しい手の指は、二月の寒さの上に、陶器の栗鼠の氷るような手ざわりを保っているが、そうしているあいだにも、中尉の逞ましい腕が延びてくる刹那を思うと、きちんと着た銘仙の裾前の同じ模様のくりかえしの下に、麗子は雪を融かす熱い果肉の潤いを感じた。

今【いま】now
愛する【あいする】love ✽
思い出【おもいで】memory
〜にすぎない be no more than 〜
心【こころ】heart, feelings
もっと more ✽
烈しい【はげしい】intense
もの thing, something
狂おしい【くるおしい】crazy
幸福【こうふく】happiness
充たす【みたす】[passive form in text] fill up
しかも moreover
麗子【れいこ】Reiko ✽
思う【おもう】think about ✽
〜だに even if
ときめく throb
〜て来る【〜てくる】indicates a condition coming into effect

日夜【にちや】day and night
肉の悦び【にくのよろこび】joys of the flesh
快楽【かいらく】pleasure
名【な】name
呼ぶ【よぶ】call
こと act, action
一度もない【いちどもない】not even once, never
美しい【うつくしい】beautiful
手【て】hand
指【ゆび】finger
二月【にがつ】February
寒さ【さむさ】cold, chill
〜の上に【〜のうえに】in addition to
陶器【とうき】china, ceramics
栗鼠【りす】squirrel
氷る【こおる】freeze

Now she only loved the memory of having once loved them, for her heart was filled with a more fierce, more frenzied happiness. . . . Reiko had never once considered the frequent joys of the flesh—the very thought of which sent a thrill through her—as mere sensual pleasure. The fingers of her lovely hand were numb from the February cold and the icy touch of the china squirrel, and yet, when she imagined the moment when the lieutenant's sturdy arms would embrace her, she felt a hot moistness in the soft, pink flesh beneath the repetitive pattern on the front of her neat Meisen kimono. It was a moistness that could melt snow.

手ざわり 【てざわり】 touch, feel
保つ 【たもつ】 hold, keep in an unchanged condition
中尉 【ちゅうい】 lieutenant
逞ましい 【たくましい】 sturdy, strong
腕 【うで】 arm
延びる 【のびる】 stretch out, extend
～てくる indicates movement toward the narrator
刹那 【せつな】 moment
きちんと punctiliously
着る 【きる】 put on, wear
銘仙 【めいせん】 Meisen silk kimono
裾前 【すそまえ】 skirt front (of a kimono)
同じ 【おなじ】 the same
模様 【もよう】 pattern
くりかえし repetition
～の下に 【～のしたに】 beneath

雪 【ゆき】 snow
融かす 【とかす】 melt
熱い 【あつい】 hot
果肉 【かにく】 flesh of a fruit
潤い 【うるおい】 moistness
感じる 【かんじる】 feel

15 ▶ 　脳裡にうかぶ死はすこしも怖くはなく、良人の今感じていること、考えていること、その悲嘆、その苦悩、その思考のすべてが、留守居の麗子には、彼の肉体と全く同じように、自分を快適な死へ連れ去ってくれるのを固く信じた。その思想のどんな破片にも、彼女の体はらくらくと溶け込んで行けると思った。

16 ▶ 　麗子はそうして、刻々のラジオのニュースに耳を傾け、良人の親友の名の幾人かが、蹶起の人たちの中に入っているのを知った。これは死のニュースだった。

Unafraid of the thoughts of death that hovered in her mind, Reiko, alone in the house, was convinced that whatever her husband was now feeling and thinking—the grief, the anguish—it would all carry her away, just as his body had, to an easeful death. She felt that her own body could comfortably melt and merge into any fragment of his thoughts.

Listening to the news bulletins on the radio minute by minute, Reiko recognized the names of several of her husband's close friends that were listed among the insurgents. It was news of her own death.

体【からだ】body
らくらくと comfortably
溶け込む【とけこむ】melt into
～て行く【～ていく】[potential form in text] indicates progression away from the narrator
思う【おもう】think

16

そうして in that way
刻々【こくこく】every moment
ラジオ radio
ニュース news ⊛
耳を傾ける【みみをかたむける】prick up one's ears, listen carefully (lit., "lean one's ear")
親友【しんゆう】close friends
名【な】name
幾人か【いくにんか／いくたりか】several people

蹶起【けっき】insurgency
人たち【ひとたち】people
～の中に【～のなかに】among
入る【はいる】join, become a member
知る【しる】learn, know

そして事態が日ましにのっぴきならぬ形をとるのを、勅命がいつ下るかもしれず、はじめ維新のための蹶起と見られたものが、叛乱の汚名を着せられつつあるのを、つぶさに知った。聯隊からは何の連絡もなかった。雪ののこる市内に、いつ戦がはじまるか知れなかった。

17 ▶ 　二十八日の日暮れ時、玄関の戸をはげしく叩く音を、麗子はおそろしい思いできいた。走り寄って、慄える手で鍵をあけた。磨硝子のむこうの影は、ものも言わなかったが、良人にちがいないことがよくわかった。麗子がその引戸の鍵を、これほどまだるっこしく感じたことはなかった。そのために鍵はなお手に逆らい、引戸はなかなか開かない。

事態【じたい】state of things

日ましに【ひましに】by the day

のっぴきならぬ irreversible

形をとる【かたちをとる】take shape

勅命【ちょくめい】Imperial edict

下る【くだる】be handed down (from on high)

〜かもしれず＝〜かもしれなくて maybe

はじめ at the start

維新【いしん】restoration

〜のための for the purpose of

蹶起【けっき】uprising

見る【みる】[passive form in text] see, view, perceive

もの thing, something

叛乱【はんらん】mutiny

汚名【おめい】stigma, disgrace

着せる【きせる】[passive form in text] fasten (a stigma on)

〜つつある continue to

つぶさに in detail

知る【しる】learn, know

聯隊【れんたい】regiment

何の〜もない【なんの〜もない】no . . . whatsoever

連絡【れんらく】contact, message

雪【ゆき】snow

のこる linger, remain

市内【しない】within the city

戦【いくさ】fight, battle

はじまる start

知れない【しれない】be impossible to tell

17

二十八日【にじゅうはちにち】the 28th

日暮れ時【ひぐれどき】nightfall, sunset

She heard the details of how the situation was becoming more irrevocable by the day. The movement that had begun as an uprising to achieve a restoration, and in reaction to which it was hoped an Imperial ordinance would be issued, had gradually come to be branded with the infamous name of mutiny. There was no word from the regiment. In the snow-blanketed city, it seemed as though battle could be joined at any time.

At dusk on the twenty-eighth, Reiko was terrified to hear the sound of someone pounding on the front door. Running down, she undid the lock, her hands trembling. The shadow on the other side of the ground glass said nothing, but she knew very well it was her husband. The door lock had never felt so awkward to Reiko before. The lock fought back against her hand and the door refused to slide open.

玄関【げんかん】entrance hall
戸【と】door
はげしく fiercely
叩く【たたく】thump, pound
音【おと】sound, noise
麗子【れいこ】Reiko ⊛
おそろしい frightening
思い【おもい】thought
きく hear
走り寄る【はしりよる】run toward
慄える【ふるえる】tremble
手【て】hand ⊛
鍵【かぎ】key, lock ⊛
あける open
磨硝子【すりガラス】ground glass
むこう other side
影【かげ】shadow

ものも言わない【ものもいわない】not say a word
良人【おっと】husband
〜にちがいない definitely be
よく well
わかる understand, know
引戸【ひきど】sliding door ⊛
これほど to this extent
まだるっこしい slow, sluggish
感じる【かんじる】feel
そのために accordingly, therefore
なお yet more
逆らう【さからう】disobey, oppose
なかなか〜ない not readily
開く【あく】open

18 ▶ 　戸があくより早く、カーキいろの外套に包まれた中尉の体が、雪の泥濘に重い長靴を踏み入れて、玄関の三和土に立った。中尉は引戸を閉めると共に、自分の手で又鍵を捩ってかけた。それがどういう意味でしたことか、麗子にはわからなかった。

19 ▶ 「お帰りあそばせ」

20 ▶ 　と麗子は深く頭を下げたが、中尉は答えない。軍刀を外し外套を脱ぎかけたので、麗子がうしろに廻って手つだった。うけとる外套は冷たく湿って、それが日向で立てる馬糞くさい匂いを消して、麗子の腕に重くのしかかった。これを外套掛にかけ、軍刀を抱いて、彼女は長靴を脱いだ良人に従って茶の間へ上った。階下の六畳である。

18

戸【と】door

あく open

〜より早く【〜よりはやく】sooner than 〜

カーキいろ khaki

外套【がいとう】overcoat ⊛

包む【つつむ】[passive form in text] wrap up (in)

中尉【ちゅうい】lieutenant ⊛

体【からだ】body

雪【ゆき】snow

泥濘【でいねい】mud, slush

重い【おもい】heavy

長靴【ちょうか】boot ⊛

踏み入れる【ふみいれる】set foot in

玄関【げんかん】entrance hall

三和土【たたき】cement floor

立つ【たつ】stand

引戸【ひきど】sliding door

閉める【しめる】shut

〜と共に【〜とともに】at the same time as

自分【じぶん】oneself, himself

手【て】hand

又【また】again

鍵【かぎ】key, lock

捩る【ねじる】turn, screw

かける＝鍵をかける lock (a door)

どういう what kind of

意味【いみ】significance

こと action

麗子【れいこ】Reiko ⊛

わかる understand

19

お帰りあそばせ【おかえりあそばせ】HON-ORIFIC, FEMININE welcome home

Almost before the door had opened, the lieutenant, wrapped in a khaki greatcoat, his boots heavy with muddy snow, strode in and stood on the cement floor of the entrance hall. As he closed the sliding door, he turned the key and locked it himself. Reiko did not know what it meant.

"Welcome back home."

Said Reiko, and bowed deeply, but the lieutenant did not reply. As he had taken off his sword and was starting to remove his greatcoat, Reiko went around behind to help him. The coat she took off him was cold and damp, smothering the smell of horse dung that it gave off in the sunlight, and it weighed heavily on her arm. She hung it on the coat stand, and clutching the sword followed her husband, who had removed his boots, up into the parlor. It was the six-mat room downstairs.

20

深く【ふかく】deeply
頭を下げる【あたまをさげる】bow one's head
答える【こたえる】reply
軍刀【ぐんとう】military sword ✪
外す【はずす】take off, remove
脱ぎかける【ぬぎかける】start to take off
うしろ behind
廻る【まわる】turn around
手つだう【てつだう】help
うけとる receive, take into one's hands
冷たい【つめたい】cold
湿る【しめる】become damp
日向【ひなた】sunshine
立てる【たてる】give off, emit
馬糞くさい【ばふんくさい】smelling of horse dung

匂い【におい】odor
消す【けす】extinguish, smother
腕【うで】arm
重く【おもく】heavily
のしかかる weigh, rest heavy
外套掛【がいとうかけ】coatrack, coat stand
かける hang
抱く【だく】hold with both hands
彼女【かのじょ】she
脱ぐ【ぬぐ】take off (shoes)
良人【おっと】husband
従う【したがう】follow
茶の間【ちゃのま】living room
上る【あがる】enter (by mounting a step)
階下【かいか】downstairs
六畳【ろくじょう】six-mat room

21▶　　明るい灯の下で見る良人の顔は、無精髭に覆われて、別人のようにやつれている。頬が落ちて、光沢と張りを失っている。機嫌のよいときは帰るなりすぐ普段着に着かえて晩飯の催促をするのに、軍服のまま、卓袱台に向って、あぐらをかいて、うなだれている。麗子は夕食の仕度をすべきかどうか訊くことを差控えた。

22▶　　ややあって、中尉はこう言った。

23▶「俺は知らなかった。あいつ等は俺を誘わなかった。おそらく俺が新婚の身だったのを、いたわったのだろう。加納も、本間も、山口もだ」

21

明るい【あかるい】bright

灯【ひ】light, lamp

〜の下で【〜のしたで】beneath

見る【みる】see, look

良人【おっと】husband

顔【かお】face

無精髭【ぶしょうひげ】five o'clock shadow

覆う【おおう】[passive form in text] cover

別人【べつじん】different person

やつれる become gaunt, become haggard

頬【ほお】cheek

落ちる【おちる】fall, sink

光沢【こうたく】glow, sheen

張り【はり】firmness, tension

失う【うしなう】lose

機嫌のよい【きげんのよい】be in a good mood

帰る【かえる】come home

〜なり as soon as 〜

すぐ immediately

普段着【ふだんぎ】casual clothes

着かえる【きかえる】change (into)

晩飯【ばんめし】evening meal

催促をする【さいそくをする】call for, request

〜のに although, in spite of the fact that 〜

軍服【ぐんぷく】military uniform

〜のまま in the unchanged state of

卓袱台【ちゃぶだい】low dining table

向う【むかう】position oneself so as to face

あぐらをかく sit cross-legged

うなだれる loll, droop

When she saw her husband's face beneath the bright light, it was covered in several days' growth of beard and so gaunt that he no longer looked like himself. His cheeks were sunken and had lost their glow and their tautness. When he was in a good mood, the instant he got home he would change into casual clothes and urge her to serve dinner, but now, still dressed in his uniform, he sat cross-legged before the low dining table and just slumped. Reiko thought it best not to ask whether to prepare any food.

After an interval, the lieutenant said:

"I had no idea. The chaps didn't ask me to join them. Maybe they just meant to be nice to me, seeing as I'd just got married. Kanō and Honma and Yamaguchi too."

麗子【れいこ】Reiko
夕食【ゆうしょく】evening meal
仕度をする【したくをする】make preparations
〜べき should, ought to
訊く【きく】ask
差控える【さしひかえる】refrain from

22

ややあって after a while
中尉【ちゅうい】lieutenant
言う【いう】say

23

俺【おれ】MASCULINE I ⊛
知る【しる】know
あいつ等【あいつら】BRUSQUE, AFFECTIONATE those fellows, they
誘う【さそう】invite, ask
おそらく perhaps, probably

新婚の身【しんこんのみ】married person
いたわる treat kindly, be considerate toward
加納【かのう】Kanō (surname)
本間【ほんま】Honma (surname)
山口【やまぐち】Yamaguchi (surname)

24 ▶ 　麗子は良人の親友であり、たびたびこの家へも遊びに来た元気な青年将校の顔を思い浮べた。

25 ▶ 　「おそらく明日にも勅命が下るだろう。奴等は叛乱軍の汚名を着るだろう。俺は部下を指揮して奴らを討たねばならん。……俺にはできん。そんなことはできん」

26 ▶ 　そして又言った。

27 ▶ 　「俺は今警備の交代を命じられて、今夜一晩帰宅を許されたのだ。明日の朝はきっと、奴らを討ちに出かけなければならんのだ。俺にはそんなことはできんぞ、麗子」

28 ▶ 　麗子は端座して目を伏せていた。よくわかるのだが、良人はすでにただ一つの死の言葉を語っている。

24

麗子【れいこ】Reiko ⊗
良人【おっと】husband ⊗
親友【しんゆう】close friend
たびたび a number of times
家【いえ】house
遊びに来る【あそびにくる】come over to visit
元気な【げんきな】energetic, cheerful
青年将校【せいねんしょうこう】young officer
顔【かお】face
思い浮べる【おもいうかべる】recall

25

おそらく perhaps, probably
明日【あした／あす】tomorrow ⊗
勅命【ちょくめい】Imperial edict

下る【くだる】be handed down (from on high)
奴等【やつら】BRUSQUE my chums, they ⊗
叛乱軍【はんらんぐん】mutinous army
汚名【おめい】stigma, disgrace
着る【きる】wear (a stigma)
俺【おれ】MASCULINE I ⊗
部下【ぶか】subordinates
指揮する【しきする】command
討つ【うつ】shoot, open fire on ⊗
〜ねばならん MASCULINE have to
できん MASCULINE can't ⊗
そんなこと that kind of thing ⊗

26

又【また】again
言う【いう】say, speak

27

今【いま】now

Reiko recalled the faces of the cheerful young officers who were such dear friends of her husband and had often paid social visits to the house.

"The Imperial ordinance will probably be issued tomorrow. The chaps will be branded as mutineers. I'll be in command of my men and we'll have to fire on 'em. I just can't. I can't do a thing like that."

Then he spoke again.

"I was ordered off guard duty just now and given home leave for the night. I know that tomorrow morning I'll have to go out and attack my chums. There's no way I'm going to do it, Reiko."

Reiko was sitting erect, looking down at the floor. She understood clearly that everything her husband had said was equivalent to a single word—death.

警備【けいび】guard duty
交代【こうたい】change (of guard)
命じる【めいじる】[passive form in text] order
今夜【こんや】tonight
一晩【ひとばん】duration of one night
帰宅【きたく】returning home
許す【ゆるす】[passive form in text] permit, allow
朝【あさ】morning
きっと for sure, most certainly
出かける【でかける】go out
～なければならん MASCULINE have to
ぞ MASCULINE particle used to emphatically express a feeling or conviction

28

端座する【たんざする】sit erect
目を伏せる【めをふせる】look down
よく well

わかる understand
すでに already
ただ一つ【ただひとつ】just one
死【し】death
言葉【ことば】word, remark
語る【かたる】talk about, speak of

中尉の心はもう決っている。言葉の一つ一つは死に裏附けられ、この黒い堅固な裏打のために、言葉が動かしがたい力を際立たせている。中尉は悩みを語っているのに、そこにはもう逡巡がないのである。

29 ▶　しかし、こうしているあいだの沈黙の時間には、雪どけの渓流のような清洌さがあった。中尉は二日にわたる永い懊悩の果てに、我家で美しい妻の顔と対座しているとき、はじめて心の安らぎを覚えた。言わないでも、妻が言外の覚悟を察していることが、すぐわかったからである。

中尉【ちゅうい】lieutenant ❀
心【こころ】heart, mind ❀
決る【きまる】be decided, be fixed
言葉【ことば】word, remark ❀
一つ一つ【ひとつひとつ】each and every one
死【し】death
裏附ける【うらづける】[passive form in text] back up
黒い【くろい】black
堅固な【けんごな】firm, hard
裏打【うらうち】lining, backing
〜のために owing to
動かしがたい【うごかしがたい】hard, solid, difficult to shake or alter
力【ちから】strength, power
際立つ【きわだつ】[causative form in text] stand out
悩み【なやみ】worries, anxieties

語る【かたる】speak of, relate
〜のに although, in spite of
逡巡【しゅんじゅん】hesitation

29

しかし however
沈黙【ちんもく】silence
時間【じかん】time
雪どけ【ゆきどけ】thaw, melting snow
渓流【けいりゅう】mountain torrent
清洌さ【せいれつさ】clarity, limpidity
二日【ふつか】two days
〜にわたる for a period of
永い【ながい】long
懊悩【おうのう】anguish
〜の果てに【〜のはてに】at the end of
我家【わがや】one's own home
美しい【うつくしい】beautiful
妻【つま】wife ❀

The lieutenant's mind was already made up. Each and every word was buttressed by death, and this hard, black support only made their immovable strength stand out the more. The lieutenant may have been explaining his worries, but there was no indecision about him.

As they sat there, the silence was as clear as a snow-fed mountain torrent. At the end of two long days of anguish, the lieutenant felt peace of mind for the first time as he sat across from his beautiful wife in his own home. It was because he knew at once that his wife, though she said nothing, had sensed his unspoken resolve.

顔 【かお】 face
対座する 【たいざする】 sit face to face
はじめて for the first time
安らぎ 【やすらぎ】 peace of mind
覚える 【おぼえる】 feel
言わないでも 【いわないでも】 though she would not say anything
言外の 【げんがいの】 unspoken, implied
覚悟 【かくご】 resolve
察する 【さっする】 infer, perceive
すぐ quickly
わかる understand

30▶ 「いいな」と中尉は重なる不眠にも澄んだ雄々しい目をあけて、はじめて妻の目をまともに見た。「俺は今夜腹を切る」

31▶ 麗子の目はすこしもたじろがなかった。

32▶ そのつぶらな目は強い鈴の音のような張りを示していた。そしてこう言った。

33▶ 「覚悟はしておりました。お供をさせていただきとうございます」

34▶ 中尉はほとんどその目の力に圧せられるような気がした。言葉は讒言のようにすらすらと出て、どうしてこんな重大な許諾が、かるがるしい表現をとるのかわからなかった。

"All right, then. . . ." Opening his eyes wide—they were strong and clear despite his not having slept for days—he looked straight into his wife's eyes for the first time. "Tonight I will cut my stomach."

Reiko's eyes showed no sign of flinching.

Her round eyes showed a firmness of will as strong as the sound of a bell. Then she said:

"I was ready for this. Pray allow me to accompany you."

The lieutenant felt himself almost overwhelmed by the power of her gaze. The words tumbled out of him like the ravings of delirium, and he could not understand why so weighty a permission should assume so flippant a turn of phrase.

力【ちから】strength, power
圧する【あっする】[passive form in text] overwhelm
〜ような気がする【〜ようなきがする】feel as though
言葉【ことば】word, remark
譫言【うわごと】delirious nonsense
すらすらと freely, fluently
出る【でる】come out
こんな this kind of
重大な【じゅうだいな】momentous
許諾【きょだく】permission, approval
かるがるしい thoughtless, flippant
表現【ひょうげん】expression
とる adopt, take
わかる understand

35▶ 「よし。一緒に行こう。但し、俺の切腹を見届けてもらいたいんだ。いいな」

36▶ こう言いおわると、二人の心には、俄かに解き放たれたような油然たる喜びが湧いた。

37▶ 麗子は良人のこの信頼の大きさに胸を搏たれた。中尉としては、どんなことがあっても死に損ってはならない。そのためには見届けてくれる人がなくてはならぬ。それに妻を選んだというのが第一の信頼である。共に死ぬことを約束しながら、妻を先に殺さず、妻の死を、もう自分には確かめられない未来に置いたということは、第二のさらに大きな信頼である。もし中尉が疑り深い良人であったら、並の心中のように、妻を先に殺すことを選んだであろう。

35
よし right, good, okay then
一緒に 【いっしょに】 together
行く 【いく】 go
但し 【ただし】 but
俺 【おれ】 MASCULINE I
切腹 【せっぷく】 cutting one's stomach
見届ける 【みとどける】 watch to the end ⊛
いいな all right

36
言いおわる 【いいおわる】 finish speaking
二人 【ふたり】 the two of them, they
心 【こころ】 heart, mind
俄かに 【にわかに】 suddenly
解き放つ 【ときはなつ】 [passive form in text] set free
油然たる 【ゆうぜんたる】 freely, abundantly

喜び 【よろこび】 joy
湧く 【わく】 gush forth, spring forth

37
麗子 【れいこ】 Reiko
良人 【おっと】 husband ⊛
信頼 【しんらい】 trust, confidence ⊛
大きさ 【おおきさ】 magnitude
胸を搏つ 【むねをうつ】 [passive form in text] move
中尉 【ちゅうい】 lieutenant ⊛
〜としては as for, for his part
どんなことがあっても no matter what happens
死に損う 【しにそこなう】 fail to die
〜てはならない must not 〜
そのためには to that end
人 【ひと】 person
なくてはならぬ there had to be

"Right-ho, then. Let's do the deed together. But I want you to witness my suicide. All right?"

As he finished speaking, a flood of joy suddenly welled up in both their hearts as though a dam had broken.

Reiko was moved by the greatness of her husband's faith in her. The lieutenant, for his part, was determined not to fail to die. That was why there had to be someone to act as witness on his behalf. The fact that he had chosen his wife for the task was the first sign of his faith. And the second—and even greater—sign of that faith was that, while they had promised to die together, rather than kill his wife first, he had set his wife's death in the future where it could no longer be verified by him. Had the lieutenant been a suspicious husband, he would most likely have opted to kill his wife first, as in the ordinary run of suicide pacts.

妻 【つま】 wife ⊛
選ぶ 【えらぶ】 choose ⊛
〜というの the fact that 〜
第一 【だいいち】 the first
共に 【ともに】 together
死ぬ 【しぬ】 die
約束する 【やくそくする】 promise
先に 【さきに】 before ⊛
殺さず 【ころさず】 without killing
死 【し】 death
自分 【じぶん】 oneself, himself
確かめる 【たしかめる】 [potential form in text]
　　make sure of
未来 【みらい】 future
置く 【おく】 place, put
〜ということ the fact that 〜
第二 【だいに】 the second
さらに again, more

大きな 【おおきな】 big
もし if
疑り深い 【うたぐりぶかい】 doubting, distrustful
並の 【なみの】 standard, average, run-of-the-mill
心中 【しんじゅう】 love suicide
殺す 【ころす】 kill

38▶　　中尉は麗子が「お供をする」と言った言葉を、新婚の夜から、自分が麗子を導いて、この場に及んで、それを澱みなく発音させたという大きな教育の成果と感じた。これは中尉の自恃を慰め、彼は愛情が自発的に言わせた言葉だと思うほど、だらけた己惚れた良人ではなかった。

39▶　　喜びはあまり自然にお互いの胸に湧き上ったので、見交わした顔が自然に微笑した。麗子は新婚の夜が再び訪れたような気がした。

40▶　　目の前には苦痛も死もなく、自由な、ひろびろとした野がひろがるように思われた。

41▶　「お風呂が湧いております。お召しになりますか」

42▶　「ああ」

38

中尉【ちゅうい】lieutenant ⊛
麗子【れいこ】Reiko ⊛
お供をする【おともをする】HUMBLE accompany
言う【いう】say
言葉【ことば】word, remark ⊛
新婚【しんこん】marriage ⊛
夜【よる】night ⊛
自分【じぶん】oneself, himself
導く【みちびく】lead, guide
この場【このば】this place, time
及ぶ【およぶ】reach, extend to
澱みなく【よどみなく】without hesitating
発音する【はつおんする】[causative form in text] pronounce
大きな【おおきな】big, great
教育【きょういく】education

成果【せいか】result, fruit
感じる【かんじる】feel
自恃【じじ】self-reliance, self-assurance
慰める【なぐさめる】comfort
彼【かれ】he
愛情【あいじょう】love
自発的に【じはつてきに】spontaneously
言わせる【いわせる】cause to say
思う【おもう】think
〜ほど to the extent of
だらけた idle, lazy
己惚れた【うぬぼれた】vain, conceited
良人【おっと】husband

39

喜び【よろこび】joy
あまり too much
自然に【しぜんに】naturally ⊛
お互い【おたがい】each other

When Reiko said the words "allow me to accompany you," the lieutenant felt that her being able to speak them without hesitation was the splendid fruit of the education he had imparted to her from the first night of their marriage up until this moment. It bolstered his faith in himself: he was not so conceited a husband as to think it was affection for him that had prompted her to speak out so readily.

Such a natural abundance of joy welled up in their hearts that when they looked at one another their faces broke naturally into smiles. Reiko felt that the joy of their wedding night had returned to them.

It felt as though it was not agony and death, but an unobstructed, wide-open plain spreading itself out before her eyes.

"The bath is ready. Will you take one?"

"Yes."

胸 【むね】 chest, heart
湧き上る 【わきあがる】 well up
見交わす 【みかわす】 look at one another
顔 【かお】 face
微笑する 【びしょうする】 smile
再び 【ふたたび】 again
訪れる 【おとずれる】 come, visit
〜ような気がする 【〜ようなきがする】
  feel as though

40
目の前 【めのまえ】 before one's eyes
苦痛 【くつう】 pain, agony
死 【し】 death
自由な 【じゆうな】 free
ひろびろとした broad, wide
野 【の】 plain, field
ひろがる stretch out
思う 【おもう】 [spontaneous form in text] think

41
お風呂 【おふろ】 bath
湧く 【わく】 be ready (lit., "boil")
お召しになりますか 【おめしになりますか】 HONORIFIC will you take a bath?

42
ああ uh-huh

43▶　「お食事は？」

44▶　この言葉は実に平淡に家庭的に発せられ、中尉は危うく錯覚に陥ろうとした。

45▶　「食事は要らんだろう。酒の燗をしといてくれんか」

46▶　「はい」

47▶　麗子は立って良人の湯上りの丹前を出すときに、あけた抽斗へ良人の注意を惹いた。中尉は立って行って、箪笥の抽斗の中をのぞいた。整理された畳紙の上に一つ一つ形見の宛名が読まれた。こうして健気な覚悟を示された中尉は、悲しみが少しもなく、心は甘い情緒に充たされた。

43

お食事【おしょくじ】POLITE meal, dinner ✕

44

言葉【ことば】words
実に【じつに】really, truly
平淡に【へいたんに】simply, plainly
家庭的に【かていてきに】in a domestic manner
発する【はっする】[passive form in text] say
中尉【ちゅうい】lieutenant ✕
危うく【あやうく】dangerously
錯覚【さっかく】illusion
陥る【おちいる】[volitional form in text] lapse into
～（ろ）うとする be about to ~

45

食事【しょくじ】meal, dinner

要る【いる】need, want
酒の燗をする【さけのかんをする】heat up saké
～ておく and leave it that way (for a future purpose)
～てくれんか MASCULINE won't you … (as a favor) for me?

47

麗子【れいこ】Reiko
立つ【たつ】stand up ✕
良人【おっと】husband ✕
湯上り【ゆあがり】after the bath
丹前【たんぜん】large padded kimono
出す【だす】take out
あけた open
抽斗【ひきだし】drawer ✕
注意を惹く【ちゅういをひく】draw attention

"And dinner?"

The words were said in so straightforward and homey a manner that the lieutenant was in danger of yielding to the illusion.

"Don't think we'll be needing any dinner. Warm up some saké for me, will you?"

"As you wish."

When Reiko stood up to take out a large padded kimono for her husband to wear after his bath, she drew his attention to the open drawer. The lieutenant got to his feet to go over and look inside the chest. On the paper wrappings of the neatly arranged packages were the names and addresses of the keepsakes' recipients. He could read each one of them. His heart was filled with the sweetest emotions—no vestige of sadness—at this laudable display of resolve.

行く 【いく】 go
箪笥 【たんす】 chest of drawers
中 【なか】 inside
のぞく look inside, peek into
整理する 【せいりする】 [passive form in text] tidy up
畳紙 【たとう】 folding paper case
〜の上に 【〜のうえに】 on top of
一つ一つ 【ひとつひとつ】 each and every one
形見 【かたみ】 keepsake
宛名 【あてな】 name and address
読む 【よむ】 [passive form in text] read
健気な 【けなげな】 praiseworthy, manly
覚悟 【かくご】 resolve
示す 【しめす】 [passive form in text] show
悲しみ 【かなしみ】 sorrow

少しもなく 【すこしもなく】 not even a little
心 【こころ】 heart, emotions
甘い 【あまい】 sweet
情緒 【じょうしょ／じょうちょ】 emotion
充たす 【みたす】 [passive form in text] fill

若い妻の子供らしい買物を見せられた良人のように、中尉はいとしさのあまり、妻をうしろから抱いて首筋に接吻した。

48▶ 麗子は首筋に中尉の髭のこそばゆさを感じた。この感覚はただ現世的なものである以上に、麗子にとって現実そのものだったが、それが間もなく失われるという感じは、この上もなく新鮮だった。一瞬一瞬がいきいきと力を得、体の隅々までがあらたに目ざめる。麗子は足袋の爪先に力を沁み入らせて、背後からの良人の愛撫を受けた。

49▶ 「風呂へ入って、酒を呑んだら……いいか、二階に床をとっておいてくれ……」

50▶ 中尉は妻の耳もとでこう言った。麗子は黙ってうなずいた。

若い【わかい】young
妻【つま】wife ❀
子供らしい【こどもらしい】childlike
買物【かいもの】shopping
見せる【みせる】[passive form in text] to show
良人【おっと】husband ❀
中尉【ちゅうい】lieutenant ❀
いとしさ tenderness, affection
〜のあまり out of an excess of
うしろ behind
抱く【だく】embrace
首筋【くびすじ】nape of the neck ❀
接吻する【せっぷんする】kiss

48
麗子【れいこ】Reiko ❀
髭【ひげ】beard, stubble
こそばゆさ ticklishness
感じる【かんじる】feel

感覚【かんかく】sensation
ただ just, only
現世的な【げんせいてきな】of this life
もの thing, something
〜以上に【〜いじょうに】insofar as, since, to the extent that 〜
〜にとって as far as 〜 is concerned
現実【げんじつ】reality
〜そのもの the very thing, itself
間もなく【まもなく】soon
失う【うしなう】[passive form in text] lose
感じ【かんじ】feeling
この上もなく【このうえもなく】unsurpassably
新鮮な【しんせんな】fresh, new
一瞬一瞬【いっしゅんいっしゅん】each and every moment
いきいきと vividly, vigorously

As if he were a husband whose young wife had just paraded her childish purchases before him, the lieutenant embraced his wife from behind, planting a kiss on the back of her neck in an uncontrollable burst of tenderness.

Reiko felt the lieutenant's beard tickling her nape. This sensation was more than just a part of her present life; as far as Reiko was concerned, it was reality in its entirety, and the feeling that in a short while it would be lost was vivid beyond anything. Every single moment took on a vigorous life, and every fiber of her body awoke anew. Tensing her toes in her tabi, Reiko let her husband fondle her from behind.

"I'll have a bath, then a drink. . . . Oh, and lay out the futons upstairs, would you?"

The lieutenant whispered into his wife's ear. Reiko nodded silently.

力を得る【ちからをえる】gain strength

体【からだ】body

隅々まで【すみずみまで】to every nook and cranny

あらたに anew, over again

目ざめる【めざめる】wake up

足袋【たび】tabi sock

爪先【つまさき】tip of one's toe

力【ちから】strength, power

沁み入る【しみいる】[causative form in text] soak, steep

背後【はいご】back

愛撫【あいぶ】caress

受ける【うける】accept, receive

49

風呂へ入る【ふろへはいる】take a bath

酒【さけ】saké

呑む【のむ】drink

いいか all right? understand?

二階【にかい】second floor

床をとる【とこをとる】take a futon (from a futon closet) and lay it out on the floor

〜ておく and leave it that way (for a future purpose)

〜てくれ [imperative form] BLUNT, MASCULINE please

50

耳もとで【みみもとで】close to one's ear

言う【いう】say

黙る【だまる】keep quiet, say nothing

うなずく nod

51▶ 　中尉は荒々しく軍服を脱ぎ、風呂場へ入った。その遠い湯のはねかえる音をききながら、麗子は茶の間の火鉢の火加減を見、酒の燗の仕度に立った。

52▶ 　丹前と帯と下着を持って風呂場へゆき、湯の加減をきいた。ひろがる湯気の中に、中尉はあぐらをかいて髭を剃っており、その濡れた逞ましい背中の肉が、腕の動きにつれて機敏に動くのがおぼろに見えた。

53▶ 　ここには何ら特別の時間はなかった。麗子はいそがしく立ち働らき、即席の肴を作っていた。手も慄えず、ものごとはいつもよりきびきびと小気味よく運んだ。それでもときどき、胸の底をふしぎな鼓動が走る。

51

中尉【ちゅうい】lieutenant ❋

荒々しく【あらあらしく】roughly, wildly

軍服【ぐんぷく】military uniform

脱ぐ【ぬぐ】take off (clothes)

風呂場【ふろば】bathroom

入る【はいる】enter

遠い【とおい】distant

湯【ゆ】hot water

はねかえる bounce back up

音【おと】sound

きく hear

麗子【れいこ】Reiko ❋

茶の間【ちゃのま】living room

火鉢【ひばち】charcoal brazier

火加減【ひかげん】the state of the fire

酒の燗【さけのかん】warm saké

仕度【したく】preparations

立つ【たつ】start

52

丹前【たんぜん】large padded kimono

帯【おび】sash

下着【したぎ】underwear

持つ【もつ】carry

ゆく go

湯【ゆ】hot water

加減【かげん】degree

きく ask about, inquire about

ひろがる spread out, billow out

湯気【ゆげ】steam

〜の中に【〜のなかに】amidst

あぐらをかく sit cross-legged

髭【ひげ】beard

剃る【そる】shave

濡れる【ぬれる】get wet

The lieutenant tore off his uniform and went into the bathroom. To the faraway plash of the bathwater, Reiko checked the fire in the charcoal brazier in the parlor, then started to prepare the saké.

Carrying the padded kimono, sash, and underwear, she went to the bathroom and inquired about the water temperature. In the billowing steam, the lieutenant sat cross-legged, shaving, and she could vaguely make out the rippling of the wet skin of his muscular back whenever he moved his arm.

Nothing in the house hinted at the present unusual circumstances. Reiko went busily about her work, improvising some dishes to go with the saké. Her hands did not tremble, and her preparations proceeded more briskly and easily than ever. Nonetheless, at times an extraordinary throbbing would break out in the depths of her chest.

逞ましい 【たくましい】 strong, muscular
背中 【せなか】 back
肉 【にく】 flesh
腕 【うで】 arm
動き 【うごき】 movement
〜につれて together with
機敏に 【きびんに】 nimbly, briskly
動く 【うごく】 move
おぼろに vaguely, hazily
見える 【みえる】 be visible

53

何ら〜ない 【なんら〜ない】 no . . . whatsoever
特別の 【とくべつの】 special, extraordinary
時間 【じかん】 time
いそがしく busily
立ち働らく 【たちはたらく】 go about
one's work
即席の 【そくせきの】 improvised, extempore
肴 【さかな】 side dishes for saké
作る 【つくる】 make
手 【て】 hand
慄えず 【ふるえず】 without trembling
ものごと things
いつもより more than usual
きびきびと briskly, energetically
小気味よく 【こきみよく】 comfortably
運ぶ 【はこぶ】 proceed, go
ときどき at times, occasionally
胸 【むね】 chest, heart
底 【そこ】 bottom
ふしぎな extraordinary
鼓動 【こどう】 throbbing, pulsating
走る 【はしる】 run

遠い稲妻のように、それがちらりと強烈に走って消える。そのほかは何一つふだんと変りがない。

54 ▶ 　風呂場の中尉は髭を剃りながら、一度温められた体は、あの遣場のない苦悩の疲労がすっかり癒やされ、死を前にしながら、たのしい期待に充たされているのを感じた。妻の立ち働らく音がほのかにきこえる。すると二日の間忘れていた健康な欲望が頭をもたげた。

55 ▶ 　二人が死を決めたときのあの喜びに、いささかも不純なもののないことに中尉は自信があった。あのとき二人は、もちろんそれとはっきり意識はしていないが、ふたたび余人の知らぬ二人の正当な快楽が、大義と神威に、一分の隙もない完全な道徳に守られたのを感じたのである。

遠い【とおい】distant
稲妻【いなずま】lightning
ちらりと for an instant
強烈に【きょうれつに】strongly
走る【はしる】run
消える【きえる】vanish
そのほか otherwise
何一つ〜ない【なにひとつ〜ない】nothing
ふだん usual
変り【かわり】difference

54
風呂場【ふろば】bathroom
中尉【ちゅうい】lieutenant ✳
髭【ひげ】beard
剃る【そる】shave
一度【いちど】once
温める【あたためる】[potential form in text] warm up

体【からだ】body
遣場のない【やりばのない】with no outlet
苦悩【くのう】mental torment
疲労【ひろう】exhaustion
すっかり completely
癒やす【いやす】[passive form in text] heal
死【し】death
〜を前にする【〜をまえにする】have in prospect
たのしい enjoyable
期待【きたい】expectation
充たす【みたす】[passive form in text] fill
感じる【かんじる】feel
妻【つま】wife
立ち働らく【たちはたらく】go about one's work
音【おと】sound

Like far-off lightning, it made a brief, intense surge, then vanished. That aside, nothing was different from normal.

As the lieutenant shaved in the bathroom, he warmed up. The exhaustion brought on by his bottled-up anxieties was soothed away and his body overflowed with happy expectations, despite the imminence of death. He could hear the faint sounds of his wife bustling about. The healthy, natural desire he had not had time to think about for the last two days reared its head.

The lieutenant was confident that there was not the slightest impurity in the joy they had felt when they resolved to die. Although the two of them were not, of course, completely conscious of it at the time, they both felt that the private pleasures to which they were entitled were once again under the aegis of Noble Duty and Divine Power and flawless and immaculate Morality.

ほのかに faintly
きこえる be audible
すると whereupon
二日【ふつか】two days
〜の間【〜のあいだ】during
忘れる【わすれる】forget
健康な【けんこうな】healthy
欲望【よくぼう】desire
頭をもたげる【あたまをもたげる】rear one's head

55

二人【ふたり】the two of them, they ⊛
死【し】death
決める【きめる】decide on
喜び【よろこび】joy
いささかも〜ない not the slightest bit
不純な【ふじゅんな】impure
自信【じしん】self-confidence

あのとき at that time
もちろん of course
はっきり clearly
意識する【いしきする】be conscious of
ふたたび again
余人【よにん／よじん】other people
知らぬ【しらぬ】not know
正当な【せいとうな】just, right
快楽【かいらく】pleasure
大義【たいぎ】great duty, noble cause
神威【しんい】power of the gods
一分の隙もない【いちぶのすきもない】without a chink, flawless
完全な【かんぜんな】perfect
道徳【どうとく】morality
守る【まもる】[passive form in text] protect
感じる【かんじる】feel

二人が目を見交わして、お互いの目のなかに正当な死を見
出したとき、ふたたび彼らは何者も破ることのできない鉄
壁に包まれ、他人の一指も触れることのできない美と正義
に鎧われたのを感じたのである。中尉はだから、自分の肉
の欲望と憂国の至情のあいだに、何らの矛盾や撞着を見な
いばかりか、むしろそれを一つのものと考えることさえで
きた。

56▶　　暗いひびわれた、湯気に曇りがちな壁鏡の中に、中尉は
顔をさし出して丹念に髭を剃った。これがそのまま死顔に
なる。見苦しい剃り残しをしてはならない。剃られた顔は
ふたたび若々しく輝やき、暗い鏡を明るませるほどになっ
た。この晴れやかな健康な顔と死との結びつきには、云っ
てみれば或る瀟洒なものがあった。

二人【ふたり】the two of them, they
目を見交わす【めをみかわす】look at one
　another
お互い【おたがい】each other
目【め】eyes
正当な【せいとうな】just, right
死【し】death ❀
見出す【みいだす】find, discover
ふたたび again
彼ら【かれら】they
何者も～ない【なにものも～ない】
　nobody
破る【やぶる】destroy
鉄壁【てっぺき】iron wall
包む【つつむ】[passive form in text] envelop
他人【たにん】other people, strangers
一指【いっし】one finger
触れる【ふれる】touch

美【び】beauty
正義【せいぎ】justice, righteousness
鎧う【よろう】[passive form in text] wear
　armor
感じる【かんじる】feel
中尉【ちゅうい】lieutenant ❀
自分【じぶん】oneself, himself
肉【にく】flesh, body
欲望【よくぼう】desire
憂国【ゆうこく】patriotism
至情【しじょう】true feelings, sincerity
～のあいだに between
何ら～ない【なんら～ない】no . . . what-
　soever
矛盾【むじゅん】contradiction
撞着【どうちゃく】conflict
見る【みる】see
～ばかりか not only . . .

When they looked at one other and discovered righteous death in each other's eyes, they both felt they were once again surrounded by a wall of steel that nobody could pierce, girt in an armor of Beauty and Righteousness upon which no stranger could lay so much as a finger. That was why, as far as the lieutenant was concerned, he not only saw no incompatibility or conflict between the yearnings of his flesh and the sincerity of his patriotism, but was even able to think of them as one and the same thing.

Thrusting his face toward the dark, cracked and steamed-up wall mirror, the lieutenant shaved with care. This would be his face in death. He could not leave any unsightly patches of stubble. His shaven face shone once again with youth, illuminating the dark mirror. Perhaps there was even something chic about the link between this gleaming, healthy face and death.

むしろ rather, if anything
一つのもの 【ひとつのもの】 the same thing
考える 【かんがえる】 think
〜さえ even

暗い 【くらい】 dark ❈
ひびわれた cracked
湯気 【ゆげ】 steam
曇りがちな 【くもりがちな】 tends to fog up
壁鏡 【かべかがみ】 wall mirror
〜の中に 【〜のなかに】 inside
顔 【かお】 face ❈
さし出す 【さしだす】 push forward
丹念に 【たんねんに】 carefully
髭 【ひげ】 beard
剃る 【そる】 shave ❈
そのまま in that state

死顔 【しにがお】 face in death
見苦しい 【みぐるしい】 ugly, unsightly
剃り残し 【そりのこし】 unshaven patch
〜てはならない must not 〜
ふたたび again
若々しく 【わかわかしく】 youthfully
輝やく 【かがやく】 gleam, shine
鏡 【かがみ】 mirror
明るむ 【あかるむ】 [causative form in text] become bright
〜ほど to the extent that 〜
晴れやかな 【はれやかな】 bright, radiant
健康な 【けんこうな】 healthy
結びつき 【むすびつき】 union, linkage
云ってみれば 【いってみれば】 if you will, if I do say so myself
或る 【ある】 a kind of, a certain
瀟洒な 【しょうしゃな】 elegant, refined

57 ▶ 　　これがそのまま死顔になる！　もうその顔は正確には半ば中尉の所有を離れて、死んだ軍人の記念碑上の顔になっていた。彼はためしに目をつぶってみた。すべては闇に包まれ、もう彼はものを見る人間ではなくなっていた。

58 ▶ 　　風呂から上った中尉は、つやややかな頬に青い剃り跡を光らせて、よく熾った火鉢のかたわらにあぐらをかいた。忙しいあいだに麗子が手早く顔を直したのを中尉は知った。頬は花やぎ、唇は潤いをまし、悲しみの影もなかった。若い妻のこんな烈しい性格のしるしを見て、彼は本当に選ぶべき妻を選んだと感じた。

57
そのまま as it is, unchanged
死顔【しにがお】face in death
顔【かお】face ⊛
正確には【せいかくには】precisely speaking, in fact
半ば【なかば】half
中尉【ちゅうい】lieutenant ⊛
所有【しょゆう】possession
離れる【はなれる】part from
死んだ【しんだ】dead
軍人【ぐんじん】soldier
記念碑【きねんひ】tombstone
〜上【〜じょう】on
彼【かれ】he ⊛
ためしに as a test
目をつぶる【めをつぶる】shut one's eyes
〜てみる and see what it is like

すべて everything
闇【やみ】darkness
包む【つつむ】[passive form in text] envelop
もの thing
見る【みる】see ⊛
人間【にんげん】human being
58
風呂【ふろ】bath
上る【あがる】get out of (a bath)
つややかな lustrous, shiny
頬【ほお】cheek ⊛
青い【あおい】blue
剃り跡【そりあと】shaved-down stubble
光らせる【ひからせる】cause to shine
よく well
熾る【おこる】start to burn, catch fire
火鉢【ひばち】charcoal brazier
〜のかたわらに next to

This—just as it was now—would be his face in death! In fact, the face had already half passed from the lieutenant's possession and become the carved likeness on the memorial stone of a dead soldier. As an experiment, he tried closing his eyes. Everything was enveloped in darkness; he was no longer a being who saw the material world.

The lieutenant got out of the bath and sat down cross-legged by the well-kindled brazier, his healthy cheeks glowing blue after shaving. He noticed that Reiko, despite being busy, had deftly touched up her face. With bright cheeks and moistened lips, there was no shadow of sadness about her. As he saw these proofs of his young wife's strong character, he felt that truly he had chosen the wife that he ought to have chosen.

あぐらをかく sit cross-legged
忙しい【いそがしい】busy
〜あいだに while
麗子【れいこ】Reiko
手早く【てばやく】nimbly
顔を直す【かおをなおす】fix one's face
知る【しる】know, realize
花やぐ【はなやぐ】be cheerful, be bright
唇【くちびる】lip
潤い【うるおい】moisture
ます increase
悲しみ【かなしみ】sorrow
影【かげ】shadow
若い【わかい】young
妻【つま】wife ⊛
こんな this kind of
烈しい【はげしい】intense, fierce
性格【せいかく】character

しるし sign, evidence
本当に【ほんとうに】really, truly
選ぶ【えらぶ】choose ⊛
〜べき should, ought to
感じる【かんじる】feel

59▶ 　中尉は杯を干すと、それをすぐ麗子に与えた。一度も酒を呑んだことのない麗子が、素直に杯をうけて、おそるおそる口をつけた。

60▶「ここへ来い」

61▶ 　と中尉は言った。麗子は良人のかたわらへ行って、斜めに抱かれた。その胸ははげしく波打ち、悲しみの情緒と喜悦とが、強い酒をまぜたようになった。中尉は妻の顔を眺め下ろした。これが自分がこの世で見る最後の人の顔、最後の女の顔である。旅人が二度と来ない土地の美しい風光にそそぐ旅立ちの眼差で、中尉は仔細に妻の顔を点検した。いくら見ても見倦かぬ美しい顔は、整っていながら冷たさがなく、唇はやわらかい力でほのかに閉ざされていた。

59

中尉【ちゅうい】lieutenant ✺
杯【さかずき】cup ✺
干す【ほす】drink up, drain
すぐ immediately, quickly
麗子【れいこ】Reiko ✺
与える【あたえる】give, hand over
一度も〜ない【いちども〜ない】not even once, never
酒【さけ】saké ✺
呑む【のむ】drink
素直に【すなおに】meekly, obediently
うける take, receive
おそるおそる timidly
口をつける【くちをつける】put one's mouth to, begin consuming

60

来い【こい】[imperative form] BLUNT, MASCULINE come ✺

61

言う【いう】say
良人【おっと】husband
かたわら side
行く【いく】go
斜めに【ななめに】diagonally, sideways
抱く【だく】[passive form in text] embrace
胸【むね】chest, heart
はげしく【はげしく】intensely, fiercely
波打つ【なみうつ】beat, surge
悲しみ【かなしみ】sorrow
情緒【じょうしょ／じょうちょ】emotion
喜悦【きえつ】joy
強い【つよい】strong
まぜる mix

As soon as the lieutenant had emptied his cup, he offered it to Reiko. Though she had never once drunk saké before, Reiko obediently took the cup and timidly put her lips to it.

"Come over to me."

The lieutenant said. Reiko moved to the lieutenant's side and was embraced across his lap. Her chest heaved as feelings of sadness and of joy commingled like strong liquors. The lieutenant looked down at his wife's face. This was the last human face—the last woman's face—he would see in this world. The lieutenant scrutinized its every detail, his gaze like that of a parting traveler contemplating a beautiful landscape to which he will never return. It was a beautiful face that he never tired of looking at, no matter how much he looked; while well formed, it was not cold, and the lips were delicately pressed together with a gentle strength.

～ようになる be as though
妻【つま】wife ❀
顔【かお】face ❀
眺め下ろす【ながめおろす】gaze down on
自分【じぶん】oneself, himself
この世【よ】this world, this life
見る【みる】see ❀
最後の【さいごの】final ❀
人【ひと】person
女【おんな】woman
旅人【たびびと】traveler
二度と～ない【にどと～ない】never again
来る【くる】come
土地【とち】piece of land
美しい【うつくしい】beautiful ❀
風光【ふうこう】beautiful natural scenery
そそぐ pour
旅立ち【たびだち】setting out on a journey

眼差【まなざし】gaze, look
仔細に【しさいに】minutely
点検する【てんけんする】scrutinize
いくら～ても no matter how much
見倦かぬ【みあかぬ】not tire of looking at
整う【ととのう】be regular, be perfectly
    formed
冷たさ【つめたさ】coldness
唇【くちびる】lip
やわらかい soft
力【ちから】strength, power
ほのかに faintly, slightly
閉ざす【とざす】[passive form in text] shut,
    close

中尉は思わずその唇に接吻した。やがて気がつくと、顔はすこしも歔欷の醜さに歪んではいないのに、閉ざされた目の長い睫のかげから、涙の滴が次々と溢れ出て眼尻から光って流れた。

62▶　やがて中尉が二階の寝室へ上ろう促すと、妻は風呂に入ってから行くと言った。そこで中尉は一人で二階へ行き、瓦斯ストーヴに温められた寝室に入って、蒲団の上に大の字に寝ころんだ。こうして妻の来るのを待っている時間まで、何一ついつもと渝らなかった。

63▶　彼は頭の下に両手を組み、スタンドの光の届かぬおぼろげに暗い天井の板を眺めた。

中尉【ちゅうい】lieutenant ❀
思わず【おもわず】without thinking
唇【くちびる】lip
接吻する【せっぷんする】kiss
やがて presently, soon ❀
気がつく【きがつく】realize something
顔【かお】face
すこしも～ない not the slightest bit
歔欷【きょき】sobbing, weeping
醜さ【みにくさ】ugliness
歪む【ゆがむ】distort, deform
～のに despite the fact that ~
閉ざす【とざす】[passive form in text] close, shut
目【め】eye
長い【ながい】long
睫【まつげ】eyelash
～のかげから from behind

涙【なみだ】tears
滴【しずく】drop
次々【つぎつぎ】one after another
溢れ出る【あふれでる】well up
眼尻【めじり】corner of the eye
光る【ひかる】shine
流れる【ながれる】flow, stream

62

二階【にかい】second floor ❀
寝室【しんしつ】bedroom ❀
上る【あがる】[volitional form in text] go up
～（ろ）うと let's ~
促す【うながす】urge, prompt
妻【つま】wife ❀
風呂に入る【ふろにはいる】take a bath
行く【いく】go ❀
言う【いう】say
一人で【ひとりで】alone

On an impulse, the lieutenant kissed those lips. Presently he became aware that although the face had none of the hideous distortion that accompanies sobbing, teardrops were welling up from beneath the long lashes of her closed eyes and sliding in a glistening trail down from the corners of her eyes.

When in due course the lieutenant proposed going up to the second-floor bedroom, his wife replied that she would come after taking a bath. The lieutenant therefore went up to the second floor by himself, and entering the bedroom that was warmed by a gas stove, flung himself down on the futon with his arms and legs splayed out. Even down to the time he spent waiting for his wife to join him, nothing was different from any other day.

Interlacing his fingers behind his head, he gazed up at the ceiling boards, dim and dark beyond the range of the light from the floor lamp.

瓦斯ストーヴ 【ガスストーヴ】 gas stove
温ためる 【あたためる】 [passive form in text] warm up
入る 【はいる】 enter, go into
蒲団 【ふとん】 futon, bedding
〜の上に 【〜のうえに】 on top of
大の字に 【だいのじに】 in the shape of 大 (i.e., legs and arms flung out)
寝ころぶ 【ねころぶ】 throw oneself down
来る 【くる】 come
待つ 【まつ】 wait for
時間 【じかん】 time
何一つ〜ない 【なにひとつ〜ない】 not a single thing
いつも usual
渝る 【かわる】 be different

63

彼 【かれ】 he

頭 【あたま】 head
〜の下に 【〜のしたに】 beneath
両手 【りょうて】 both hands
組む 【くむ】 link, join
スタンド floor lamp
光 【ひかり】 light
届かぬ 【とどかぬ】 not reach
おぼろげに dimly
暗い 【くらい】 dark
天井 【てんじょう】 ceiling
板 【いた】 board, plank
眺める 【ながめる】 gaze at

彼が今待っているのは死なのか、狂おしい感覚の喜びなのか、そこのところが重複して、あたかも肉の欲望が死に向っているようにも感じられる。いずれにしろ、中尉はこれほどまでに渾身の自由を味わったことはなかった。

64 ▶ 　窓の外に自動車の音がする。道の片側に残る雪を蹴立てるタイヤのきしみがきこえる。近くの塀にクラクションが反響する。……そういう音をきいていると、あいかわらず忙しく往来している社会の海の中に、ここだけは孤島のように屹立して感じられる。自分が憂える国は、この家のまわりに大きく雑然とひろがっている。自分はそのために身を捧げるのである。しかし自分が身を滅ぼしてまで諫めようとするその巨大な国は、果たしてこの死に一顧を与えてくれるかどうかわからない。

彼【かれ】he
今【いま】now
待つ【まつ】wait
死【し】death ⊛
〜なのか〜なのか is it . . . or . . . ?
狂おしい【くるおしい】crazy
感覚【かんかく】sensation
喜び【よろこび】joy
そこのところ those two things
重複する【じゅうふくする】overlap
あたかも just as
肉【にく】flesh, sensual things
欲望【よくぼう】desires
〜に向う【〜にむかう】head for
感じる【かんじる】[potential form in text]
　feel ⊛
いずれにしろ either way
中尉【ちゅうい】lieutenant

これほどまでに to this extent
渾身【こんしん】whole body
自由【じゆう】free
味わう【あじわう】taste, savor

64

窓【まど】window
〜の外【〜のそと】outside
自動車【じどうしゃ】automobile
音がする【おとがする】make noise
道【みち】road, street
片側【かたがわ】one side
残る【のこる】be left, remain
雪【ゆき】snow
蹴立てる【けたてる】kick up
タイヤ tire
きしみ squeak, squeal
きこえる be audible
近くの【ちかくの】nearby

Was he waiting now for death, or for frenzied pleasure of the senses? The two overlapped, and it felt as though his physical desires were headed straight for death. Either way, the lieutenant had never before enjoyed such an absolute sense of freedom.

There was the sound of a car outside the window. He heard the squeal of the tires churning up the snow that still lay on one side of the road. The car's horn echoed off the nearby walls. . . . Listening to these noises, he felt as though this house was like a lone island protruding from the ocean of society that was flowing hither and thither, just as busily as ever. The country about which he was so concerned sprawled out messily far away on every side of the house. He was going to give his life for it. But although he was prepared to annihilate himself to express his disapproval of this vast country, he had no idea whether it would even deign to notice to his death.

塀 【へい】 wall, fence
クラクション car horn
反響する 【はんきょうする】 echo
音 【おと】 sound, noise
きく listen
あいかわらず as usual
忙しく 【いそがしく】 busily
往来する 【おうらいする】 come and go
社会 【しゃかい】 society
海 【うみ】 sea
〜の中に 【〜のなかに】 inside
孤島 【ことう】 solitary island
屹立する 【きつりつする】 rise up
自分 【じぶん】 oneself, himself ✽
憂える 【うれえる】 feel anxious about
国 【くに】 country ✽
家 【いえ】 house
〜のまわりに around

大きく 【おおきく】 on a large scale
雑然と 【ざつぜんと】 higgledy-piggledy
ひろがる spread out, extend
そのために for it
身を捧げる 【みをささげる】 sacrifice oneself
しかし however
身を滅ぼす 【みをほろぼす】 destroy oneself
諫める 【いさめる】 [volitional form in text] expostulate, admonish
〜（よ）うとする be about to 〜
巨大な 【きょだいな】 huge
果たして 【はたして】 even (used to emphasize a doubt)
一顧 【いっこ】 notice, consideration
与える 【あたえる】 give
わかる know

それでいいのである。ここは華々しくない戦場、誰にも勲しを示すことのできぬ戦場であり、魂の最前線だった。

65▶ 　麗子が階段を上ってくる足音がする。古い家の急な階段はよくきしんだ。このきしみは懐しく、何度となく中尉は寝床に待っていて、この甘美なきしみを聴いたのである。二度とこれを聴くことがないと思うと、彼は耳をそこに集中して、貴重な時間の一瞬一瞬を、その柔らかい蹠が立てるきしみで隈なく充たそうと試みた。そうして時間は燦めきを放ち、宝石のようになった。

華々しい【はなばなしい】splendid, glorious
戦場【せんじょう】battleground ✿
誰にも〜ない【だれにも〜ない】nobody
勲し【いさおし】meritorious deeds
示す【しめす】show
できぬ＝できない
魂【たましい】soul
最前線【さいぜんせん】front line

65
麗子【れいこ】Reiko
階段【かいだん】stairs ✿
上る【あがる】go up
〜てくる indicates movement toward the narrator
足音【あしおと】footstep
古い【ふるい】old
家【いえ】house

急な【きゅうな】steep
きしむ squeak, creak
きしみ creaking sound ✿
懐しい【なつかしい】familiar, nostalgic
何度となく【なんどとなく】on many occasions
中尉【ちゅうい】lieutenant
寝床【ねどこ】bedroom
待つ【まつ】wait
甘美な【かんびな】sweet, lovely
聴く【きく】hear, listen to ✿
二度と〜ない【にどと〜ない】never again
思う【おもう】think, consider
彼【かれ】he
耳【みみ】ear
集中する【しゅうちゅうする】focus
貴重な【きちょうな】precious
時間【じかん】time ✿

That was as it should be. This was a battlefield without glory, a battlefield where no one could display heroic deeds. It was the front line of the soul.

There came the sound of Reiko's footsteps ascending the stairs. The steep staircase of the old house creaked a great deal. The creaking reminded the lieutenant of the good old days—countless times while waiting in bed he had heard that same delicious creaking sound. When he realized he would never hear it again, he focused his ears in an effort to fill every fragment of every instant of his precious time with the creaks that the soft soles of her feet inspired. Time itself came to resemble a glimmering and sparkling jewel.

一瞬一瞬【いっしゅんいっしゅん】each and every moment
柔らかい【やわらかい】soft
蹠【あしのうら】sole of the foot
立てる【たてる】make (a noise)
隈なく【くまなく】throughout, in every nook and cranny
充たす【みたす】[volitional form in text] fill
〜(そ)うと to〜
試みる【こころみる】try
燦めき【きらめき】glitter, sparkle
放つ【はなつ】emit
宝石【ほうせき】jewel
〜のようになる come to be like

66 ▶ 　麗子は浴衣に名古屋帯を締めていたが、その帯の紅いは薄闇のなかに黒ずんで、中尉がそれに手をかけると、麗子の手の援ける力につれて、帯はゆるめきながら走って畳に落ちた。まだ着ている浴衣のまま、中尉は妻の両脇に手を入れて抱こうとしたが、八ツ口の腋の温かい肌に指が挟まれたとき、中尉はその指先の感触に、全身が燃えるような心地がした。

67 ▶ 　二人はストーヴの火明りの前で、いつのまにか自然に裸かになった。

68 ▶ 　口には出さなかったけれど、心も体も、さわぐ胸も、これが最後の営みだという思いに湧き立っていた。その「最後の営み」という文字は、見えない墨で二人の全身に隈なく書き込まれているようであった。

66

麗子【れいこ】Reiko ⊛
浴衣【ゆかた】light cotton kimono ⊛
名古屋帯【なごやおび】Nagoya sash
締める【しめる】wear (around the waist)
帯【おび】sash ⊛
紅い【くれない】red, crimson
薄闇【うすやみ】half-light, near darkness
黒ずむ【くろずむ】darken
中尉【ちゅうい】lieutenant ⊛
手をかける【てをかける】touch, put one's hand to
手【て】hand ⊛
援ける【たすける】help
力【ちから】strength, power
〜につれて together with
ゆるめく quiver, flutter
走る【はしる】run

畳【たたみ】tatami mat
落ちる【おちる】fall
着る【きる】wear
〜のまま as is, unchanged
妻【つま】wife
両脇【りょうわき】both underarms
入れる【いれる】insert
抱く【だく】[volitional form in text] embrace
〜（こ）うとする be about to 〜
八ツ口【やつくち】opening in the under-arms of a *yukata*
腋【わき】armpits
温かい【あたたかい】warm
肌【はだ】skin
指【ゆび】finger
挟む【はさむ】[passive form in text] insert, slip (something) in
指先【ゆびさき】fingertip

Reiko had done up her cotton *yukata* with a Nagoya sash. When the lieutenant put his hand to the sash, its crimson color black in the half-darkness, Reiko's hand joined in to help, and the sash, unraveling, slid down to the tatami. Thrusting his hands through the sleeve vents, the lieutenant made as if to embrace her while still in her *yukata*; but the sensation in his fingertips when his fingers were caught in the warmth of her underarms made him feel that his whole body was on fire.

Effortlessly and almost before they knew it, the two of them were naked before the fiery glow of the stove.

Although they did not verbalize it, their hearts, their bodies and their pounding chests were seething at the thought that this would be their final act of love. It was as if the characters for "The Final Act" had been written over every inch of their bodies in invisible ink.

感触 【かんしょく】 touch, feel
全身 【ぜんしん】 whole body ⊗
燃える 【もえる】 burn
～ような心地がする 【～ようなここちがする】 feel as though, have the sensation that ~

67
二人 【ふたり】 the two of them, they ⊗
ストーヴ stove
火明り 【ひあかり】 firelight
～の前で 【～のまえで】 before, in front of
いつのまにか before one knew it
自然に 【しぜんに】 naturally
裸かになる 【はだかになる】 get naked

68
口に出す 【くちにだす】 say, utter
心 【こころ】 heart, mind
体 【からだ】 body

さわぐ be in turmoil
胸 【むね】 chest, heart
最後の 【さいごの】 final ⊗
営み 【いとなみ】 act ⊗
思い 【おもい】 thought
湧き立つ 【わきたつ】 boil, seethe
文字 【もじ】 character
見える 【みえる】 be visible
墨 【すみ】 India ink
隈なく 【くまなく】 all over
書き込む 【かきこむ】 [passive form in text] write in

69▶ 　中尉は烈しく若い妻を掻き抱いて接吻した。二人の舌は相手のなめらかな口の中の隅々までたしかめ合い、まだどこにも兆していない死苦が、感覚を灼けた鉄のように真赤に鍛えてくれるのを感じた。まだ感じられない死苦、この遠い死苦は、彼らの快感を精錬したのである。

70▶ 「お前の体を見るのもこれが最後だ。よく見せてくれ」

71▶ 　と中尉は言った。そしてスタンドの笠を向うへ傾け、横たわった麗子の体へ明りが棚引くようにしつらえた。

72▶ 　麗子は目を閉じて横たわっていた。低い光りが、この厳そかな白い肉の起伏をよく見せた。中尉はいささか利己的な気持から、この美しい肉体の崩壊の有様を見ないですむ倖せを喜んだ。

69

中尉【ちゅうい】lieutenant ⊛
烈しく【はげしく】intensely, fiercely
若い【わかい】young
妻【つま】wife
掻き抱く【かきだく】grab
接吻する【せっぷんする】kiss
二人【ふたり】the two of them, they
舌【した】tongue
相手【あいて】partner
なめらかな smooth
口【くち】mouth
中【なか】inside
隅々まで【すみずみまで】to every nook and cranny
たしかめ合う【たしかめあう】check one another, mutually explore and verify
どこにも〜ない nowhere

兆す【きざす】show signs of
死苦【しく】pain of death ⊛
感覚【かんかく】sensation
灼ける【やける】make red hot
鉄【てつ】iron, steel
真赤【まっか／まあか】deep red
鍛える【きたえる】forge, temper
感じる【かんじる】feel ⊛ (NOTE: Next usage is in the potential form.)
遠い【とおい】distant
彼ら【かれら】they
快感【かいかん】pleasure
精錬する【せいれんする】refine, smelt

70

お前【おまえ】MASCULINE, FAMILIAR you
体【からだ】body ⊛
見る【みる】see ⊛
最後【さいご】last time

The lieutenant drew his young wife roughly to him, and kissed her. Their tongues delved into the smooth depths of each other's mouths, and they felt that the agonies of death, of which there was still no sign, had tempered their senses to the red heat of molten steel. It was these still-unfelt agonies of death, these distant agonies of death, that heightened their pleasure.

"This is the last time I'll get to see your body. Give me a good look."

The lieutenant said. He tilted the shade of the lamp to one side so that Reiko's supine body was bathed in light.

Reiko was lying down with her eyes shut. The low light brought out the undulations of her stern, pale flesh. With a touch of self-centeredness, the lieutenant rejoiced that he would never have to see this beautiful body in a state of ruin.

よく well, properly ⊛
見せる【みせる】show ⊛
〜てくれ [imperative form] BLUNT, MASCULINE please

71

言う【いう】say
スタンド floor lamp
笠【かさ】lampshade
向う【むこう】other side
傾ける【かたむける】tip, incline
横たわる【よこたわる】lie down ⊛
麗子【れいこ】Reiko ⊛
明り【あかり】light
棚引く【たなびく】hang over (like mist)
しつらえる beautifully decorate

72

目を閉じる【めをとじる】shut one's eyes
低い【ひくい】low

光り【ひかり】light
厳そかな【おごそかな】stern, severe
白い【しろい】white
肉【にく】flesh
起伏【きふく】ups and downs
いささか slightly
利己的な【りこてきな】selfish, egoistic
気持【きもち】feeling
美しい【うつくしい】beautiful
肉体【にくたい】body
崩壊【ほうかい】collapse, destruction
有様【ありさま】sight, spectacle
見る【みる】see
〜ないですむ get by without doing
倖せ【しあわせ】happiness
喜ぶ【よろこぶ】rejoice in

73 ▶　　中尉は忘れがたい風景をゆっくりと心に刻んだ。片手で髪を弄びながら、片手でしずかに美しい顔を撫で、目の赴くところに一つ一つ接吻した。富士額のしずかな冷たい額から、ほのかな眉の下に長い睫に守られて閉じている目、形のよい鼻のたたずまい、厚みの程のよい端正な唇のあいだからかすかにのぞいている歯のきらめき、やわらかな頬と怜悧な小さい顎、……これらが実に晴れやかな死顔を思わせ、中尉はやがて麗子が自ら刺すだろう白い咽喉元を、何度も強く吸ってほの赤くしてしまった。

73

中尉【ちゅうい】lieutenant ⊛

忘れがたい【わすれがたい】hard to forget

風景【ふうけい】scene

ゆっくりと leisurely

心【こころ】heart, mind

刻む【きざむ】engrave, etch

片手【かたて】one hand ⊛

髪【かみ】hair

弄ぶ【もてあそぶ】play with

しずかに gently ⊛

美しい【うつくしい】beautiful

顔【かお】face

撫でる【なでる】caress

目【め】eye ⊛

赴く【おもむく】proceed, tend

ところ place

一つ一つ【ひとつひとつ】each and every one

接吻する【せっぷんする】kiss

富士額【ふじびたい】forehead with a hair-line that tapers down into a peak thus resembling the upside-down silhouette of Mt. Fuji; widow's peak

しずかな gentle, calm

冷たい【つめたい】cold

額【ひたい】forehead

ほのかな faint, indistinct

眉【まゆ】eyebrows

〜の下に【〜のしたに】beneath

長い【ながい】long

睫【まつげ】eyelash

守る【まもる】[passive form in text] protect

閉じる【とじる】close, shut

形のよい【かたちのよい】shapely

鼻【はな】nose

Slowly the lieutenant etched the unforgettable scene onto his heart. Toying with her hair with one hand and softly caressing her exquisite face with the other, he planted kisses wherever his eye roamed. The cool, quiet forehead with its elegant outline; the closed eyes, guarded by long eyelashes beneath delicate brows; the shape of the chiseled nose; the glint of the teeth, barely visible between the delectably plump and well-formed lips; the soft cheeks; the clever little chin . . . they conjured up the radiance of her face as it would look in death, and the lieutenant planted countless fierce kisses on the white throat that Reiko was soon to stab, until it flushed a faint red.

たたずまい form, shape
厚み 【あつみ】 fullness
程のよい 【ほどのよい】 suitable
端正な 【たんせいな】 neat
唇 【くちびる】 lip
〜のあいだから from between
かすかに dimly, faintly
のぞく peep
歯 【は】 tooth
きらめき glitter, sparkle
やわらかな soft
頬 【ほお】 cheek
怜悧な 【れいりな】 clever-looking
小さい 【ちいさい】 small
顎 【あご】 chin
これら these
実に 【じつに】 really, truly
晴れやかな 【はれやかな】 clear

死顔 【しにがお】 face in death
思う 【おもう】 [causative form in text] think of, imagine
やがて presently, shortly
麗子 【れいこ】 Reiko
自ら 【みずから】 on one's own initiative
刺す 【さす】 stab
白い 【しろい】 white
咽喉元 【のどもと】 base of the throat
何度も 【なんども】 repeatedly
強く 【つよく】 strongly
吸う 【すう】 suck
ほの赤い 【ほのあかい】 faintly red
〜てしまう thoroughly, completely

唇に戻って、唇を軽く圧し、自分の唇をその唇の上に軽い舟のたゆたいのように揺れ動かした。目を閉じると、世界が揺籃のようになった。

74　中尉の目の見るとおりを、唇が忠実になぞって行った。その高々と息づく乳房は、山桜の花の蕾のような乳首を持ち、中尉の唇に含まれて固くなった。胸の両脇からなだらかに流れ落ちる腕の美しさ、それが帯びている丸みがそのままに手首のほうへ細まってゆく巧緻なすがた、そしてその先には、かつて結婚式の日に扇を握っていた繊細な指があった。指の一本一本は中尉の唇の前で、羞らうようにそれぞれの指のかげに隠れた。

唇【くちびる】lip ❀
戻る【もどる】return
軽く【かるく】lightly
圧する【あっする】press
自分【じぶん】oneself, himself
〜の上に【〜のうえに】upon
軽い【かるい】light
舟【ふね】boat
たゆたい swaying
揺れ動かす【ゆれうごかす】rock to and fro
目を閉じる【めをとじる】shut one's eyes
世界【せかい】world
揺籃【ようらん】cradle
〜のようになる come to be like

74
中尉【ちゅうい】lieutenant ❀
目【め】eye

見る【みる】look at
〜とおりを as
忠実に【ちゅうじつに】faithfully
なぞる follow, trace
〜て行く【〜ていく】indicates movement away from the narrator
高々と【たかだかと】proudly, pertly
息づく【いきづく】breathe
乳房【ちぶさ】breast
山桜【やまざくら】mountain cherry
花【はな】flower
蕾【つぼみ】bud
乳首【ちくび】nipple
持つ【もつ】have
含む【ふくむ】[passive form in text] keep in one's mouth
固い【かたい】hard
胸【むね】breast, chest

Returning to her mouth, he pressed his lips gently against hers and rolled them back and forth with a motion like the swaying of a small boat. He shut his eyes, and the whole world became a cradle.

Wherever the lieutenant's eyes went, his lips would faithfully follow. The proud, panting breasts had nipples like the buds of the flower of the mountain cherry, and they hardened as they were taken into his lips. The beauty of the arms, which flowed down so gracefully from either side of the chest, and their exquisite roundness tapering down to the wrists; then, beyond them, were the delicate fingers that had clasped the fan on their wedding day. Confronted by the lieutenant's lips, each finger hid in the shadow of its neighbor as if ashamed. . . .

両脇【りょうわき】both sides
なだらかに gently
流れ落ちる【ながれおちる】slide away
腕【うで】arm
美しさ【うつくしさ】beauty
帯びる【おびる】have (a quality)
丸み【まるみ】roundness
そのままに in that state
手首【てくび】wrist
〜のほうへ toward
細まる【ほそまる】taper, grow thin
〜てゆく indicates an increase in tendency
巧緻な【こうちな】elaborate, exquisite
すがた shape, figure
その先に【そのさきに】beyond that
かつて previously
結婚式【けっこんしき】wedding ceremony

日【ひ】day
扇【おうぎ】fan
握る【にぎる】grip, hold
繊細な【せんさいな】delicate, fine
指【ゆび】finger ❀
一本一本【いっぽんいっぽん】each one (of long, thin objects)
〜の前で【〜のまえで】before, in front of
差らう【はじらう】be shy, be coy
それぞれの each, respective
かげ shadow, behind
隠れる【かくれる】hide

……胸から腹へと辿る天性の自然な括れは、柔らかなままに弾んだ力をたわめていて、そこから腰へひろがる豊かな曲線の予兆をなしながら、それなりに些かもだらしなさのない肉体の正しい規律のようなものを示していた。光りから遠く隔たったその腹と腰の白さと豊かさは、大きな鉢に満々と湛えられた乳のようで、ひときわ清らかな凹んだ臍は、そこに今し一粒の雨滴が強く穿った新鮮な跡のようであった。影の次第に濃く集まる部分に、毛はやさしく敏感に叢れ立ち、香りの高い花の焦げるような匂いは、今は静まってはいない体のとめどもない揺動と共に、そのあたりに少しずつ高くなった。

胸【むね】breast, chest
腹【はら】belly, stomach ⊛
辿る【たどる】make one's way, meander
天性の【てんせいの】of nature, natural
自然な【しぜんな】natural (= uncorsetted)
括れ【くびれ】narrow part (= waist)
柔らかな【やわらかな】soft
〜ままに at the same time as being
弾んだ【はずんだ】springy, firm
力【ちから】strength, power
たわめる bend, cause to arc
腰【こし】loins, middle ⊛
ひろがる spread, broaden
豊かな【ゆたかな】rich, abundant, lush
曲線【きょくせん】curve
予兆【よちょう】foretaste
なす give form to

それなりに in its own way
些かも〜ない【いささかも〜ない】not the slightest bit
だらしなさ slovenliness
肉体【にくたい】body
正しい【ただしい】correct
規律【きりつ】discipline, order (NOTE: 規律正しい regular)
示す【しめす】show
光り【ひかり】light
遠く【とおく】far
隔たる【へだたる】be distant, be apart
白さ【しろさ】whiteness
豊かさ【ゆたかさ】richness, abundance
大きな【おおきな】big
鉢【はち】bowl
満々と【まんまんと】overflowingly
湛える【たたえる】[passive form in text] fill

Going down from the chest to the stomach, the naturally narrow waist was soft but curved with a springy firmness, and while presaging the generous curves that swelled down to the loins, it also displayed the proper disciplined quality of a body with no trace of slackness. Well removed from the light, the rich whiteness of her stomach and her loins was like milk brimming over in a big bowl, and the conspicuous, clean indent of her navel looked as if it were the fresh mark left by a single powerful raindrop that had bored its way into her just a moment ago. In the part where the shadows gradually gathered and thickened, the hair rose in a gentle, sensitive cluster, and there an odor like the burning of fragrant flowers gradually grew more intense, together with the ceaseless writhing of her aroused body.

乳【ちち】milk
ひときわ conspicuously
清らかな【きよらかな】pure, clear
凹んだ【くぼんだ】concave, indented
臍【へそ】navel
今し【いまし】just now, at that moment
一粒【ひとつぶ】one drop
雨滴【うてき】raindrop
強く【つよく】strongly
穿つ【うがつ】drill, bore
新鮮な【しんせんな】fresh
跡【あと】trace, mark
影【かげ】shadow
次第に【しだいに】gradually
濃く【こく】thickly
集まる【あつまる】gather
部分【ぶぶん】part
毛【け】hair

やさしく gently, softly
敏感に【びんかんに】sensitively
叢れ立つ【むれたつ】stand in a clump
香りの高い【かおりのたかい】fragrant
花【はな】flower
焦げる【こげる】burn
匂い【におい】smell
今は【いまは】now
静まる【しずまる】become quiet
は（in 静まってはいない）particle used for emphasis
体【からだ】body
とめどもない ceaseless
揺動【ようどう】swaying motion
〜と共に【〜とともに】together with
そのあたり that area
少しずつ【すこしずつ】little by little
高い【たかい】strong, piercing

75 ▶ 　ついに麗子は定かでない声音でこう言った。

76 ▶ 　「見せて……私にもお名残によく見せて」

77 ▶ 　こんな強い正当な要求は、今まで一度も妻の口から洩れたことがなく、それはいかにも最後まで慎しみが隠していたものが迸ったように聞かれたので、中尉は素直に横たわって妻に体を預けた。白い揺蕩していた肉体はしなやかに身を起し、良人にされたとおりのことを良人に返そうという愛らしい願いに熱して、じっと彼女を見上げている中尉の目を、二本の白い指で流れるように撫でて瞑らせた。

78 ▶ 　麗子は瞼も赤らむ上気に頬をほてらせて、いとしさに堪えかねて、中尉の五分刈の頭を抱きしめた。

75
ついに finally
麗子【れいこ】Reiko
定かでない【さだかでない】not certain, not sure
声音で【こわねで／せいおんで】tone of voice
言う【いう】say

76
見せる【みせる】show ⊛
私【わたし】I
お名残【おなごり】POLITE keepsake, remembrance
よく well, properly

77
強い【つよい】strong
正当な【せいとうな】justified, right
要求【ようきゅう】demand, request

今まで【いままで】until now
一度も〜ない【いちども〜ない】not even once, never
妻【つま】wife ⊛
口【くち】mouth
洩れる【もれる】escape (one's lips)
いかにも truly
最後まで【さいごまで】until the end
慎しみ【つつしみ】modesty
隠す【かくす】hide
もの thing, something
迸る【ほとばしる】gush forth
聞く【きく】[spontaneous form in text] hear
中尉【ちゅうい】lieutenant ⊛
素直に【すなおに】meekly, obediently
横たわる【よこたわる】lie down
体【からだ】body
預ける【あずける】entrust, give over

Eventually Reiko spoke in an unsteady voice.

"Show me . . . Show me everything so I can remember."

His wife had never before made this kind of forceful demand for her rights; and because it sounded just like the bursting forth of a feeling that modesty had concealed until the very end, the lieutenant meekly lay down and gave himself over to his wife. She gracefully raised her white, quivering torso, and excited by a sweet eagerness to do to her husband what he had done to her, with two white fingers gently stroked the lieutenant's eyes shut as they gazed up at her.

Reiko's cheeks flushed with a dizzying rush of feeling, and she reddened to her very eyelids. Unable to contain her affection, she embraced the lieutenant's close-shorn head.

白い 【しろい】 white ❀
揺蕩する 【ようとうする】 sway, quiver
肉体 【にくたい】 body
しなやかに lithely, with suppleness
身を起す 【みをおこす】 raise oneself
良人 【おっと】 husband ❀
〜とおり exactly as
返す 【かえす】 [volitional form in text] give back, return
愛らしい 【あいらしい】 sweet
願い 【ねがい】 desire, wish
熱する 【ねっする】 get hot, get excited
じっと MIMETIC fixedly
彼女 【かのじょ】 she
見上げる 【みあげる】 look up at
目 【め】 eye
二本 【にほん】 two (long, thin objects)
指 【ゆび】 finger

流れる 【ながれる】 flow
撫でる 【なでる】 stroke, caress
瞑る 【つぶる】 [causative form in text] shut, close (eyes)

78

瞼 【まぶた】 eyelid
赤らむ 【あからむ】 redden
上気 【じょうき】 rush of blood to the head
頬 【ほお】 cheek
ほてる [causative form in text] burn, flush
いとしさ tenderness
堪えかねる 【たえかねる】 be unable to endure
五分刈 【ごぶがり】 buzz cut
頭 【あたま】 head
抱きしめる 【だきしめる】 embrace, hug

乳房には短かい髪の毛が痛くさわり、良人の高い鼻は冷た
くめり込み、息は乳房に熱くかかっていた。彼女は引き離
して、その男らしい顔を眺めた。凛々しい眉、閉ざされた
目、秀でた鼻梁、きりりと結んだ美しい唇、……青い剃り
跡の頬は灯を映して、なめらかに輝いていた。麗子はその
おのおのに、ついで太い首筋に、強い盛り上がった肩に、
二枚の楯を張り合わせたような逞ましい胸とその樺色の乳
首に接吻した。胸の肉附のよい両脇が濃い影を落している
腋窩には、毛の繁りに甘い暗鬱な匂いが立ち迷い、この匂
いの甘さには何かしら青年の死の実感がこもっていた。

乳房【ちぶさ】breast
短かい【みじかい】short
髪の毛【かみのけ】hair (on the head)
痛く【いたく】painfully
さわる touch, prickle
良人【おっと】husband
高い【たかい】high, prominent
鼻【はな】nose (NOTE: 鼻が高い proud)
冷たく【つめたく】coldly
めり込む【めりこむ】sink into
息【いき】breath
熱く【あつく】hotly
かかる spill over
彼女【かのじょ】she
引き離す【ひきはなす】pull away
男らしい【おとこらしい】manly
顔【かお】face
眺める【ながめる】gaze at

凛々しい【りりしい】commanding
眉【まゆ】eyebrow
閉ざす【とざす】[passive form in text] close, shut
目【め】eyes
秀でる【ひいでる】superior, magnificent
鼻梁【びりょう】bridge of the nose
きりりと tightly
結ぶ【むすぶ】shut, join
美しい【うつくしい】beautiful
唇【くちびる】lip
青い【あおい】blue
剃り跡【そりあと】shaved-down stubble
頬【ほお】cheek
灯【あかり／あかし／ともしび／ひ】light, lamp
映す【うつす】reflect
なめらかに smoothly

Against her breasts, her husband's close-cropped hair felt painful; his proud nose was cold as it sank into them; and his breath felt hot. She pulled him away from her and gazed at his manly visage. The commanding eyebrows, the closed eyes, the magnificent bridge of the nose, the beautiful lips pressed tightly together . . . and the blue-tinged, close-shaven cheeks that caught the lamplight and glowed so sleekly: Reiko kissed all of these, then she kissed the thick nape of the neck, the strong, burly shoulders, the muscular chest that resembled twin shields placed side by side, and its russet nipples. A sweet but melancholy smell rose from the clumps of hair in the armpits, where the sides of the well-muscled chest cast deep shadows, and the sweetness of this smell seemed somehow heavy with the reality of young death.

輝く 【かがやく】 shine
麗子 【れいこ】 Reiko
おのおの each one
ついで and then
太い 【ふとい】 thick
首筋 【くびすじ】 nape of the neck
強い 【つよい】 strong
盛り上がる 【もりあがる】 swell, rise
肩 【かた】 shoulder
二枚 【にまい】 two (flat objects)
楯 【たて】 shields
張り合わせる 【はりあわせる】 stick together
逞ましい 【たくましい】 strong, muscular
胸 【むね】 chest ⊛
樺色 【かばいろ】 russet, brownish
乳首 【ちくび】 nipple
接吻する 【せっぷんする】 kiss

肉附のよい 【にくづきのよい】 fleshed out
両脇 【りょうわき】 both sides
濃い 【こい】 thick
影 【かげ】 shadow
落す 【おとす】 cast
腋窩 【えきか】 armpits
毛 【け】 hair
繁り 【しげり】 clump, thick growth
甘い 【あまい】 sweet
暗鬱な 【あんうつな】 melancholy, gloomy
匂い 【におい】 smell ⊛
立ち迷う 【たちまよう】 rise, float up
甘さ 【あまさ】 sweetness
何かしら 【なにかしら】 somehow
青年 【せいねん】 youth, young man
死 【し】 death
実感 【じっかん】 feeling, reality, sense
こもる fill, hang (in the air)

中尉の肌は麦畑のような輝やきを持ち、いたるところの筋肉はくっきりとした輪郭を露骨にあらわし、腹筋の筋目の下に、つつましい臍窩を絞っていた。麗子は良人のこの若々しく引き締った腹、さかんな毛におおわれた謙虚な腹を見ているうちに、ここがやがてむごたらしく切り裂かれるのを思って、いとしさの余りそこに泣き伏して接吻を浴びせた。

79▶　　横たわった中尉は自分の腹にそそがれる妻の涙を感じて、どんな劇烈な切腹の苦痛にも堪えようという勇気を固めた。

80▶　　こうした経緯を経て二人がどれほどの至上の歓びを味わったかは言うまでもあるまい。

中尉【ちゅうい】lieutenant ❀
肌【はだ】skin
麦畑【むぎばたけ】field of barley
輝やき【かがやき】glow
持つ【もつ】possess
いたるところ everywhere
筋肉【きんにく】muscle
くっきりとした clearly, distinctly
輪郭【りんかく】outline
露骨に【ろこつに】plainly
あらわす show, display, reveal
腹筋【ふっきん】muscles of the abdomen
筋目【すじめ】crease, fold
〜の下に【〜のしたに】beneath
つつましい modest
臍窩【せいか】navel
絞る【しぼる】squeeze, tighten

麗子【れいこ】Reiko
良人【おっと】husband
若々しい【わかわかしい】youthful
引き締った【ひきしまった】tight, firm (of stomach)
腹【はら】belly, stomach ❀
さかんな vigorous, thriving
毛【け】hair
おおう [passive form in text] cover
謙虚な【けんきょな】modest, humble
見る【みる】look at
〜うちに while, in the course of
やがて presently, shortly
むごたらしく cruelly
切り裂く【きりさく】slit open
思う【おもう】think, imagine
いとしさ tenderness, affection
〜の余り【〜のあまり】out of an excess of

The lieutenant's skin shone like a field of barley, and the muscles all over his body revealed their firm contours without shame, pressing tight around the discreet navel beneath the serried abdominal muscles. As Reiko looked at her husband's young, hard stomach—at that modest stomach covered by thick hair—and thought that soon it would be sliced open savagely, she fell upon it in a flood of tenderness, weeping and bathing it in kisses.

As the lieutenant lay there, he felt his wife's tears falling onto his belly, and this hardened his courage to bear the agony of the stomach-cutting, no matter how excruciating it might be.

It is needless to dwell on the supreme joy they enjoyed after passing through these preliminaries.

泣き伏す 【なきふす】 throw oneself upon in tears
接吻 【せっぷん】 kiss
浴びせる 【あびせる】 shower with

79

横たわる 【よこたわる】 lie down
自分 【じぶん】 oneself, himself
そそぐ [passive form in text] pour
妻 【つま】 wife
涙 【なみだ】 tears
感じる 【かんじる】 feel
劇烈な 【げきれつな】 extreme, intense
切腹 【せっぷく】 suicide by cutting one's stomach
苦痛 【くつう】 pain, agony
堪える 【たえる】 [volitional form in text] endure
勇気 【ゆうき】 courage

固める 【かためる】 harden

80

経緯 【けいい】 course
経る 【へる】 experience, go through
二人 【ふたり】 the two of them, they
どれほど to what extent
至上の 【しじょうの】 supreme
歓び 【よろこび】 joy
味わう 【あじわう】 taste, savor
言うまでもあるまい 【いうまでもあるまい】 it need hardly be said

中尉は雄々しく身を起し、悲しみと涙にぐったりした妻の体を、力強い腕に抱きしめた。二人は左右の頬を互いちがいに狂おしく触れ合わせた。麗子の体は慄えていた。汗に濡れた胸と胸とはしっかり貼り合わされ、二度と離れることは不可能に思われるほど、若い美しい肉体の隅々までが一つになった。麗子は叫んだ。高みから奈落へ落ち、奈落から翼を得て、又目くるめく高みへまで天翔った。中尉は長駆する聯隊旗手のように喘いだ。……そして、一ト巡りがおわると又たちまち情意に溢れて、二人はふたたび相携えて、疲れるけしきもなく、一息に頂きへ登って行った。

中尉【ちゅうい】lieutenant ✪
雄々しく【おおしく】heroically, bravely
身を起す【みをおこす】raise oneself
悲しみ【かなしみ】sorrow
涙【なみだ】tears
ぐったりした dog-tired, limp
妻【つま】wife
体【からだ】body ✪
力強い【ちからづよい】strong, powerful
腕【うで】arms
抱きしめる【だきしめる】embrace
二人【ふたり】the two of them, they ✪
左右の【さゆうの】left and right, both
頬【ほお】cheek
互いちがいに【たがいちがいに】alternately
狂おしく【くるおしく】crazily
触れ合う【ふれあう】[causative form in text] press against each other

麗子【れいこ】Reiko ✪
慄える【ふるえる】shudder, tremble
汗【あせ】sweat
濡れる【ぬれる】get wet
胸【むね】chest ✪
しっかり firmly
貼り合わせる【はりあわせる】[passive form in text] stick together
二度と【にどと】ever again
離れる【はなれる】part, separate
不可能【ふかのう】impossibility
思う【おもう】[spontaneous form in text] think
～ほど to the extent that ~
若い【わかい】young
美しい【うつくしい】beautiful
肉体【にくたい】body
隅々まで【すみずみまで】to every nook and cranny

The lieutenant resolutely raised himself and took his wife—her body drooping with sorrow and with tears—in his powerful arms. They nuzzled frenziedly, cheek against cheek, now this side, now that. Reiko was trembling all over. Their sweat-drenched chests were clamped firmly together, and down to the last cell their beautiful, young bodies became so much one that it seemed they could never again be separated. Reiko uttered a cry. They plunged from the heights to the depths, and from the depths, taking wing, they flew back up to dizzying heights. The lieutenant was gasping for breath like the regimental standard bearer on a long march. . . . No sooner had one cycle come to an end than, their emotions brimming over, they would come together again and once more scale the summit in a single surge, with no sign of tiring.

一つ 【ひとつ】one
叫ぶ 【さけぶ】cry out
高み 【たかみ】high place ⊛
奈落 【ならく】infernal regions, the pit ⊛
落ちる 【おちる】fall
翼 【つばさ】wing
得る 【える】get, obtain
又 【また】and again, once again ⊛
目くるめく 【めくるめく】get dizzy
天翔る 【あまかける】fly through the heavens
長駆する 【ちょうくする】march far
聯隊旗手 【れんたいきしゅ】regimental standard bearer
喘ぐ 【あえぐ】pant
一トめぐり 【ひとめぐり】one round
おわる end
たちまち at once

情意 【じょうい】emotion
溢れる 【あふれる】abound, brim
ふたたび again
相携える 【あいたずさえる】come together, unite, join hands
疲れる 【つかれる】get tired
けしき sign
一息に 【ひといきに】in one stretch
頂き 【いただき】summit
登る 【のぼる】climb
〜て行く 【〜ていく】indicates movement away from the narrator

肆 (し)

81▶　時が経って、中尉が身を離したのは倦き果てたからではない。一つには切腹に要する強い力を減殺することを怖れたからである。一つには、あまり貪りすぎて、最後の甘美な思い出を損ねることを怖れたからである。

82▶　中尉がはっきり身を離すと、いつものように、麗子も大人しくこれに従った。二人は裸かのまま、手の指をからみあわせて仰臥して、じっと暗い天井を見つめている。汗が一時に引いてゆくが、ストーヴの火熱のために少しも寒くはない。このあたりの夜はしんとして、車の音さえ途絶えている。

肆【し】four

81

時【とき】time
経つ【たつ】pass, elapse
中尉【ちゅうい】lieutenant ✿
身を離す【みをはなす】draw one's body away ✿
倦き果てる【あきはてる】be thoroughly tired (of something), have enough
一つには【ひとつには】for one thing, on the one hand ✿
切腹【せっぷく】suicide by cutting one's stomach
要する【ようする】require
強い【つよい】strong
力【ちから】strength, power
減殺する【げんさつする】reduce
怖れる【おそれる】fear ✿
あまり too much

貪る【むさぼる】be greedy
〜すぎる (do) to excess
最後の【さいごの】final
甘美な【かんびな】sweet, lovely
思い出【おもいで】memory
損ねる【そこねる】spoil

82

はっきり clearly
いつものように as usual
麗子【れいこ】Reiko
大人しく【おとなしく】meekly
従う【したがう】follow
二人【ふたり】the two of them, they
裸かのまま【はだかのまま】naked as they were
手【て】hand
指【ゆび】finger

4

When, after some time, the lieutenant drew away it was not because he had had enough. For one thing, he was afraid of eroding the enormous strength that disemboweling himself would demand. For another, he was afraid that overindulging himself might taint his last, sweet memory.

As the lieutenant had clearly pulled away, Reiko, as always, meekly followed suit. Still naked, the fingers of their hands interlaced, and lying on their backs they gazed intently up at the dark ceiling. They soon stopped sweating, but the fire in the stove meant they were not in the least cold. Around them, the night was still; even the noise of cars had ceased.

からみあう [causative form in text] be intertwined
仰臥する 【ぎょうがする】 lie on one's back
じっと MIMETIC fixedly
暗い 【くらい】 dark
天井 【てんじょう】 ceiling
見つめる 【みつめる】 stare
汗 【あせ】 sweat
一時に 【いちじに】 temporarily, for a short while
引く 【ひく】 go away
〜てゆく indicates an increase in tendency
ストーヴ stove
火熱 【かねつ】 heat of a fire
〜のために because of
少しも〜ない 【すこしも〜ない】 not the slightest bit
寒い 【さむい】 cold

このあたり this area
夜 【よる】 night
しんとする MIMETIC be quiet, be still
車 【くるま】 car
音 【おと】 sound, noise
〜さえ even
途絶える 【とだえる】 cease

四谷駅界隈の省線電車や市電の響きも、濠の内側に谺する
ばかりで、赤坂離宮前のひろい車道に面した公園の森に遮
られ、ここまでは届いて来ない。この東京の一劃で、今
も、二つに分裂した皇軍が相対峙しているという緊迫感は
嘘のようである。

83 ▶　二人は内側に燃えている火照りを感じながら、今味わっ
たばかりの無上の快楽を思い浮べている。その一瞬一瞬、
尽きせぬ接吻の味わい、肌の感触、目くるめくような快さ
の一齣一齣を思っている。暗い天井板には、しかしすでに
死の顔が覗いている。あの喜びは最終のものであり、二度
とこの身に返っては来ない。

四谷駅【よつやえき】Yotsuya Station

界隈【かいわい】vicinity, neighborhood

省線電車【しょうせんでんしゃ】Shōsen
Densha (common name for the state-
run train)

市電【しでん】streetcars

響き【ひびき】sound, clang

濠【ほり】moat

内側【うちがわ】inner side ✪

谺する【こだまする】echo

〜ばかり only, just

赤坂離宮【あかさかりきゅう】Akasaka
Palace

〜前【〜まえ】in front of

ひろい wide, spacious

車道【しゃどう】road

面する【めんする】face

公園【こうえん】park

森【もり】trees, grove

遮る【さえぎる】[passive form in text] block

届く【とどく】reach

〜て来る【〜てくる】indicates movement
toward the narrator

東京【とうきょう】Tokyo

一劃【いっかく】area, corner

今も【いまも】even now

二つ【ふたつ】two

分裂する【ぶんれつする】split

皇軍【こうぐん】Imperial Army

相対峙する【あいたいじする】confront

緊迫感【きんぱくかん】tension, strain

嘘【うそ】lie, falsehood

83

二人【ふたり】the two of them, they

燃える【もえる】burn

火照り【ほてり】heat, burning sensation

The rumblings of the trains and streetcars near Yotsuya station echoed in the area bounded by the moat, but blocked out by the trees in the park facing the broad boulevards in front of Akasaka Palace, did not reach this far. The tension in this corner of Tokyo, even now, with the Imperial Army split into two factions engaged in a standoff, seemed like an illusion.

As they felt the fire smoldering within them, they remembered the supreme ecstasy that they had just enjoyed. They recalled every single moment—the taste of endless kisses, the feel of each other's flesh—picture after picture of intoxicating delight. But the face of death was already visible upon the dark boards of the ceiling planks. Those joys had been their last and would never again revisit them.

感じる【かんじる】feel

今【いま】now

味わう【あじわう】taste

〜ばかり just now

無上の【むじょうの】unsurpassed, supreme

快楽【かいらく】pleasure

思い浮べる【おもいうかべる】call to mind

一瞬一瞬【いっしゅんいっしゅん】each and every moment

尽きせぬ【つきせぬ】endless

接吻【せっぷん】kiss

味わい【あじわい】taste

肌【はだ】skin

感触【かんしょく】touch, feel

目くるめく【めくるめく】get dizzy

快さ【こころよさ】delight

一齣一齣【ひとこまひとこま】each and every frame

思う【おもう】think of, picture

暗い【くらい】dark

天井板【てんじょういた】ceiling plank

しかし however

すでに already

死【し】death

顔【かお】face

覗く【のぞく】be visible, show oneself

喜び【よろこび】joy

最終【さいしゅう】the end

二度と〜ない【にどと〜ない】never again

身【み】body

返って来る【かえってくる】return

が、思うのに、これからいかに長生きをしても、あれほど
の歓喜に到達することが二度とないことはほぼ確実で、そ
の思いは二人とも同じである。

84▶　　からめ合った指さきの感触、これもやがて失われる。
今見ている暗い天井板の木目の模様でさえ、やがて失われ
る。死がひたと身をすり寄せて来るのが感じられる。時を
移してはならない。勇気をふるって、こちらからその死に
つかみかからねばならないのだ。

85▶「さあ、仕度をしよう」

86▶　　と中尉が言った。それはたしかに決然たる調子で言われ
たが、麗子は良人のこれほどまでに温かい優しい声をきい
たことがなかった。

思うのに【おもうのに】one can imagine
いかに〜も no matter how
長生きをする【ながいきをする】live long
あれほど to that extent
歓喜【かんき】rapture
到達する【とうたつする】attain, arrive at
二度とない【にどとない】never again
ほぼ virtually
確実【かくじつ】certainty
思い【おもい】thought
二人【ふたり】the two of them, they
〜とも for both
同じ【おなじ】the same

84

からめ合う【からめあう】intertwine
指さき【ゆびさき】fingertips
感触【かんしょく】feel, touch

やがて presently, shortly ❀
失う【うしなう】[passive form in text] lose ❀
今【いま】now
見る【みる】see, look at
暗い【くらい】dark
天井板【てんじょういた】ceiling plank
木目【もくめ】grain of wood
模様【もよう】pattern
〜さえ even
死【し】death ❀
ひたと up close to
身をすり寄せる【みをすりよせる】
　snuggle up close
〜て来る【〜てくる】indicates movement
　toward the narrator
感じる【かんじる】[potential form in text] feel
時を移す【ときをうつす】pass the time,
　allow time to go by

But then, it was almost certain they would never again attain such rapture, no matter how long they lived—so they both thought.

The sensations of their intertwined fingertips would fade away. Even the wood-grain pattern they were looking at on the dark ceiling boards—that, too, would soon be lost. They could feel death creeping up on them, closer and closer. They could not put it off. They had to exercise courage, go forth and seize that death with vigor.

"Right. Let's get ready."

The lieutenant said. The remark was delivered in a resolute tone, but Reiko had never heard her husband sound so warm and kind.

～てはならない must not ～

勇気をふるう 【ゆうきをふるう】 wield courage

こちらから themselves taking the initiative

つかみかかる go and grab hold of

～ねばならない have to, must

85

さあ right, well then

仕度をする 【したくをする】 [volitional form in text] make preparations

86

中尉 【ちゅうい】 lieutenant

言う 【いう】 say ⊕ (NOTE: Next usage is in the passive form.)

たしかに certainly

決然たる 【けつぜんたる】 determined

調子 【ちょうし】 tone, manner

麗子 【れいこ】 Reiko

良人 【おっと】 husband

これほどまでに to this extent

温かい 【あたたかい】 warm, friendly

優しい 【やさしい】 gentle, kind

声 【こえ】 voice

きく hear

87▶　　身を起こすと、忙しい仕事が待っていた。

88▶　　中尉は今まで一度も、床の上げ下げを手つだったことはなかったが、快活に押入れの襖をあけて、手ずから蒲団を運んで納めた。

89▶　　ガス・ストーヴの火を止め、スタンドを片附けると、中尉の留守中に麗子がこの部屋の整理をすませ、すがすがしく掃除をしておいたので、片隅に引き寄せられた紫檀の卓のほかには、八畳の間は、大事な客を迎える前の客間のけしきと渝らなかった。

90▶　「ここでよく呑んだもんだなあ、加納や本間や山口と」

91▶　「よくお呑みになりましたのね、皆さん」

87
身を起こす【みをおこす】raise oneself
忙しい【いそがしい】busy
仕事【しごと】work
待つ【まつ】wait

88
中尉【ちゅうい】lieutenant ⊛
今まで【いままで】until now
一度も〜ない【いちども〜ない】not even once, never
床の上げ下げ【とこのあげさげ】putting in and taking out the futons
手つだう【てつだう】help with
快活【かいかつに】cheerfully
押入れ【おしいれ】closet
襖【ふすま】sliding door
あける open
手ずから【てずから】with one's own hands
蒲団【ふとん】bedding, futon
運ぶ【はこぶ】carry
納める【おさめる】put away

89
ガス・ストーヴ gas stove
火を止める【ひをとめる】turn off
スタンド floor lamp
片附ける【かたづける】put away
留守中【るすちゅう】while someone was away
麗子【れいこ】Reiko
部屋【へや】room
整理【せいり】tidying
すませる finish, take care of
すがすがしく freshly, refreshingly
掃除をする【そうじをする】clean

Once they got up, there was a great deal of work to be done.

The lieutenant, who until this moment had never once helped with laying out or putting away the bedding, cheerfully slid open the closet door and picked up the futon and put it in.

They then turned off the gas stove and put the lamp away. Since Reiko had already tidied and cleaned the room during the lieutenant's absence until it was spic-and-span, aside from the rosewood table that had been dragged off into a corner, the eight-mat room looked exactly like as it did when serving as their reception room about to welcome an important guest.

"We had good times drinking here, with Kanō, Honma and Yamaguchi."

"Yes, they all enjoyed a good drink."

〜ておく and leave it that way (for a future purpose)
片隅【かたすみ】one corner (of several)
引き寄せる【ひきよせる】[passive form in text] pull to one side
紫檀【したん】rosewood
卓【たく】table
〜のほかに other than
八畳の間【はちじょうのま】eight-mat room
大事な【だいじな】important
客【きゃく】guest
迎える【むかえる】play host to
〜前【〜まえ】before
客間【きゃくま】parlor, sitting room
けしき appearance
渝る【かわる】be different

90
よく plenty ⊛
呑む【のむ】drink
〜もん＝〜もの used with emotive particle な to express admiration
加納【かのう】Kanō
本間【ほんま】Honma
山口【やまぐち】Yamaguchi

91
お呑みになる【おのみになる】HONORIFIC drink
〜のね FEMININE particle combination used to draw attention to a reality
皆さん【みなさん】POLITE everybody

92▶ 「あいつ等とも近いうちに冥途で会えるさ。お前を連れて来たのを見たら、さぞ奴等にからかわれるだろう」

93▶ 　階下へ下りるとき、中尉は今あかあかと電燈をつけたこの清浄な部屋へ振向いた。そこで呑んで、騒いで、無邪気な自慢話をしていた青年将校たちの顔が浮ぶ。そのときはこの部屋で自分が腹を切ることになろうとは夢にも思わなかった。

94▶ 　階下の二間で、夫婦は水の流れるように淡々とそれぞれの仕度にいそしんだ。中尉は手水に立ち、ついで体を清めに風呂場へ入り、そのあいだ麗子は良人の丹前を畳み、軍服の上下と切り立ての晒の六尺を風呂場へ置き、

92

あいつ等 【あいつら】 BRUSQUE, AFFECTION-ATE those fellows

近いうちに 【ちかいうちに】 soon

冥途 【めいど】 the other world

会う 【あう】 [potential form in text] meet

〜さ particle used to give emphasis to an assertion

お前 【おまえ】 MASCULINE, FAMILIAR you

連れて来る 【つれてくる】 bring (someone somewhere)

見る 【みる】 see

さぞ no doubt (used when empathizing with the experience of another)

奴等 【やつら】 BRUSQUE, AFFECTIONATE those fellows

からかう [passive form in text] tease

93

階下 【かいか】 downstairs ❀

下りる 【おりる】 descend

中尉 【ちゅうい】 lieutenant ❀

今 【いま】 now

あかあかと brightly

電燈をつける 【でんとうをつける】 turn on (electric) lights

清浄な 【せいじょうな】 spotless, pure

部屋 【へや】 room ❀

振向く 【ふりむく】 look back at

呑む 【のむ】 drink

騒ぐ 【さわぐ】 get boisterous

無邪気な 【むじゃきな】 guileless

自慢話 【じまんばなし】 boastful talk

青年将校 【せいねんしょうこう】 young officer

顔 【かお】 face

浮ぶ 【うかぶ】 come to mind

自分 【じぶん】 oneself, himself

"I'll be meeting 'em over in the other world in no time. Bet they'll give me a ribbing when they see I've brought you along."

As he went down the stairs, the lieutenant turned around to look at the immaculate room under the brightness of the newly switched-on electric light. The faces of the young officers drinking, merrymaking, and innocently bragging appeared in his mind's eye. He had never then dreamed he would end up cutting his stomach in this room.

In the two downstairs rooms, the couple busied themselves with their respective preparations as tranquilly as flowing water. The lieutenant went to the toilet, then to the bathroom to make himself pure and clean; Reiko, meanwhile, folded up her husband's padded kimono and laid out the jacket and trousers of his uniform together with a loincloth of freshly cut bleached cotton in the bathroom;

腹を切る 【はらをきる】 cut one's stomach
夢にも思わない 【ゆめにもおもわない】 never imagine in one's wildest dreams

94

二間 【ふたま】 two rooms
夫婦 【ふうふ】 couple
水 【みず】 water
流れる 【ながれる】 flow
淡々と 【たんたんと】 calmly, coolly, unconcernedly
それぞれの each, respective
仕度 【したく】 preparations
いそしむ busy oneself
手水に立つ 【ちょうずにたつ】 go to the toilet
ついで next, while one is at it
体 【からだ】 body
清める 【きよめる】 purify, wash

風呂場 【ふろば】 bathroom ❀
入る 【はいる】 go into
そのあいだ meanwhile
麗子 【れいこ】 Reiko
良人 【おっと】 husband
丹前 【たんぜん】 large padded kimono
畳む 【たたむ】 fold up
軍服 【ぐんぷく】 military uniform
上下 【じょうげ】 jacket and trousers
切り立ての 【きりたての】 freshly cut
晒の 【さらしの】 bleached
六尺 【ろくしゃく】 *fundoshi*, loincloth
置く 【おく】 place, put

遺書を書くための半紙を卓袱台の上に揃え、さて硯箱の蓋
をとって墨を磨った。遺書の文句はすでに考えてあった。

95▶ 　麗子の指は墨の冷たい金箔を押し、硯の海が黒雲のひろ
がるように忽ち曇って、彼女はこんな仕草の反復が、この
指の圧力、このかすかな音の往来が、ひたすら死のためだ
と考えることを罷めた。死がいよいよ現前するまでは、
それは時間を平淡に切り刻む家常茶飯の仕事にすぎなかっ
た。しかし磨るにつれて滑らかさを増す墨の感触と、つの
る墨の匂いには、言おうようのない暗さがあった。

96▶ 　素肌の上に軍服をきちんと着た中尉が風呂場からあらわ
れた。

遺書【いしょ】final note ❊
書く【かく】write
〜ための for the purpose of
半紙【はんし】writing paper
卓袱台【ちゃぶだい】low dining table
〜の上に【〜のうえに】on ❊
揃える【そろえる】arrange
さて and then
硯箱【すずりばこ】inkstone box
蓋【ふた】lid
とる take off, remove
墨【すみ】stick of India ink ❊
磨る【する】prepare (ink) by grinding (an
　ink stick) ❊
文句【もんく】phrase
すでに already
考える【かんがえる】think of

95
麗子【れいこ】Reiko
指【ゆび】finger ❊
冷たい【つめたい】cold
金箔【きんぱく】gold leaf (of characters
　written on an ink stick)
押す【おす】press
硯の海【すずりのうみ】well of an inkstone
黒雲【くろくも／こくうん】black cloud
ひろがる spread out
忽ち【たちまち】at once
曇る【くもる】become cloudy
彼女【かのじょ】she
仕草【しぐさ】action
反復【はんぷく】repetition
圧力【あつりょく】pressure
かすかな faint
音【おと】sound

on the dining table she set out the paper for writing their final messages, then, having taken the lid off the inkstone case, ground down the ink stick. She had already made up her mind about the phrasing of her final message.

Reiko's fingers pressed the cold gilt characters on the ink stick, and the well of the inkstone soon darkened, as if a black cloud were spreading across it. She willed herself not to think that this repetitive action—the pressure of her fingers, the faint noise rising and falling—was for the sole purpose of death. It was no more than an everyday domestic task to casually break up the time until death finally appeared before her. But there was darkness beyond words in the sensation of the ink tablet growing smoother the more she rubbed it, and in the intensifying smell of ink.

The lieutenant emerged from the bathroom, his uniform neatly worn over his nakedness.

往来【ゆきき】coming and going
ひたすら solely
死【し】death ⊗
〜のためだと that (something) would be for the purpose of
考える【かんがえる】think, consider
罷める【やめる】stop
いよいよ finally, really
現前する【げんぜんする】be right before one
時間【じかん】time
平淡に【へいたんに】simply, plainly
切り刻む【きりきざむ】cut to pieces
家常茶飯【かじょうさはん】everyday occurrence
仕事【しごと】work
〜にすぎない be no more than
しかし however

〜につれて as
滑らかさ【なめらかさ】smoothness
増す【ます】increase
感触【かんしょく】touch, feel
つのる intensify
匂い【におい】smell
言おうようのない【いおうようのない】unspeakable
暗さ【くらさ】darkness

96

素肌【すはだ】bare skin
軍服【ぐんぷく】military uniform
きちんと properly, neatly
着る【きる】put on, wear
中尉【ちゅうい】lieutenant
風呂場【ふろば】bathroom
あらわれる appear

そして黙って、卓袱台の前に正座をして、筆をとって、紙を前にしてためらった。

97▶ 麗子は白無垢の一揃えを持って風呂場へゆき、身を清め、薄化粧をして、白無垢の姿で茶の間へ出て来たときには、燈下の半紙に、黒々と、

98▶ 「皇軍万歳　陸軍歩兵中尉武山信二」

99▶ とだけ書いた遺書が見られた。

100▶ 麗子がその向いに坐って遺書を書くあいだ、中尉は黙って、真剣な面持で、筆を持つ妻の白い指の端正な動きを見詰めていた。

黙る【だまる】say nothing ❀
卓袱台【ちゃぶだい】low dining table
〜の前に【〜のまえに】in front of
正座をする【せいざをする】sit straight upright (with legs folded underneath oneself) on tatami matting
筆【ふで】brush ❀
とる pick up
紙【かみ】paper
〜を前にする【〜をまえにする】put in front of oneself
ためらう hesitate

97

麗子【れいこ】Reiko ❀
白無垢【しろむく】white silk kimono ❀
一揃え【ひとそろえ】single set
持つ【もつ】carry, hold
風呂場【ふろば】bathroom

ゆく go
身を清める【みをきよめる】wash oneself
薄化粧をする【うすげしょうをする】put on light make-up
姿【すがた】dress, appearance
茶の間【ちゃのま】living room
出て来る【でてくる】come out
燈下【とうか】under the lamplight
半紙【はんし】writing paper
黒々と【くろぐろと】very black

98

皇軍【こうぐん】Imperial Army
万歳【ばんざい】long live . . . !
陸軍歩兵【りくぐんほへい】army infantry
中尉【ちゅうい】lieutenant ❀
武山信二【たけやましんじ】Takeyama Shinji

Then, without saying a word, he seated himself rigidly upright by the low dining table, picked up a brush and paused over the paper before him.

Reiko went into the bathroom carrying a white silk kimono, washed, and put on some light make-up. When she came back out into the parlor dressed in the white kimono, written on the paper in the lamplight she saw the bold black strokes of the final note. . . .

"Long Live the Imperial Army! Army Infantry Lieutenant Takeyama Shinji."

. . . was all it said.

While Reiko was sitting opposite him and writing her final message, the lieutenant, silent and grave-faced, stared at the precise movements of his wife's white fingers as they held the brush.

99
書く 【かく】 write ❀
遺書 【いしょ】 final note ❀
見る 【みる】 [potential form in text] see

100
向い 【むかい】 front
坐る 【すわる】 sit
あいだ while
真剣な 【しんけんな】 serious
面持 【おももち】 look, face
持つ 【もつ】 hold, carry
妻 【つま】 wife
白い 【しろい】 white
指 【ゆび】 finger
端正な 【たんせいな】 neat, precise
動き 【うごき】 movement
見詰める 【みつめる】 stare

101▶ 　中尉は軍刀を携え、麗子は白無垢の帯に懐剣をさしはさみ、遺書を持って、神棚の前に並んで黙禱したのち、階下の電気を皆消した。二階へ上る階段の途中で振向いた中尉は、闇の中から伏目がちに彼に従って昇ってくる妻の白無垢の姿の美しさに目をみはった。

102▶ 　遺書は二階の床の間に並べて置かれた。掛軸を外すべきであろうが、仲人の尾関中将の書で、しかも「至誠」の二字だったので、そのままにした。たとえ血しぶきがこれを汚しても、中将は諒とするであろう。

101

中尉【ちゅうい】lieutenant ✸
軍刀【ぐんとう】military sword
携える【たずさえる】hold
麗子【れいこ】Reiko
白無垢【しろむく】white silk kimono ✸
帯【おび】sash
懐剣【かいけん】dagger
さしはさむ insert
遺書【いしょ】final note
持つ【もつ】hold
神棚【かみだな】household altar
～の前に【～のまえに】in front of
並ぶ【ならぶ】stand side by side
黙禱する【もくとうする】pray silently
～のち after
階下【かいか】downstairs
電気【でんき】electric light

皆【みな】all
消す【けす】extinguish
二階【にかい】second floor ✸
上る【あがる】go up
階段【かいだん】stairs
途中【とちゅう】halfway
振向く【ふりむく】look back
闇【やみ】darkness
～の中から【～のなかから】from within
伏目がちに【ふしめがちに】with downcast eyes
彼【かれ】he
従う【したがう】follow
昇る【のぼる】climb
～てくる indicates movement toward the narrator
妻【つま】wife
姿【すがた】figure, appearance

The lieutenant held his sword in his hand and Reiko thrust the dagger into the sash of her kimono, and, clasping their final messages, they stood side by side before the household altar, praying in silence. Then they turned off all the downstairs lights. Turning around halfway up the staircase leading to the second floor, the lieutenant gazed in awe at the beautiful white-robed figure of his wife as, eyes modestly downcast, she climbed after him up the stairs and on out of the darkness.

Their final messages were placed side-by-side in the alcove upstairs. They felt it would be appropriate to take down the hanging scroll, but since it was the work of their go-between, Lieutenant General Ozeki, and, more importantly, consisted of the two characters for "sincerity," they left it as it was. They imagined that, even were splashes of their blood to soil it, the lieutenant general would understand.

美しさ 【うつくしさ】 beauty
目をみはる 【めをみはる】 open one's eyes in wonder

102

床の間 【とこのま】 alcove
並べる 【ならべる】 arrange side-by-side
置く 【おく】 put, place
掛軸 【かけじく】 hanging scroll
外す 【はずす】 take down
〜べき should, ought to
仲人 【なこうど】 go-between, matchmaker
尾関 【おぜき】 Ozeki
中将 【ちゅうじょう】 lieutenant general ❀
書 【しょ】 penmanship
しかも moreover
至誠 【しせい】 sincerity
二字 【にじ】 two characters
そのままにする leave as is

たとえ even supposing
血しぶき 【ちしぶき】 splash of blood
汚す 【けがす／よごす】 make dirty
諒とする 【りょうとする】 understand, excuse

103▶　　中尉は床柱を背に正座をして、軍刀を膝の前に横たえた。

104▶　　麗子は畳一畳を隔てたところに端座した。すべてが白いので、唇に刷いた薄い紅が大そう艶やかに見える。

105▶　　二人は畳一畳を隔てて、じっと目を見交わしている。中尉の膝の前には軍刀がある。これを見ると麗子は初夜のことを思い出して、悲しみに堪えなくなった。中尉が押し殺した声でこう言った。

106▶　「介錯がないから、深く切ろうと思う。見苦しいこともあるかもしれないが、恐がってはいかん。どのみち死というものは、傍から見たら怖ろしいものだ。それを見て挫けてはならん。いいな」

107▶　「はい」

108▶　と麗子は深くうなずいた。

103

中尉【ちゅうい】lieutenant ⊕

床柱【とこばしら】alcove post

〜を背に【〜をせに】putting (something) behind one

正座をする【せいざをする】sit straight upright on tatami

軍刀【ぐんとう】military sword ⊕

膝【ひざ】knee ⊕

〜の前に【〜のまえに】in front of ⊕

横たえる【よこたえる】lay down

104

麗子【れいこ】Reiko ⊕

畳一畳【たたみいちじょう】one tatami mat's width ⊕

隔てる【へだてる】be distant from ⊕

ところ place

端座する【たんざする】sit upright

すべて everything

白い【白い】white

唇【くちびる】lip

刷く【はく】put on, paint

薄い【うすい】pale, light

紅【べに】lipstick, rouge

大そう【たいそう】very

艶やかな【あでやかな】seductive

見える【みえる】look, seem

105

二人【ふたり】the two of them, they

じっと MIMETIC fixedly

目を見交わす【めをみかわす】look at one another

見る【みる】see, look at ⊕

初夜【しょや】wedding night

思い出す【おもいだす】recall

悲しみ【かなしみ】sorrow

Sitting upright with the alcove post behind him, the lieutenant lay the sword down before his knees.

Reiko sat stiffly at one tatami mat's remove. She was clad entirely in white, so the thin film of rouge she had applied to her lips looked particularly alluring.

Separated by a single tatami mat they gazed intently at one another. The lieutenant's sword lay before his knees. The sight reminded Reiko of their wedding night and she found the sorrow of it unbearable. The lieutenant said in a muffled voice:

"As I have no second, I plan to cut deep. It may look ugly, but you must not be afraid. Death, after all, is a fearful thing when seen from the outside. When you see it, you must not waver. Understand?"

"Yes."

Reiko nodded deeply.

堪える【たえる】bear, put up with
押し殺した【おしころした】hoarse, strangled
声【こえ】voice
言う【いう】say

106

介錯【かいしゃく】second (assistant at ritual suicide)
深く【ふかく】deeply ⊛
切る【きる】[volitional form in text] cut
～（ろ）うと思う【～（ろ）うとおもう】intend to
見苦しい【みぐるしい】unsightly
～かもしれない probably
恐がる【こわがる】be afraid
～てはいかん MASCULINE mustn't
どのみち either way
死【し】death

もの thing, something ⊛
傍から【はたから】from outside
怖ろしい【おそろしい】fearful
見る【みる】see
挫ける【くじける】lose heart
～てはならん MASCULINE mustn't
いいな MASCULINE all right? got that?

108

うなずく nod

その白いなよやかな風情を見ると、死を前にした中尉はふしぎな陶酔を味わった。今から自分が着手するのは、嘗て妻に見せたことのない軍人としての公けの行為である。戦場の決戦と等しい覚悟の要る、戦場の死と同等同質の死である。自分は今戦場の姿を妻に見せるのだ。

これはつかのまのふしぎな幻想に中尉を運んだ。戦場の孤独な死と目の前の美しい妻と、この二つの次元に足をかけて、ありえようのない二つの共在を具現して、今自分が死のうとしているというこの感覚には、言いしれぬ甘美なものがあった。これこそは至福というものではあるまいかと思われる。妻の美しい目に自分の死の刻々を看取られるのは、香りの高い微風に吹かれながら死に就くようなものである。そこでは何かが宥されている。

109

白い【しろい】white
なよやかな slender, willowy
風情【ふぜい】appearance
見る【みる】see
死【し】death ⊛
〜を前にする【〜をまえにする】put in front of oneself
中尉【ちゅうい】lieutenant ⊛
ふしぎな strange, extraordinary ⊛
陶酔【とうすい】intoxication, rapture
味わう【あじわう】taste, feel
今から【いまから】from now
自分【じぶん】oneself, himself ⊛
着手する【ちゃくしゅする】undertake
嘗て【かつて】previously
妻【つま】wife ⊛
見せる【みせる】show ⊛

軍人【ぐんじん】soldier
〜として in one's role as
公け【おおやけ】public
行為【こうい】act, deed
戦場【せんじょう】battlefield ⊛
決戦【けっせん】decisive battle
等しい【ひとしい】equal
覚悟【かくご】resolve
要る【いる】need, require
同等同質【どうとうどうしつ】equal in quality
自分【じぶん】oneself, himself ⊛
今【いま】now ⊛
姿【すがた】figure, appearance

110

つかのまの fleeting
幻想【げんそう】fantasy
運ぶ【はこぶ】bear away

When he looked at her willowy white elegance, the lieutenant, his death before him, felt a curious intoxication. What he was about to carry out was a public act of himself as a soldier—something he had never before shown his wife. It was a death equal in rank and quality to death in combat, a death that demanded as much determination as any battlefield confrontation. It was his battlefield persona he was about to reveal to his wife.

This briefly swept the lieutenant into a bizarre fantasy. A solitary death on the battlefield and the presence of his beautiful wife—there was something inexpressibly sweet in the sense of being about to die straddling these two dimensions, and embodying their unrealizable union. It seemed to him that this must be the highest form of bliss. To have every second of his death observed by his wife's lovely eyes was to be wafted to death upon a fragrant breeze. In that he was somehow blessed.

孤独な 【こどくな】 lonely
目の前 【めのまえ】 before one's eyes
美しい 【うつくしい】 beautiful ❋
二つ 【ふたつ】 two ❋
次元 【じげん】 dimension
足をかける 【あしをかける】 stand
ありえようのない unfeasible
共在 【きょうざい】 coexistence
具現する 【ぐげんする】 embody, personify
死ぬ 【しぬ】 [volitional form in text] die
〜（の）うとする be about to 〜
感覚 【かんかく】 sensation
言いしれぬ 【いいしれぬ】 inexpressible
甘美な 【かんびな】 sweet, lovely
もの thing, something ❋
〜こそ the very, indeed
至福 【しふく】 bliss, nirvana

〜ではあるまいか＝〜ではないか
思う 【おもう】 [spontaneous form in text] think
目 【め】 eye
刻々 【こくこく】 every moment
看取る 【みとる】 [passive form in text] look after
香りの高い 【かおりのたかい】 fragrant
微風 【びふう】 breeze
吹く 【ふく】 [passive form in text] blow
就く 【つく】 set about (a course of action)
何か 【なにか】 something
宥す 【ゆるす】 [passive form in text] grant, bestow

何かわからないが、余人の知らぬ境地で、ほかの誰にも許されない境地がゆるされている。中尉は目の前の花嫁のような白無垢の美しい妻の姿に、自分が愛しそれに身を捧げてきた皇室や国家や軍旗や、それらすべての花やいだ幻を見るような気がした。それらは目の前の妻と等しく、どこからでも、どんな遠くからでも、たえず清らかな目を放って、自分を見詰めていてくれる存在だった。

111▶ 麗子も亦、死に就こうとしている良人の姿を、この世にこれほど美しいものはなかろうと思って見詰めていた。軍服のよく似合う中尉は、その凛々しい眉、そのきりっと結んだ唇と共に、今死を前にして、おそらく男の至上の美しさをあらわしていた。

何か【なにか】what

わかる know

余人【よじん／よにん】other people

知らぬ【しらぬ】not know

境地【きょうち】state ❀

ほかの other

誰にも～ない【だれにも～ない】to nobody else

許す【ゆるす】[passive form in text] grant ❀

中尉【ちゅうい】lieutenant ❀

目の前【めのまえ】before one's eyes ❀

花嫁【はなよめ】bride

白無垢【しろむく】white silk kimono

美しい【うつくしい】beautiful ❀

妻【つま】wife ❀

姿【すがた】figure, appearance ❀

自分【じぶん】oneself, himself ❀

愛す／愛する【あいす／あいする】love

身を捧げる【みをささげる】devote one's life to

～てくる indicates progression up to a point

皇室【こうしつ】Imperial Family

国家【こっか】nation

軍旗【ぐんき】military flag

それらすべて all those things

花やぐ【はなやぐ】be cheerful, be bright

幻【まぼろし】vision, dream

見る【みる】see

～ような気がする【～ようなきがする】feel as though

それら those things

～と等しく【～とひとしく】equal to

遠くから【とおくから】from afar

たえず ceaselessly

清らかな【きよらかな】pure

A state—he was not quite sure of its nature—had been granted to him that was unknown to anyone else, and vouchsafed to no one but him. In the bridelike figure of his beautiful wife in her white kimono, the lieutenant felt as though he were seeing a glorious composite vision of the Imperial Family, the Nation and the Army Flag that he loved and to which he had devoted his life. All these—as much as the wife before him—were presences that watched over him, regarding him with a pure and unblinking gaze, no matter from where or from how far.

Reiko, too, looked at him intently. She felt there could be nothing in this life so beautiful as her husband about to meet his death. The lieutenant always looked his best in uniform, but now as he stood on the verge of death with his commanding brows and tightly pressed lips, he seemed to be giving expression to male beauty at its highest.

目を放つ 【めをはなつ】 gaze far into the
　distance
見詰める 【みつめる】 stare ⊛
存在 【そんざい】 being, presence

111

麗子 【れいこ】 Reiko
亦 【また】 also, and, again
死 【し】 death ⊛
就く 【つく】 [volitional form] set about (a
　course of action)
〜（こ）うとする be about to 〜
良人 【おっと】 husband
この世 【このよ】 this present life
これほど to this extent
もの thing
〜なかろう = 〜ないだろう
思う 【おもう】 think
軍服 【ぐんぷく】 military uniform

よく well
似合う 【にあう】 suit
凛々しい 【りりしい】 commanding,
　imposing
眉 【まゆ】 eyebrow
きりっと MIMETIC tightly
結ぶ 【むすぶ】 shut, join
唇 【くちびる】 lip
〜と共に 【〜とともに】 together with
今 【いま】 now
〜を前にする 【〜をまえにする】 put
　before oneself
おそらく perhaps
男 【おとこ】 man
至上 【しじょう】 supremacy
美しさ 【うつくしさ】 beauty
あらわす show, express

112▶ 「じゃあ、行くぞ」

113▶ とついに中尉（ちゅうい）が言った。麗子（れいこ）は畳に深く身を伏せてお辞儀をした。どうしても顔が上げられない。涙で化粧を崩したくないと思っても、涙を禦（とど）めることができない。

114▶ ようやく顔をあげたとき、涙ごしにゆらいで見えるのは、すでに引抜いた軍刀の尖（さき）を五六寸あらわして、刀身に白布を巻きつけている良人（おっと）の姿である。

115▶ 巻きおわった軍刀を膝（ひざ）の前に置くと、中尉は膝を崩してあぐらをかき、軍服の襟（えり）のホックを外した。その目はもう妻を見ない。平らな真鍮（しんちゅう）の釦（ボタン）をひとつひとつゆっくり外した。浅黒い胸があらわれ、ついで腹があらわれる。

112

じゃあ well, right (exclamation of resolve)

行く【いく】go

ぞ MASCULINE particle used to emphatically voice one's resolve

113

ついに at last

中尉【ちゅうい】lieutenant ✻

言う【いう】say

麗子【れいこ】Reiko

畳【たたみ】tatami mat

深く【ふかく】deeply

身を伏せる【みをふせる】prostrate one-self

お辞儀をする【おじぎをする】bow

どうしても～ない by no means

顔を上げる【かおをあげる】[potential form in

text] look up ✻

涙【なみだ】tears ✻

化粧【けしょう】make-up

崩す【くずす】ruin

思う【おもう】think, intend

禦める【とどめる】stop

114

ようやく finally

～ごしに through

ゆらぐ flicker, waver

見える【みえる】be visible

すでに already

引抜く【ひきぬく】unsheathe

軍刀【ぐんとう】military sword ✻

尖【さき】tip (of a blade)

五六寸【ごろくすん】five or six *sun* (1 *sun* = 1.19 inches)

あらわす expose, show

"Right. Here goes."

Said the lieutenant eventually. Reiko bowed, pressing her body deeply down toward the tatami. She could not bring herself to look up. Though she did not want to ruin her make-up with tears, she was unable to hold them back.

When she finally looked up she saw through tears the blurry image of her husband wrapping a white cloth around the blade of his sword, which he had already unsheathed from its scabbard. He left six or seven inches exposed.

Placing the wrapped sword before his knees, the lieutenant shifted off his knees, sat cross-legged on the floor and unfastened the hooks on the collar of his uniform. His eyes no longer saw his wife. Slowly he undid the flat brass buttons, one by one. His dusky chest emerged, then his stomach was exposed.

刀身 【とうしん】 blade
白布 【しろぬの】 white cloth
巻きつける 【まきつける】 wind onto, fold around
良人 【おっと】 husband
姿 【すがた】 figure, appearance
115
巻きおわる 【まきおわる】 finish winding
膝 【ひざ】 knee
〜の前に 【〜のまえに】 in front of
置く 【おく】 place, put
膝を崩す 【ひざをくずす】 shift off one's knees
あぐらをかく sit cross-legged
軍服 【ぐんぷく】 military uniform
襟 【えり】 collar
ホック hook, clip
外す 【はずす】 undo ⊛

目 【め】 eye
妻 【つま】 wife
見る 【みる】 see
平らな 【たいらな】 flat
真鍮 【しんちゅう】 brass
釦 【ボタン】 button
ひとつひとつ one by one
ゆっくり slowly
浅黒い 【あさぐろい】 dusky
胸 【むね】 chest
あらわれる appear, become visible ⊛
ついで next
腹 【はら】 belly, stomach

バンドの留金を外し、ズボンの釦を外した。六尺褌の純白
が覗き、中尉はさらに腹を寛ろげて、褌を両手で押し下
げ、右手に軍刀の白布の握りを把った。そのまま伏目で自
分の腹を見て、左手で下腹を揉み柔らげている。

116▶　　中尉は刀の切れ味が心配になったので、ズボンの左方を
折り返して、腿を少しあらわし、そこへ軽く刃を滑らせ
た。たちまち傷口には血がにじみ、数条の細い血が、明る
い光りに照り輝きながら、股のほうへ流れた。

117▶　　はじめて良人の血を見た麗子は、怖ろしい動悸がした。
良人の顔を見る。中尉は平然とその血を見つめている。

バンド belt
留金【とめがね】clasp, buckle
外す【はずす】undo ⊛
ズボン trousers ⊛
釦【ボタン】button
六尺褌【ろくしゃくふんどし】*fundoshi*,
　loincloth (*rokushaku* refers to its
　unwound length of six *shaku* [1 *shaku* =
　11.93 inches])
純白【じゅんぱく】pure white
覗く【のぞく】be visible
中尉【ちゅうい】lieutenant ⊛
さらに again, more
腹【はら】waistline of one's trousers
寛ろげる【くつろげる】loosen
褌【ふんどし】loincloth
両手【りょうて】both hands
押し下げる【おしさげる】push down

右手【みぎて】right hand
軍刀【ぐんとう】military sword
白布【しろぬの】white cloth
握り【にぎり】grip
把る【とる】take hold of
そのまま in that position
伏目で【ふしめで】with eyes downcast
自分【じぶん】oneself, himself
腹【はら】belly, stomach ⊛
見る【みる】look at, see ⊛
左手【ひだりて】left hand
下腹【したはら】lower belly
揉み柔らげる【もみやわらげる】soften up
　by massaging

116

刀【かたな】sword
切れ味【きれあじ】sharpness

He undid the clasp of his belt, and loosened the buttons of his trousers. The pure-white color of his loincloth was visible. The lieutenant further loosened the front of his trousers, pushed the loincloth down with his hands, then clasped the white-cloth grip of the sword in his right hand. Keeping that position, he looked down at his middle and massaged his lower belly with his left hand to make it soft.

The lieutenant was concerned about the sharpness of his sword, so he folded down the left flap of his trousers to expose a little of his thigh, and ran the blade lightly over it. Straightaway blood oozed out of the wound, and a few thin trickles glistened in the strong light as they ran down toward his crotch.

Reiko, who was seeing her husband's blood for the first time, felt her heart throb violently. She looked at her husband's face. The lieutenant was contemplating his blood without emotion.

心配になる【しんぱいになる】become worried about

左方【さほう】left side

折り返す【おりかえす】fold over

腿【もも】thigh

少し【すこし】slightly

あらわす【あらわす】expose

軽く【かるく】lightly

刃【やいば】blade

滑る【すべる】[causative form in text] slide

たちまち immediately

傷口【きずぐち】wound

血【ち】blood, drop of blood ⊛

にじむ ooze

数条【すうじょう】several streaks

細い【ほそい】thin, fine

明るい【あかるい】bright

光り【ひかり】light

照り輝やく【てりかがやく】shine brightly

股【また】crotch

〜のほうへ toward

流れる【ながれる】flow, stream

117

はじめて for the first time

良人【おっと】husband ⊛

麗子【れいこ】Reiko

怖ろしい【おそろしい】intense, violent

動悸【どうき】throbbing, palpitation

顔【かお】face

平然と【へいぜんと】impassively, unfazed

見つめる【みつめる】stare

姑息な安心だと思いながら、麗子はつかのまの安堵を味わった。

118▶　そのとき中尉は鷹のような目つきで妻をはげしく凝視した。刀を前へ廻し、腰を持ち上げ、上半身が刃先へのしかかるようにして、体に全力をこめているのが、軍服の怒った肩からわかった。中尉は一思いに深く左脇腹へ刺そうと思ったのである。鋭い気合の声が、沈黙の部屋を貫ぬいた。

119▶　中尉は自分で力を加えたにもかかわらず、人から太い鉄の棒で脇腹を痛打されたような感じがした。一瞬、頭がくらくらし、何が起ったのかわからなかった。五六寸あらわした刃先はすでにすっかり肉に埋まって、拳が握っている布がじかに腹に接していた。

姑息な【こそくな】superficial, short-term
安心【あんしん】peace of mind
思う【おもう】think ⊛
麗子【れいこ】Reiko
つかのまの fleeting
安堵【あんど】relief
味わう【あじわう】taste, feel

118
中尉【ちゅうい】lieutenant ⊛
鷹【たか】hawk
目つき【めつき】look, expression in one's eyes
妻【つま】wife
はげしく intensely, fiercely
凝視する【ぎょうしする】stare
刀【かたな】sword
前【まえ】front
廻す【まわす】bring around

腰【こし】loin, hip
持ち上げる【もちあげる】raise
上半身【じょうはんしん】upper body
刃先【はさき】tip (of a blade) ⊛
のしかかる lean onto
体【からだ】body
全力【ぜんりょく】all one's strength
こめる put in
軍服【ぐんぷく】military uniform
怒る【いかる】angulate, become pointed
肩【かた】shoulder (NOTE: 怒り肩 square shoulders)
わかる understand
一思いに【ひとおもいに】resolutely
深く【ふかく】deeply
左脇腹【ひだりわきばら】left flank
刺す【さす】[volitional form in text] stab
鋭い【するどい】sharp

She knew the respite was only temporary, but Reiko nonetheless enjoyed a fleeting sense of relief.

At that moment the lieutenant glared fiercely at his wife with the eyes of a hawk. He swung the sword around in front of him and raised his hips so that his torso hung over the tip of the blade. From the pointed shoulders of his uniform, it was clear that he was gathering all his strength. The lieutenant planned to make a deep and determined stab into his left side. His martial shout rang through the silent room.

The lieutenant had himself made the thrust, but he felt as though someone else had dealt him an excruciating blow on the side with a thick iron bar. Lightheaded for a moment, he could not understand what was going on. The six or seven inches of exposed blade were now embedded deep in his flesh, and the cloth, clasped in his clenched fist, was pressing up against his stomach.

気合 【きあい】 battle cry
声 【こえ】 voice
沈黙 【ちんもく】 silence
部屋 【へや】 room
貫ぬく 【つらぬく】 pierce

119

自分で 【じぶんで】 himself
力 【ちから】 strength, force
加える 【くわえる】 add
〜にもかかわらず despite
人 【ひと】 person
太い 【ふとい】 thick
鉄の棒 【てつのぼう】 iron bar
脇腹 【わきばら】 flank
痛打する 【つうだする】 [passive form in text]
  strike painfully
感じがする 【かんじがする】 feel
一瞬 【いっしゅん】 momentarily

頭 【あたま】 head
くらくらする MIMETIC feel dizzy
何 【なに】 what
起る 【おきる】 happen
わかる understand
五六寸 【ごろくすん】 five or six *sun* (1 *sun*
  = 1.19 inches)
あらわす expose, appear
すでに already
すっかり completely
肉 【にく】 flesh
埋まる 【うまる】 be buried
拳 【こぶし】 fist
握る 【にぎる】 grip, hold
布 【ぬの】 cloth
じかに directly
腹 【はら】 belly, stomach
接する 【せっする】 come into contact

　意識が戻る。刃はたしかに腹膜を貫ぬいたと中尉は思った。呼吸が苦しく胸がひどい動悸を打ち、自分の内部とは思えない遠い遠い深部で、地が裂けて熱い熔岩が流れ出したように、怖ろしい劇痛が湧き出して来るのがわかる。その劇痛が怖ろしい速度でたちまち近くへ来る。中尉は思わず呻きかけたが、下唇を嚙んでこらえた。

　これが切腹というものかと中尉は思っていた。それは天が頭上に落ち、世界がぐらつくような滅茶滅茶な感覚で、切る前はあれほど鞏固に見えた自分の意志と勇気が、今は細い針金の一線のようになって、一途にそれに縋ってゆかねばならない不安に襲われた。

120

意識【いしき】consciousness

戻る【もどる】return

刃【やいば】blade

たしかに certainly

腹膜【ふくまく】membrane lining the abdominal cavity

貫ぬく【つらぬく】pierce

中尉【ちゅうい】lieutenant ✪

思う【おもう】think ✪ (NOTE: Next usage is in the potential form.)

呼吸【こきゅう】breathing

苦しい【くるしい】painful

胸【むね】chest

ひどい terrible

動悸【どうき】throbbing

打つ【うつ】beat

自分【じぶん】oneself, himself ✪

内部【ないぶ】innards

遠い【とおい】distant ✪

深部【しんぶ】deep part

地【ち】earth, ground

裂ける【さける】split, rip open

熱い【あつい】hot

熔岩【ようがん】lava

流れ出す【ながれだす】flow out

怖ろしい【おそろしい】intense, violent ✪

劇痛【げきつう】acute pain ✪

湧き出す【わきだす】surge up

〜て来る【〜てくる】indicates progression in the direction of the narrator

わかる realize, feel

速度【そくど】speed

たちまち immediately

近く【ちかく】close

来る【くる】come

He came to. The lieutenant was convinced that the blade had punctured the peritoneal membrane. He had difficulty breathing, his chest was pounding madly, and deep down inside—so far, far away that he could hardly believe it was part of him—he felt a terrifyingly intense pain erupt, as if the ground had split open and hot lava were streaming forth. Searing pain closed in on him at frightening speed. Despite himself, the lieutenant emitted the beginnings of a groan, but stifled it by biting his lip.

So this is ritual suicide? the lieutenant was thinking to himself. It was a sense of total and utter chaos as if the sky had crashed down on his head and the whole world was reeling around him. His courage and his strength of will—seemingly so strong before he cut himself—had now been reduced to something like a single, fine length of wire, and he was overcome with anxiety at the thought of having only that to depend on.

思わず 【おもわず】 involuntarily
呻きかける 【うめきかける】 start to groan
下唇 【したくちびる】 lower lip
噛む 【かむ】 bite
こらえる suppress

121

切腹 【せっぷく】 suicide by cutting one's stomach
もの thing
天 【てん】 sky, the heavens
頭上に 【ずじょうに】 onto one's head
落ちる 【おちる】 fall
世界 【せかい】 world
ぐらつく reel, totter
滅茶滅茶な 【めちゃめちゃな】 shambolic
感覚 【かんかく】 sensation
切る 【きる】 cut
前 【まえ】 before

あれほど to that extent
鞏固な 【きょうこな】 strong, firm
見える 【みえる】 seem, appear
意志 【いし】 will, determination
勇気 【ゆうき】 courage
今は 【いまは】 now
細い 【ほそい】 thin
針金 【はりがね】 wire
一線 【いっせん】 single line
一途に 【いちずに】 blindly
縋る 【すがる】 rely on, cling to
〜てゆく indicates an increase in tendency
〜ねばならない have to
不安 【ふあん】 anxiety, uneasiness
襲う 【おそう】 [passive form in text] attack

拳がぬるぬるして来る。見ると白布も拳もすっかり血に塗れそぼっている。褌もすでに真紅に染っている。こんな烈しい苦痛の中でまだ見えるものが見え、在るものが在るのはふしぎである。

122▶

　麗子は中尉が左脇腹に刀を突っ込んだ瞬間、その顔から忽ち幕を下ろしたように血の気が引いたのを見て、駈け寄ろうとする自分と戦っていた。とにかく見なければならぬ。見届けねばならぬ。それが良人の麗子に与えた職務である。畳一枚の距離の向うに、下唇を嚙みしめて苦痛をこらえている良人の顔は、鮮明に見えている。その苦痛は一分の隙もない正確さで現前している。麗子にはそれを救う術がないのである。

拳【こぶし】fist ✦

ぬるぬるする MIMETIC become slimy

〜て来る【〜てくる】indicates a condition coming into effect

見る【みる】look

白布【しろぬの】white cloth

すっかり completely

血【ち】blood

塗れそぼる【ぬれそぼる】become soaked

褌【ふんどし】loincloth

すでに already

真紅【しんく】pure crimson

染る【そまる】be dyed

烈しい【はげしい】intense, fierce

苦痛【くつう】pain, agony ✦

〜の中で【〜のなかで】amid

見える【みえる】be visible ✦

もの thing ✦

在る【ある】be, exist ✦

ふしぎ marvel, miracle

122

麗子【れいこ】Reiko ✦

中尉【ちゅうい】lieutenant

左脇腹【ひだりわきばら】left flank

刀【かたな】sword

突っ込む【つっこむ】plunge

瞬間【しゅんかん】moment

顔【かお】face ✦

忽ち【たちまち】immediately

幕を下ろす【まくをおろす】bring down the curtain

血の気が引く【ちのけがひく】blood drains from one's face

見る【みる】see, watch ✦

駈け寄る【かけよる】[volitional form in text] rush over to

His clenched fists were now slimy and wet. He looked down to see that the white cloth and his hands were completely drenched in blood. His loincloth was already dyed a deep crimson color. He was amazed that, even amidst this intense agony, visible things were still visible, and things that existed, existed still.

The instant the lieutenant drove the sword into his left flank, Reiko wrestled with her desire to rush to his side as she saw the blood drain out of his face like a hastily lowered curtain. She had to watch no matter what. She had to bear witness. It was the duty her husband had assigned her. Opposite her, one tatami away, she could clearly see her husband's face as he bit down on his lip to stifle his agony. His pain was there to see, evident down to the very last detail. There was nothing Reiko could do to help him.

~（ろ）うとする be about to ~
自分【じぶん】oneself, herself
戦う【たたかう】fight
とにかく in any circumstances
見届ける【みとどける】watch to the end
~ねばならぬ must, have to
良人【おっと】husband ⊛
与える【あたえる】assign
職務【しょくむ】duty, task
畳一枚【たたみいちまい】one tatami mat
距離【きょり】distance
向う【むこう】other side
下唇【したくちびる】lower lip
噛みしめる【かみしめる】bite down on
こらえる suppress
鮮明に【せんめいに】vividly
一分の隙もない【いちぶのすきもない】
  solid, faultless

正確さ【せいかくさ】accuracy, precision
現前する【げんぜんする】appear right
  before one
救う【すくう】help
術【すべ】way, means

　良人の額にはにじみ出した汗が光っている。中尉は目をつぶり、又ためすように目をあける。その目がいつもの輝やきを失って、小動物の目のように無邪気でうつろに見える。

　苦痛は麗子の目の前で、麗子の身を引き裂かれるような悲嘆にはかかわりなく、夏の太陽のように輝やいている。その苦痛がますます背丈を増す。伸び上る。良人がすでに別の世界の人になって、その全存在を苦痛に還元され、手をのばしても触れられない苦痛の檻の囚人になったのを麗子は感じる。しかも麗子は痛まない。悲嘆は痛まない。それを思うと、麗子は自分と良人との間に、何者かが無情な高い硝子の壁を立ててしまったような気がした。

良人【おっと】husband ✿

額【ひたい】forehead

にじみ出す【にじみだす】ooze out

汗【あせ】sweat

光る【ひかる】shine

中尉【ちゅうい】lieutenant

目をつぶる【めをつぶる】shut one's eyes

又【また】also, and, again

ためす【ためす】experiment

目をあける【めをあける】open one's eyes

目【め】eyes ✿

いつも always

輝やき【かがやき】glow

失う【うしなう】lose

小動物【しょうどうぶつ】small animal

無邪気な【むじゃきな】innocent

うつろな blank, vacant

見える【みえる】appear

苦痛【くつう】pain, agony ✿

麗子【れいこ】Reiko ✿

目の前【めのまえ】before one's eyes

身【み】body

引き裂く【ひきさく】[passive form in text] rip open

悲嘆【ひたん】grief ✿

かかわりなく heedlessly, indifferently

夏【なつ】summer

太陽【たいよう】sun

輝やく【かがやく】shine

ますます more and more

背丈【せたけ】stature

増す【ます】increase

伸び上る【のびあがる】stretch up

すでに already

The sweat beading her husband's forehead glistened. The lieutenant was shutting his eyes, then opening them again as if to try them out. They had lost their usual gleam and looked innocent and vacant like the eyes of a small animal.

Despite the grief that seemed to be tearing her body apart, the agony in front of Reiko's eyes shone like the summer sun. The pain grew ever taller in stature. It loomed up. Reiko felt that her husband had already become a man of a different world—his whole existence distilled into pain, a prisoner in a cage of pain, unreachable even to her outstretched hand. But Reiko herself felt no pain. Grief does not hurt. As the thought came to her, Reiko felt as though someone had built a cruel and high glass wall between herself and her husband.

別の世界【べつのせかい】another world
人【ひと】person
全存在【ぜんそんざい】whole existence
還元する【かんげんする】[passive form in text] resolve into
手をのばす【てをのばす】stretch out a helping hand
触れる【ふれる】[potential form in text] touch
檻【おり】cage
囚人【しゅうじん】prisoner
感じる【かんじる】feel
しかも moreover
痛む【いたむ】hurt ✪
思う【おもう】think about, consider
自分【じぶん】oneself, herself
〜の間に【〜のあいだに】between
何者か【なにものか】somebody
無情な【むじょうな】heartless

高い【たかい】high
硝子【ガラス】glass
壁【かべ】wall
立てる【たてる】build
〜てしまう expresses with regret the completion of action
〜ような気がする【〜ようなきがする】feel as though

125 ▶ 　結婚以来、良人が存在していることは自分が存在していることであり、良人の息づかいの一つ一つはまた自分の息づかいでもあったのに、今、良人は苦痛のなかにありありと存在し、麗子は悲嘆の裡に、何一つ自分の存在の確証をつかんでいなかった。

126 ▶ 　中尉は右手でそのまま引き廻そうとしたが、刃先は腸にからまり、ともすると刀は柔らかい弾力で押し出されて来て、両手で刃を腹の奥深く押えつけながら、引廻して行かねばならぬのを知った。引廻した。思ったほど切れない。中尉は右手に全身の力をこめて引いた。三四寸切れた。

125

結婚【けっこん】wedding, marriage
〜以来【〜いらい】since
良人【おっと】husband ⊛
存在する【そんざいする】exist ⊛
自分【じぶん】oneself, herself ⊛
息づかい【いきづかい】breathing ⊛
一つ一つ【ひとつひとつ】each and every one
また also, again
〜のに although, in spite of
今【いま】now
苦痛【くつう】pain, agony
〜のなかに amidst
ありありと clearly, vividly
麗子【れいこ】Reiko
悲嘆【ひたん】grief
〜の裡に【〜のうちに】inside

何一つ〜ない【なにひとつ〜ない】nothing
存在【そんざい】existence
確証【かくしょう】confirmation, proof
つかむ grasp, grab hold of

126

中尉【ちゅうい】lieutenant ⊛
右手【みぎて】right hand ⊛
そのまま in that position
引き廻す【ひきまわす】[volitional form in text] pull across
〜（そ）うとする try to 〜
刃先【はさき】tip (of a blade)
腸【ちょう】intestines
からまる get entangled
ともすると at times
刀【かたな】sword
柔らかい【やわらかい】soft

Since their marriage, her husband's existence had been her existence, her husband's each and every breath her own breathing. Now, as her husband drew breath amidst palpable pain, within her own grief Reiko could find no proof of her own existence.

Using his right hand, the lieutenant attempted to pull the sword across at the same depth; but the tip got caught in his intestines and was propelled outward by their soft springiness. He realized he would have to slice across with both hands pressing the blade deep into his stomach. He pulled sideways. It did not cut as much as he had expected. The lieutenant concentrated the strength of his entire body into his right arm and pulled again. It cut a little more than three or four inches.

弾力【だんりょく】elasticity

押し出す【おしだす】[passive form in text] push out

〜て来る【〜てくる】indicates a situation or phenomenon emerging

両手【りょうて】both hands

刃【やいば】blade

腹【はら】belly, stomach

奥深く【おくぶかく】deeply

押えつける【おさえつける】hold down

〜て行く【〜ていく】indicates an increase in tendency

〜ねばならぬ have to

知る【しる】realize

思ったほど【おもったほど】as one had thought

切れる【きれる】cut ✳

全身の力【ぜんしんのちから】all one's strength

こめる put into play

引く【ひく】pull

三四寸【さんよんすん】three or four *sun* (1 *sun* = 1.19 inches)

127▶　　　苦痛は腹の奥から徐々にひろがって、腹全体が鳴り響いているようになった。それは乱打される鐘のようで、自分のつく呼吸の一息一息、自分の打つ脈搏の一打ち毎に、苦痛が千の鐘を一度に鳴らすかのように、彼の存在を押しゆるがした。中尉はもう呻きを抑えることができなくなった。しかし、ふと見ると、刃がすでに臍の下まで切り裂いているのを見て、満足と勇気をおぼえた。

128▶　　　血は次第に図に乗って、傷口から脈打つように迸った。前の畳は血しぶきに赤く濡れ、カーキいろのズボンの襞からは溜った血が畳に流れ落ちた。ついに麗子の白無垢の膝に、一滴の血が遠く小鳥のように飛んで届いた。

127

苦痛【くつう】pain, agony ✿

腹【はら】belly, stomach ✿

奥【おく】depths

徐々に【じょじょに】gradually

ひろがる spread out

～全体【～ぜんたい】entire ~

鳴り響く【なりひびく】resonate

乱打する【らんだする】[passive form in text] hit repeatedly

鐘【かね】bell ✿

自分【じぶん】oneself, himself ✿

つく take (a breath)

呼吸【こきゅう】breathing

一息一息【ひといきひといき】each and every breath

打つ【うつ】beat

脈搏【みゃくはく】pulse

一打ち【ひとうち】one stroke

～毎に【～ごとに】each, every

千【せん】1,000

一度に【いちどに】at once

鳴らす【ならす】sound, ring

彼【かれ】he

存在【そんざい】existence

押しゆるがす【おしゆるがす】push and shake

中尉【ちゅうい】lieutenant

呻き【うめき】groan

抑える【おさえる】suppress, stifle

しかし however

ふと fleetingly, briefly

見る【みる】see, look ✿

刃【やいば】blade

すでに already

臍【へそ】navel

The pain slowly spread from the depths of his stomach until it seemed his whole abdomen reverberated with it. It was like a bell that was being struck frenziedly; and with every breath he took and every beat of his pulse, the pain—like a thousand bells being sounded at once—convulsed his very existence. The lieutenant was no longer able to stifle his groans. But when he glanced down and saw that the blade had already ripped him open to beneath his navel, he felt mingled pride and courage.

Gaining confidence, the blood started squirting from the wound with the beating of his pulse. The tatami before him was soaked red with splashing blood, and pooled blood streamed down to the tatami from the folds in his khaki trousers. A single drop of blood had even flown, like a small bird, to land all the way over on the lap of Reiko's white kimono.

〜の下 【〜のした】beneath
切り裂く 【きりさく】be cut open
満足 【まんぞく】satisfaction
勇気 【ゆうき】courage
おぼえる feel

128

血 【ち】blood ⊛
次第に 【しだいに】gradually
図に乗る 【ずにのる】get in the swing
傷口 【きずぐち】wound
脈打つ 【みゃくうつ】beat (of pulse, heart)
迸る 【ほとばしる】gush forth
前の 【まえの】in front, before oneself
畳 【たたみ】tatami mat ⊛
血しぶき 【ちしぶき】splash of blood
赤く 【あかく】redly
濡れる 【ぬれる】get wet
カーキいろ khaki color

ズボン trousers
襞 【ひだ】fold
溜る 【たまる】collect, form puddles
流れ落ちる 【ながれおちる】flow down on
ついに at last, finally
麗子 【れいこ】Reiko
白無垢 【しろむく】white silk kimono
膝 【ひざ】knee
一滴 【いってき】one drop
遠く 【とおく】far
小鳥 【ことり】little bird
飛ぶ 【とぶ】fly
届く 【とどく】reach

　中尉がようやく右の脇腹まで引廻したとき、すでに刃は
やや浅くなって、膏と血に辷る刀身をあらわしていたが、
突然嘔吐に襲われた中尉は、かすれた叫びをあげた。嘔吐
が劇痛をさらに攪拌して、今まで固く締っていた腹が急に
波打ち、その傷口が大きくひらけて、あたかも傷口がせい
一ぱい吐瀉するように、腸が弾け出て来たのである。腸は
主の苦痛も知らぬげに、健康な、いやらしいほどいきいき
とした姿で、喜々として辷り出て股間にあふれた。中尉は
うつむいて、肩で息をして目を薄目にあき、口から涎の糸
を垂らしていた。肩には肩章の金がかがやいていた。

129

中尉【ちゅうい】lieutenant ✲
ようやく finally
右【みぎ】right
脇腹【わきばら】flank
引廻す【ひきまわす】pull across
すでに already
刃【やいば】blade
やや somewhat, rather
浅い【あさい】shallow
膏【あぶら】fat
血【ち】blood
辷る【すべる】slip
刀身【とうしん】blade
あらわす show, expose
突然【とつぜん】suddenly
嘔吐【おうと】vomiting ✲
襲う【おそう】[passive form in text] attack

かすれる become hoarse, go raspy
叫び【さけび】shout
あげる emit, let out
劇痛【げきつう】acute pain
さらに more
攪拌する【かくはんする】exacerbate
今まで【いままで】until now
固く【かたく】firmly, strongly
締る【しまる】be firm, be tight
腹【はら】belly, stomach
急に【きゅうに】suddenly
波打つ【なみうつ】beat, surge
傷口【きずぐち】wound ✲
大きく【おおきく】wide
ひらける open up
あたかも just as if
せい一ぱい【せいいっぱい】to one's
　utmost

By the time the lieutenant had finally dragged the sword across to his right side, the blade, somewhat shallow now inside him, was showing its length slippery with fat and blood; attacked by a sudden fit of retching, the lieutenant emitted a hoarse cry. The retching aggravated his agony still further, and suddenly his stomach, which had been tight and firm up to this point, began to heave and the wound opened wide and his innards came bounding forth as if the cut itself were vomiting them out as hard as it could. Seemingly ignorant of their master's torment, the intestines looked healthy and almost obscenely full of life as they gleefully slithered out and tumbled down into his crotch. The lieutenant's head drooped, his shoulders heaved as he breathed, his eyes narrowed down to mere slits, and a string of drool hung from his mouth. The gold of his epaulets gleamed on his shoulders.

吐瀉する 【としゃする】 vomit and have diarrhea
腸 【はらわた】 intestines ⊛
弾け出る 【はじけでる】 bounce out
〜て来る 【〜てくる】 indicates movement in the direction of the narrator
主 【あるじ】 master
苦痛 【くつう】 pain, agony
知らぬげに 【しらぬげに】 with an air of not knowing
健康な 【けんこうな】 healthy
いやらしい obscene, offensive
〜ほど to the extent of
いきいきとした full of life
姿 【すがた】 form, appearance
喜々として 【ききとして】 joyfully
辷り出る 【すべりでる】 slip out
股間 【こかん】 crotch

あふれる overflow
うつむく drop one's head
肩で息をする 【かたでいきをする】 one's shoulders heave as one breathes ⊛
息をする 【いきをする】 breathe
目 【め】 eye
薄目 【うすめ】 narrowed eyes
あく open
口 【くち】 mouth
涎 【よだれ】 saliva, drool
糸 【いと】 thread, string
垂らす 【たらす】 dribble
肩 【かた】 shoulder
肩章 【けんしょう】 epaulet
金 【きん】 gold
かがやく shine

130▶　　血はそこかしこに散って、中尉は自分の血溜りの中に膝までつかり、そこに片手をついて崩折れていた。生ぐさい匂いが部屋にこもり、うつむきながら嘔吐をくりかえしている動きがありありと肩にあらわれた。腸に押し出されたかのように、刀身はすでに刃先まであらわれて中尉の右手に握られていた。

131▶　　このとき中尉が力をこめてのけぞった姿は、比べるものがないほど壮烈だったと云えよう。あまり急激にのけぞったので、後頭部が床柱に当る音が明瞭にきこえたほどである。麗子はそれまで、顔を伏せて、ただ自分の膝もとへ寄って来る血の流れだけを一心に見つめていたが、この音におどろいて顔をあげた。

130
血【ち】blood
そこかしこに all over the place
散る【ちる】spread, spatter
中尉【ちゅうい】lieutenant ✛
自分【じぶん】himself, herself ✛
血溜り【ちだまり】pool of blood
〜の中に【〜のなかに】inside
膝【ひざ】knee
つかる be soaked
片手をつく【かたてをつく】put one hand
　to the floor
崩折れる【くずおれる】collapse, crumble
生ぐさい【なまぐさい】rank, bloody-
　smelling
匂い【におい】smell
部屋【へや】room
こもる fill

うつむく drop one's head
嘔吐【おうと】vomiting
くりかえす repeat
動き【うごき】movement
ありありと clearly, vividly
肩【かた】shoulder
あらわれる appear, show itself ✛
腸【はらわた】intestines
押し出す【おしだす】[passive form in text]
　push out
刀身【とうしん】blade
すでに already
刃先【はさき】tip (of a blade)
右手【みぎて】right hand
握る【にぎる】[passive form in text] grip, hold
131
力【ちから】strength, power
こめる put in

Blood was everywhere. The lieutenant was hunched over, propping himself up with one hand in the pool of blood that drenched his knees. A rank smell filled the room, and as he slumped forward, his repeated retching was all too evident in the movement of his shoulders. The sword, still gripped in the lieutenant's right hand, was now exposed as far as the tip, as though pushed back out by the intestines.

The sight of the lieutenant at this point, as he gathered his strength and flung his head back, was incomparably heroic. He threw his head back so violently that there was a clearly audible thud as the back of his skull hit the alcove pillar. Until that moment, Reiko had kept her head down, staring solely at the sea of blood approaching her knees, but startled by this sound, she looked up.

のけぞる throw one's head back ⊛
姿 【すがた】 figure, appearance
比べる 【くらべる】 compare
もの thing
～ほど to the extent that ~ ⊛
壮烈な 【そうれつな】 heroic, brave
云う 【いう】 [volitional form of potential form in text] say
あまり too much
急激に 【きゅうげきに】 suddenly, abruptly
後頭部 【こうとうぶ】 back of the head
床柱 【とこばしら】 alcove post
当る 【あたる】 hit
音 【おと】 sound, noise ⊛
明瞭に 【めいりょうに】 clearly
きこえる be audible
～ほど to the extent that ~
麗子 【れいこ】 Reiko

顔を伏せる 【かおをふせる】 look down
ただ only
膝もと 【ひざもと】 near one's knees
寄る 【よる】 approach
～て来る 【～てくる】 indicates movement toward the narrator
血 【ち】 blood
流れ 【ながれ】 flow
一心に 【いっしんに】 wholeheartedly
見つめる 【みつめる】 stare
おどろく be surprised
顔をあげる 【かおをあげる】 look up

　　中尉の顔は生きている人の顔ではなかった。目は凹み、肌は乾いて、あれほど美しかった頬や唇は、涸化した土いろになっていた。ただ重たげに刀を握った右手だけが、操人形のように浮薄に動き、自分の咽喉元に刃先をあてようとしていた。こうして麗子は、良人の最期の、もっとも辛い、空虚な努力をまざまざと眺めた。血と膏に光った刃先が何度も咽喉を狙う。又外れる。もう力が十分でないのである。外れた刃先が襟に当り、襟章に当る。ホックは外されているのに、軍服の固い襟はともすると窄まって、咽喉元を刃から衛ってしまう。

中尉【ちゅうい】lieutenant

顔【かお】face ⊛

生きる【いきる】live, be alive

人【ひと】person

目【め】eye

凹む【くぼむ】become hollow, become sunken

肌【はだ】skin

乾く【かわく】dry out

あれほど to that extent

美しい【うつくしい】beautiful

頬【ほお】cheek

唇【くちびる】lip

涸化する【こかする】dry up

土いろ【つちいろ】earth color

ただ only, just

重たげに【おもたげに】as though it were heavy

刀【かたな】sword

握る【にぎる】grip, hold

右手【みぎて】right hand

操人形【あやつりにんぎょう】puppet

浮薄に【ふはくに】fickly, inconstantly

動く【うごく】move

自分【じぶん】oneself, himself

咽喉元【のどもと】base of the throat ⊛

刃先【はさき】tip (of a blade) ⊛

あてる [volitional form in text] place against

～ようとする try to ～

麗子【れいこ】Reiko

良人【おっと】husband

最期【さいご】last moment (prior to death)

もっとも most

The lieutenant's face was not the face of a living man. His eyes were sunken, his skin desiccated, and his once-beautiful cheeks and lips had become the color of parched earth. Only his right hand, clumsily gripping the sword, jerked around in a puppet-like attempt to point the tip at his throat. In this way, Reiko saw every lurid detail of her husband's last, most heartbreaking and futile efforts. The sword point shining with blood and grease took repeated aim at his throat. And every time it missed. The strength was no longer there. When it missed, the point of the sword hit his collar, or the insignia on his collar. The hooks were undone, but the stiff collar of his uniform had closed up again and was shielding his throat from the blade.

辛い 【つらい】 painful, bitter
空虚な 【くうきょな】 empty, hollow
努力 【どりょく】 effort
まざまざと vividly, clearly
眺める 【ながめる】 gaze at
血 【ち】 blood
膏 【あぶら】 fat
光る 【ひかる】 shine
何度も 【なんども】 repeatedly
咽喉 【のど】 throat
狙う 【ねらう】 aim for
又 【また】 and, again
外れる 【はずれる】 miss ✦
もう〜ない no longer
力 【ちから】 strength, power
十分 【じゅうぶん】 enough
襟 【えり】 collar ✦
当る 【あたる】 hit ✦

襟章 【えりしょう】 collar badge
ホック hook, clip
外す 【はずす】 [passive form in text] undo
〜のに although, in spite of
軍服 【ぐんぷく】 military uniform
固い 【かたい】 hard
ともすると at times
窄まる 【すぼまる】 become narrower, close up
刃 【やいば】 blade
衛る 【まもる】 protect
〜てしまう expresses with regret the completion of an action

麗子はとうとう見かねて、良人に近寄ろうとしたが、立つことができない。血の中を膝行して近寄ったので、白無垢の裾は真紅になった。彼女は良人の背後にまわって、襟をくつろげるだけの手助けをした。慄えている刃先がようやく裸かの咽喉に触れる。麗子はそのとき自分が良人を突き飛ばしたように感じたが、そうではなかった。それは中尉が自分で意図した最後の力である。彼はいきなり刃へ向って体を投げかけ、刃はその項をつらぬいて、おびただしい血の迸りと共に、電燈の下に、冷静な青々とした刃先をそば立てて静まった。

133

麗子【れいこ】Reiko ⊛
とうとう finally
見かねる【みかねる】be unable to look on
良人【おっと】husband ⊛
近寄る【ちかよる】[volitional form in text] approach ⊛
〜（ろ）うとする try to 〜
立つ【たつ】stand up
血【ち】blood
〜の中を【〜のなかを】through
膝行する【しっこうする】waddle on one's knees
白無垢【しろむく】white silk kimono
裾【すそ】skirt, hem
真紅【しんく】deep crimson
彼女【かのじょ】she
〜の背後に【〜のはいごに】behind one

まわる move around
襟【えり】collar
くつろげる loosen
手助け【てだすけ】help
慄える【ふるえる】shudder, tremble
刃先【はさき】tip (of a blade) ⊛
ようやく finally
裸かの【はだかの】naked
咽喉【のど】throat
触れる【ふれる】touch
自分【じぶん】herself, oneself ⊛
突き飛ばす【つきとばす】thrust away
感じる【かんじる】feel
中尉【ちゅうい】lieutenant
自分で【じぶんで】himself
意図する【いとする】intend, will
最後の【さいごの】final, last
力【ちから】strength, power

Eventually no longer able to look on passively, Reiko tried to draw closer to her husband but was incapable of standing up. She edged toward him, waddling on her knees through the blood, and the skirts of her white silk kimono turned deep crimson. Moving around behind her husband, she helped him only by loosening his collar. The twitching tip of the blade finally made contact with his bare throat. At that moment, Reiko felt as if she had pushed her husband forward, but that was not the case. It was the last shred of the lieutenant's own strength he was to consciously exert: he abruptly flung his body onto the sword, and the blade came out through the back of his neck. There was a tremendous spurt of blood, and beneath the electric light its cold, blue tip jutted out of him and then was still.

彼【かれ】he
いきなり suddenly, abruptly
刃【やいば】blade ⊛
向う【むかう】face toward
体【からだ】body
投げかける【なげかける】throw upon
項【うなじ】nape of the neck
つらぬく pierce
おびただしい torrential, abundant
迸り【ほとばしり】gush, surge
〜と共に【〜とともに】together with
電燈【でんとう】electric light
〜の下に【〜のしたに】beneath
冷静な【れいせいな】cool
青々とした【あおあおとした】blue
そば立てる【そばだてる】stick (one end) high
静まる【しずまる】go still

伍 【ご】

134▶ 　麗子は血に辷る足袋で、ゆっくりと階段を下りた。すでに二階はひっそりしていた。

135▶ 　階下の電気をつけ、火元をしらべ、ガスの元栓をしらべ、火鉢の埋み火に、水をかけて消した。四畳半の姿見の前へ行って垂れをあげた。血が白無垢を、華麗で大胆な裾模様のように見せていた。姿見の前に坐ると、腿のあたりが良人の血に濡れて大そう冷たく、麗子は身を慄わせた。それから永いこと、化粧に時を費した。頬は濃い目に紅を刷き、唇も濃く塗った。これはすでに良人のための化粧ではなかった。

伍【ご】five

134
麗子【れいこ】Reiko ✸
血【ち】blood ✸
辷る【すべる】slip
足袋【たび】tabi sock
ゆっくりと slowly
階段【かいだん】stairs
下りる【おりる】descend
すでに already, by now ✸
二階【にかい】second floor
ひっそりする be quiet

135
階下【かいか】downstairs
電気【でんき】electric light
つける turn on
火元【ひもと】gas jet
しらべる check ✸

ガス gas
元栓【もとせん】main tap
火鉢【ひばち】charcoal brazier
埋み火【うずみび】buried ember
水をかける【みずをかける】throw water on
消す【けす】extinguish
四畳半【よじょうはん】four-and-a-half-mat room
姿見【すがたみ】full-length mirror ✸
〜の前へ【〜のまえへ】in front of
行く【いく】go
垂れ【たれ】cloth covering
あげる lift up
白無垢【しろむく】white silk kimono
華麗な【かれいな】gorgeous
大胆な【だいたんな】bold
裾模様【すそもよう】skirt pattern

5

Her tabi slippery with blood, Reiko slowly descended the stairs. The upper floor was now quiet.

Switching on the downstairs light, she checked the gas burners and the main gas tap, then poured water over the buried embers in the brazier to put them out. She then went over to the full-length mirror in the four-and-a-half-mat room and lifted the cloth that covered it. The blood made it look as though there were a gorgeous, bold pattern on her skirt. As she sat down in front of the mirror, the area around her thighs, which was clammy with her husband's blood, felt cold and she shivered. Then she spent a long time applying her make-up. She applied rouge thickly to her cheeks, and painted her lips heavily too. This was no longer make-up for the sake of her husband.

見せる 【みせる】 show
〜の前に 【〜のまえに】 in front of
坐る 【すわる】 sit
腿 【もも】 thigh
あたり area
良人 【おっと】 husband ⊛
濡れる 【ぬれる】 get wet
大そう 【たいそう】 very
冷たい 【つめたい】 cold
身を慄わせる 【みをふるわせる】 shiver
永いこと 【ながいこと】 long while
化粧 【けしょう】 make-up ⊛
時を費す 【ときをついやす】 spend time
頬 【ほお】 cheek
濃い目に 【こいめに】 thickly
紅 【べに】 rouge
刷く 【はく】 put on, brush on
唇 【くちびる】 lip

濃く 【こく】 thickly
塗る 【ぬる】 paint
すでに already
〜のための for 〜

残された世界のための化粧で、彼女の刷毛には壮大なものがこもっていた。立上ったとき、姿見の前の畳は血に濡れている。麗子は意に介しなかった。

　それから手水へゆき、最後に玄関の三和土に立った。この鍵を、昨夜良人がしめたのは、死の用意だったのである。彼女はしばらく単純な思案に耽った。鍵をあけておくべきか否か。もし鍵をかけておけば、隣り近所の人が、数日二人の死に気がつかないということがありうる。麗子は自分たちの屍が腐敗して発見されることを好まない。やはりあけておいたほうがいい。……彼女は鍵を外し、磨硝子の戸を少し引きあけた。

残す【のこす】[passive form in text] leave behind
世界【せかい】world
〜のための for 〜
化粧【けしょう】make-up
彼女【かのじょ】she ❀
刷毛【はけ】brush
壮大な【そうだいな】magnificent
もの thing, something
こもる fill
立上る【たちあがる】stand up
姿見【すがたみ】full-length mirror
〜の前の【〜のまえの】in front of
畳【たたみ】tatami mat
血【ち】blood
濡れる【ぬれる】get wet
麗子【れいこ】Reiko ❀

意に介する【いにかいする】mind, worry about

手水【ちょうず】toilet
ゆく【ゆく】go
最後に【さいごに】finally
玄関【げんかん】entrance hall
三和土【たたき】cement floor
立つ【たつ】stand
鍵【かぎ】key, lock
昨夜【さくや】last night
良人【おっと】husband
しめる shut
死【し】death ❀
用意【ようい】preparation
しばらく for a while
単純な【たんじゅんな】simple

It was make-up for the world she would leave behind her, so her brush was endowed with something exalted. When she stood up, the mat before the mirror was damp with blood. Reiko paid no heed.

She then went to the toilet, and finally stood on the cement floor of the entrance hall. Her husband's turning of this lock last night had been a part of his death preparations. For a while Reiko was preoccupied with a simple question: should she leave the door unlocked or not? If she left it locked, it was quite possible that the neighbors would not become aware of their deaths for several days. Reiko did not like the idea of their bodies being found in a putrefied state. Yes, better to leave the door open. . . . She undid the lock and slid open the glass door slightly.

思案【しあん】thought
耽る【ふける】be absorbed (in)
鍵をあける【かぎをあける】unlock
〜ておく and leave it that way (for a future purpose) ⊛
〜べき should, ought to
〜か否か【〜かいなか】whether or not
もし if
鍵をかける【かぎをかける】lock
隣り近所【となりきんじょ】neighborhood
人【ひと】person
数日【すうじつ】several days
二人【ふたり】the two of them, they
気がつく【きがつく】notice, catch on
ありうる be possible
自分たち【じぶんたち】themselves
屍【しかばね】corpse

腐敗する【ふはいする】rot, putrefy
発見する【はっけんする】[passive form in text] discover
好む【このむ】like
やはり when all is said and done
あける unlock
〜ほうがいい had better
鍵を外す【かぎをはずす】undo a lock
磨硝子の戸【すりガラスのと】glass door
少し【すこし】slightly
引きあける【ひきあける】pull open

……たちまち寒風が吹き込んだ。深夜の道には人かげもなく、向いの邸の樹立の間に氷った星がきらきらしく見えた。

137▶　麗子は戸をそのままにして階段を上った。あちこちと歩いたので、もう足袋は辷らなかった。階段の中ほどから、すでに異臭が鼻を突いた。

138▶　中尉は血の海の中に俯伏していた。項から立っている刃先が、さっきよりも秀でているような気がする。

139▶　麗子は血だまりの中を平気で歩いた。そして中尉の屍のかたわらに坐って、畳に伏せたその横顔をじっと見つめた。中尉はものに憑かれたように大きく目を見ひらいていた。

たちまち immediately
寒風【かんぷう】cold wind
吹き込む【ふきこむ】blow in
深夜【しんや】late night
道【みち】street
人かげ【ひとかげ】person, figure
向い【むかい】opposite
邸【やしき】mansion
樹立【こだち】group of trees
〜の間に【〜のあいだに】between
氷る【こおる】freeze
星【ほし】stars
きらきらしく MIMETIC brilliantly, glitteringly
見える【みえる】be visible

137

麗子【れいこ】Reiko ⊛
戸【と】door

そのままにする leave as is
階段【かいだん】stairs ⊛
上る【あがる】go up
あちこちと here and there
歩く【あるく】walk ⊛
足袋【たび】tabi sock
辷る【すべる】slip
中ほど【なかほど】around the midpoint
すでに already
異臭【いしゅう】strange smell
鼻を突く【はなをつく】accost one's nose

138

中尉【ちゅうい】lieutenant ⊛
血【ち】blood ⊛
海【うみ】sea
〜の中に【〜のなかに】in
俯伏す【うつぶす】lie face down
項【うなじ】nape of the neck

Straightaway a cold gust of wind blew in. There was no one to be seen in the nighttime streets, and the ice-cold stars glimmered brightly between the trees of the mansion opposite.

Leaving the door as it was, Reiko climbed up the stairs. As she had walked around, her tabi were no longer slippery. From about halfway up the staircase, a strange odor assailed her nostrils.

The lieutenant lay prone in a sea of blood. She had the sense that the point of the sword was jutting further out of his neck than before.

Reiko walked unconcerned through the pool of blood. She sat down beside the body of the lieutenant and gazed at one side of the face that was pressing down on the mat. The lieutenant's eyes were wide open like one possessed.

立つ 【たつ】 stand
刃先 【はさき】 tip (of a blade)
さっき before
〜よりも even more than 〜
秀でる 【ひいでる】 stick out, stand out in sharp relief
〜ような気がする 【〜ようなきがする】 feel as though

139

血だまり 【ちだまり】 pool of blood
〜の中を 【〜のなかを】 through
平気で 【へいきで】 indifferently, unfazed
屍 【しかばね】 corpse
〜のかたわらに beside
坐る 【すわる】 sit
畳 【たたみ】 tatami mat
伏せる 【ふせる】 be turned face down
横顔 【よこがお】 profile

じっと MIMETIC fixedly
見つめる 【みつめる】 stare
ものに憑かれる 【ものにつかれる】 be possessed
大きく 【おおきく】 wide
目を見ひらく 【めをみひらく】 open one's eyes

その頭を袖で抱き上げて、袖で唇の血を拭って、別れの接吻をした。

140▶　それから立って、押入れから、新らしい白い毛布と腰紐を出した。裾が乱れぬように、腰に毛布を巻き、腰紐で固く締めた。

141▶　麗子は中尉の死骸から、一尺ほど離れたところに坐った。懐剣を帯から抜き、じっと澄明な刃を眺め、舌をあてた。磨かれた鋼はやや甘い味がした。

142▶　麗子は遅疑しなかった。さっきあれほど死んでゆく良人と自分を隔てた苦痛が、今度は自分のものになると思うと、良人のすでに領有している世界に加わることの喜びがあるだけである。

頭【あたま】head

袖【そで】sleeve ✿

抱き上げる【だきあげる】lift up and embrace

唇【くちびる】lip

血【ち】blood

拭う【ぬぐう】wipe away

別れの【わかれの】parting

接吻【せっぷん】kiss

140

立つ【たつ】stand

押入れ【おしいれ】closet

新らしい【あたらしい】new, fresh

白い【しろい】white

毛布【もうふ】blanket ✿

腰紐【こしひも】waist cord ✿

出す【だす】take out

裾【すそ】skirt

乱れぬ【みだれぬ】not get messed up

腰【こし】loins, middle

巻く【まく】wrap (something) around

固く【かたく】firmly

締める【しめる】tie, tighten

141

麗子【れいこ】Reiko ✿

中尉【ちゅうい】lieutenant

死骸【しがい】corpse

一尺【いっしゃく】one *shaku* (1 *shaku* = 11.93 inches)

～ほど around

離れる【はなれる】be distant, be apart

ところ place

坐る【すわる】sit

懐剣【かいけん】dagger

帯【おび】sash

抜く【ぬく】draw, pull out

She cradled his head in her sleeve-covered arms, wiped the blood from his lips with her sleeve and gave him a farewell kiss.

Then she stood up and took out from the closet a fresh white blanket and a waist cord. To stop her skirts from becoming disordered, she wrapped the blanket around her middle and fastened it tight with the waist cord.

Reiko sat at a spot about a foot away from the lieutenant's body. She pulled the dagger from her sash, stared at the clear, bright blade and held it to her tongue. The polished steel tasted rather sweet.

Reiko did not falter. When she thought that the pain that had previously put such a distance between her and her dying husband would now be hers too, she felt only joy that she could become part of the world of which her husband already had possession.

じっと MIMETIC fixedly
澄明な【ちょうめいな】bright
刃【やいば】blade
眺める【ながめる】look at intently
舌【した】tongue
あてる place against
磨く【みがく】[passive form in text] polish
鋼【はがね】steel
やや somewhat, rather
甘い【あまい】sweet
味【あじ】taste

142

遅疑する【ちぎする】hesitate, vacillate
さっき previously
あれほど so much
死ぬ【しぬ】die
〜てゆく indicates movement away from
  the narrator

良人【おっと】husband ⊛
自分【じぶん】oneself, herself ⊛
隔てる【へだてる】separate
苦痛【くつう】pain, agony
今度は【こんどは】now
もの thing
思う【おもう】think, consider
すでに already
領有する【りょうゆうする】possess
世界【せかい】world
加わる【くわわる】join
喜び【よろこび】joy

苦しんでいる良人（おっと）の顔には、はじめて見る何か不可解なものがあった。今度は自分がその謎（なぞ）を解くのである。麗子（れいこ）は良人（おっと）の信じた大義の本当の苦味と甘味を、今こそ自分も味わえるという気がする。今まで良人（おっと）を通じて辛うじて味わってきたものを、今度はまぎれもない自分の舌で味わうのである。

143 ▶　麗子（れいこ）は咽喉元（のどもと）へ刃先をあてた。一つ突いた。浅かった。頭がひどく熱して来て、手がめちゃくちゃに動いた。刃を横に強く引く。口のなかに温かいものが迸（ほとばし）り、目先は吹き上げる血の幻で真赤になった。彼女は力を得て、刃先を強く咽喉（のど）の奥へ刺し通した。

――一九六〇、一〇、一六――

苦しむ【くるしむ】suffer
良人【おっと】husband ⊛
顔【かお】face
はじめて for the first time
見る【みる】see
何か【なにか】something
不可解な【ふかかいな】incomprehensible
もの thing, something ⊛
今度は【こんどは】now ⊛
自分【じぶん】oneself, herself ⊛
謎【なぞ】riddle, mystery
解く【とく】solve
麗子【れいこ】Reiko ⊛
信じる【しんじる】believe in
大義【たいぎ】great duty, noble cause
本当の【ほんとうの】true
苦味【にがみ】bitterness
甘味【あまみ】sweetness

今こそ【いまこそ】now for sure, this time (without fail)
味わう【あじわう】[potential form in text] taste, experience ⊛
～という気がする【～というきがする】feel as though, imagine
今まで【いままで】until now
～を通じて【～をつうじて】through, via
辛うじて【かろうじて】with difficulty
～てくる indicates a situation or phenomenon emerging
まぎれもない unmistakable
舌【した】tongue

143
咽喉元【のどもと】base of the throat
刃先【はさき】tip (of a blade) ⊛
あてる place against
一つ【ひとつ】one

On the face of her husband in his torment there had been something enigmatic that Reiko had seen for the first time. Now it was her turn to solve that riddle. Reiko felt that now she herself would be able to savor the true bitterness and sweetness of the Noble Duty in which her husband believed. What she had until now tasted only faintly through her husband she would now get to taste directly on her own tongue.

Reiko put the point of the blade to her throat. She made a single thrust. Too shallow. Her head grew terribly hot and her hands shook uncontrollably. She dragged the blade forcefully to the side. Something warm gushed up into her mouth, and before her eyes was a scarlet vision of spraying blood. She summoned up her strength and drove the point of the blade violently into the depths of her throat.

10/16/1960

突く【つく】thrust
浅い【あさい】shallow
頭【あたま】head
ひどく horribly
熱する【ねっする】grow hot
〜て来る【〜てくる】indicates a situation or phenomenon emerging
手【て】hand
めちゃくちゃに wildly
動く【うごく】move
刃【やいば】blade
横【よこ】sideways
強く【つよく】strongly ⊛
引く【ひく】pull
口【くち】mouth
温かい【あたたかい】warm
迸る【ほとばしる】gush forth
目先【めさき】before one's eyes

吹き上げる【ふきあげる】spurt up
血【ち】blood
幻【まぼろし】vision
真赤【まっか／まあか】deep red
彼女【かのじょ】she
力を得る【ちからをえる】become emboldened
咽喉【のど】throat
奥【おく】depths, interior
刺し通す【さしとおす】stab through
一九六〇【せんきゅうひゃくろくじゅう】1960
一〇、一六【じゅう（がつ）じゅうろく（にち）】October 16

谷崎潤一郎

JUN'ICHIRŌ TANIZAKI
(1886–1965)

Jun'ichirō Tanizaki was born in the Nihonbashi district of Tokyo in 1886. Although his grandfather was a prosperous merchant, Tanizaki's own father was without commercial talent, and a series of abortive business ventures meant the family was always short of money. All but one of Tanizaki's younger siblings were dispatched to foster homes, and had it not been for the intervention of family friends, Tanizaki himself would have been unable to complete his education.

Much more important to Tanizaki's development than his hapless father were the women in his life: his beautiful mother, Seiki, and his nursemaid, Miyo. The cosseted boy is reported to have suckled at his mother's breast until the age of six and his nursemaid slept at his side throughout his childhood.

Entering Tokyo Imperial University as a Japanese literature student at the age of twenty-two, Tanizaki was instrumental in establishing the literary journal *Shinshichō*, the third issue of which featured his short story *The Tattooer*. The tale of a tattoo artist who decorates the back of a young girl with a spider that enables her to dominate the opposite sex, it featured the luxuriant prose, rich descriptive detail, and risqué subject matter that were to characterize the writer throughout his career. Tanizaki was taking a deliberate stand against the literalness of the Naturalists and, according to Gessel, his influences at this time were Edgar Allan Poe, Oscar Wilde, Baudelaire, and Krafft-Ebbing's studies in sexual pathology.

As offers from magazines poured in, Tanizaki dropped out of university to devote himself to writing, publishing his first collection of stories in 1911. He married Chiyo Ishikawa in 1915, but soon started living with her younger sister, Seiko, instead. Tanizaki was so besotted with all things modern and Western at this stage that he moved to the foreign district of Yokohama in the early 1920s, and with her occidental looks and movie star ambitions, Seiko dovetailed more neatly with this obsession than her placid sister. Seiko is even thought to be the model for the promiscuous female protagonist of *Naomi*, Tanizaki's 1924 novel about Taisho Era decadence.

After the Great Kanto Earthquake of 1923, Tanizaki moved his family to Western Japan. This was originally intended as no more than a temporary expedient, but, accustomed as Tanizaki was to the relentless modernization of Tokyo, the traditional atmosphere of Kansai (the Kyoto-Osaka-Kobe area) seemed dreamlike and exotic by comparison and he was to spend the rest of his life there.

The 1928 novel *Some Prefer Nettles*, about a man trapped in a passionless marriage who finds consolation in the beauty of old Japan, was clearly autobiographical. In 1930, Tanizaki shunted his wife Chiyo off onto a poet friend of his, and in 1931 he was briefly married to a student little more than half his age, before wedding Matsuko Morita, the ex-wife of a wealthy Osaka merchant, in 1935.

Tanizaki's books from this period—*The Secret History of the Lord of Musashi*, *The Reed Cutter*, *A Portrait of Shunkin*—though set in the Japan of several centuries ago tend to deal with the modern theme of sexual obsession. This enthusiasm for the past found its logical culmination in Tanizaki's rendering of the eleventh-century *The Tale of Genji* into modern Japanese, a massive undertaking that took several years.

During the war, Tanizaki worked on his masterpiece, *The Makioka Sisters*, a psychological study of three sisters from a declining Osaka merchant family. It was one of his least sexual works but fell foul of the censors and so was not published until 1948. Partly because of his refusal to be co-opted by the militarists, Tanizaki was lionized after the war, receiving the Medal of Culture in 1949. Respectability did nothing to affect his choice of subjects, and later works such as *The Diary of a Mad Old Man* and *The Key* address the paradox of unfading sexual desire in impotent old age. Tanizaki died in 1965.

"An obsessive concern with 'lust, cleptomania, sadomasochism, homosexuality, foot-fetishism, coprophilia and Eisenbahnkrankheit (railroad phobia)' does not constitute a focus upon the concerns of the average citizen" drily observes Tanizaki biographer Gessel (1993, 69; in reference to a list by Anthony H. Chambers). Sexual deviancy may be Tanizaki's best known, but it is far from being his only subject. Aside from an artificiality worthy of Flaubert or Oscar Wilde, at different times of his career his works display an insight into female psychology worthy of Henry James, a playfulness worthy of Nabokov, and a historical knowledge worthy of Victor Hugo. Perhaps Tanizaki's overriding characteristic as a writer is his uninhibited and innocent zest for life in all its aspects.

The Secret

Love Is a Game

The story of a jaded sensualist seeking ever-stronger stimuli in an attempt to reignite his flagging zest for life, "The Secret" appeared in Tanizaki's first collection of short stories in 1911. It thus dates from his "diabolist" period when he was heavily influenced by the decadent aestheticism of late-nineteenth-century Western literature. Luxuriant, elaborate language with meticulous descriptions of everything from the labyrinthine Tokyo streetscape to fine silk kimonos; exotic themes like transvestitism and romantic gamesmanship; a pervasive tone of mischievous, waggish charm—whether in terms of style, content or attitude, "The Secret" is a perfect microcosm of Tanizaki's eccentric but beguiling universe.

Go to www.speaking-japanese.com to join an online discussion about this story and share your questions, translations and insights with other readers.

1▶　その頃私は或る気紛れな考から、今迄自分の身のまわりを裹んで居た賑やかな雰囲気を遠ざかって、いろいろの関係で交際を続けて居た男や女の圏内から、ひそかに逃れ出ようと思い、方々と適当な隠れ家を捜し求めた揚句、浅草の松葉町辺に真言宗の寺のあるのを見附けて、ようよう其処の庫裡の一と間を借り受けることになった。

2▶　新堀の溝へついて、菊屋橋から門跡の裏手を真っ直ぐに行ったところ、十二階の下の方の、うるさく入り組んだObscureな町の中にその寺はあった。

1

頃【ころ】time, period

私【わたし】I

或る【ある】a certain, one

気紛れな【きまぐれな】whimsical

考【かんがえ】thought

今迄【いままで】until now

自分【じぶん】I, myself

身のまわり【みのまわり】one's surroundings, the things around oneself

裹む【つつむ】surround

賑やかな【にぎやかな】lively

雰囲気【ふんいき】atmosphere

遠ざかる【とおざかる】get away from

いろいろの various

関係【かんけい】relationships

交際【こうさい】social intercourse

続ける【つづける】continue

男【おとこ】man

女【おんな】woman

圏内【けんない】within range

ひそかに secretly

逃れ出る【のがれでる】[volitional form in text] slip away

思う【おもう】think, intend

方々と【ほうぼうと】here and there

適当な【てきとうな】suitable

隠れ家【かくれが】hideaway

捜し求める【さがしもとめる】seek

〜揚句【〜あげく】after 〜

浅草【あさくさ】Asakusa

松葉町【まつばちょう】Matsuba-chō

辺【あたり】area

真言宗【しんごんしゅう】Shingon sect

寺【てら】temple ⊛

見附ける【みつける】find

Prompted by little more than a whim, it was then that I decided to retire from the lively milieu that had heretofore enveloped me, and slip away from the various men and women with whom I normally socialized. I had hunted high and low for a suitable hiding place before I discovered a Shingon temple in the Matsuba-chō area of Asakusa where I eventually ended up renting a room in the monks' living quarters.

The temple was in the middle of an obscure and fiendishly labyrinthine part of town near the grounds of the Twelve Story Tower. You got there by following the Shinbori Canal from Kikuya Bridge straight along behind the Higashi-Hongan Temple.

ようよう finally, eventually
其処 【そこ】 there
庫裡 【くり】 monks' living quarters
一と間 【ひとま】 one room
借り受ける 【かりうける】 rent

2
新堀 【しんぼり】 Shinbori
溝 【みぞ】 channel, canal
〜へついて along
菊屋橋 【きくやばし】 Kikuya Bridge
門跡 【もんぜき】 another name for Higashi-Hongan Temple
裏手 【うらて】 back
真っ直ぐ 【まっすぐ】 straight ahead
行く 【いく】 go
ところ place
十二階 【じゅうにかい】 Twelve Story Tower (landmark of Meiji-era Tokyo)

〜の下の方の 【〜のしたのほうの】 near the base of
うるさく in a terribly complicated way
入り組んだ 【いりくんだ】 intricate
町 【まち】 district, quarter
〜の中に 【〜のなかに】 inside

ごみ溜めの箱を覆した如く、あの辺一帯にひろがって居る貧民窟の片側に、黄橙色の土塀の壁が長く続いて、如何にも落ち着いた、重々しい寂しい感じを与える構えであった。

3▶ 私は最初から、渋谷だの大久保だのと云う郊外へ隠遁するよりも、却って市内の何処かに人の心附かない、不思議なさびれた所があるであろうと思っていた。丁度瀬の早い渓川のところどころに、澱んだ淵が出来るように、下町の雑沓する巷と巷の間に挟まりながら、極めて特殊の場合か、特殊の人でもなければめったに通行しないような閑静な一郭が、なければなるまいと思っていた。

4▶ 同時に又こんな事も考えて見た。———

On one side of the slums, which sprawled out like so much trash tipped from a bin, there ran a long, orange-colored earthen wall that projected an extraordinary atmosphere of serene and solemn isolation.

In preference to secluding myself in a suburb like Shibuya or Ōkubo, right from the start I suspected there must exist a marvelous, lonely spot that people overlooked somewhere within the city itself. Just as stagnant pools are found here and there in fast-running mountain streams, I was convinced that, squeezed between all the bustling streets of the old town, there must be a tranquil quarter through which—exceptional cases and individuals aside—people almost never passed.

Something else occurred to me too.

人【ひと】person ❀
心附く【こころづく】notice
不思議な【ふしぎな】strange, extraordinary
さびれた quiet, lonesome
所【ところ】place
思う【おもう】think ❀
丁度【ちょうど】exactly, just
瀬の早い【せのはやい】fast current
渓川【たにがわ】mountain stream
ところどころ here and there
澱んだ【よどんだ】stagnant
淵【ふち】pool
出来る【できる】be formed
下町【したまち】the low town (the low-lying eastern wards of Tokyo where merchant culture thrived in the old days)
雑沓する【ざっとうする】be crowded

巷【ちまた】streets ❀
～の間に【～のあわいに】between
挟まる【はさまる】be squeezed (between)
極めて【きわめて】extremely
特殊の【とくしゅの】unique ❀
場合【ばあい】case
めったに rarely
通行する【つうこうする】pass by
閑静な【かんせいな】tranquil
一郭【いっかく】quarter, spot
なければなるまい = なければならない

4

同時に【どうじに】at the same time
又【また】also
事【こと】thing
考える【かんがえる】think
～て見る【～てみる】to see what it is like

5▶　　己は随分旅行好きで、京都、仙台、北海道から九州までも歩いて来た。けれども未だこの東京の町の中に、人形町で生れて二十年来永住している東京の町の中に、一度も足を踏み入れた事のないと云う通りが、屹度あるに違いない。いや、思ったより沢山あるに違いない。

6▶　　そうして大都会の下町に、蜂の巣の如く交錯している大小無数の街路のうち、私が通った事のある所と、ない所では、孰方が多いかちょいと判らなくなって来た。

7▶　　何でも十一二歳の頃であったろう。父と一緒に深川の八幡様へ行った時、

5

己【おれ】 masculine I

随分【ずいぶん】very much

旅行好き【りょこうずき】fond of traveling

京都【きょうと】Kyoto

仙台【せんだい】Sendai (in northern Japan)

北海道【ほっかいどう】Hokkaidō (northernmost of Japan's four largest islands)

九州【きゅうしゅう】Kyūshū (south-westernmost of Japan's four largest islands)

歩く【あるく】walk, travel

〜て来る【〜てくる】and come back

未だ〜ない【いまだ〜ない】still have not

東京【とうきょう】Tokyo ✴

町【まち】district, quarter ✴

〜の中に【〜のなかに】among ✴

人形町【にんぎょうちょう】Ningyō-chō

生れる【うまれる】be born

二十年【にじゅうねん】20 years

〜来【〜らい】for, since

永住する【えいじゅうする】live permanently

一度も〜ない【いちども〜ない】not even once, never

足を踏み入れる【あしをふみいれる】set foot in

〜事のない【〜ことのない】have never 〜

〜と云う【〜という】of such a kind

通り【とおり】street

屹度【きっと】surely, certainly

〜に違いない【〜にちがいない】definitely be ✴

いや no

思ったより【おもったより】more than one thinks

沢山【たくさん】many

I was a great lover of traveling. I had journeyed to Kyoto and Sendai, and from Hokkaidō all the way down to Kyūshū. But there was no doubt about it: amongst the various neighborhoods of Tokyo—the very neighborhoods of Tokyo where I had lived for twenty years now since my birth in Ningyō-chō—there were still streets on which I had never set foot. Doubtless there were more such streets than I thought.

Among the countless streets great and small that crisscross one another like a honeycomb in the old town of this metropolis, I became unsure which were more numerous: streets I had walked down or streets I had not.

It must have been when I was eleven or twelve years old. I went with my father to the Hachiman Shrine in Fukagawa.

6

大都会 【だいとかい】 metropolis
下町 【したまち】 low town
蜂の巣 【はちのす】 beehive
〜の如く 【〜のごとく】 just like
交錯する 【こうさくする】 be intricate, be interlinked
大小無数 【だいしょうむすう】 all sorts
街路 【がいろ】 streets, roads
〜のうち among
私 【わたし】 I
通る 【とおる】 pass through
〜事のある 【〜ことのある】 have had the experience of
所 【ところ】 place ⊛
〜ない所 = 通ったことのない所 place one has not passed through
孰方 【どっち】 which (of two)

多い 【おおい】 numerous
ちょいと slightly, a bit
判る 【わかる】 understand
〜て来る 【〜てくる】 indicates a condition coming into effect

7

何でも 【なんでも】 probably
十一二歳 【じゅういちにさい】 11 or 12 years old
頃 【ころ】 time, period
〜であったろう = 〜であったであろう
父 【ちち】 father
〜と一緒に 【〜といっしょに】 together with
深川 【ふかがわ】 Fukagawa
八幡様 【はちまんさま】 Hachiman Shrine
行く 【いく】 go
〜時 【〜とき】 when

「これから渡しを渡って、冬木の米市で名代のそばを御馳走してやるかな。」

　こう云って、父は私を境内の社殿の後の方へ連れて行った事がある。其処には小網町や小舟町辺の掘割と全く趣の違った、幅の狭い、岸の低い、水の一杯にふくれ上っている川が、細かく建て込んでいる両岸の家々の、軒と軒とを押し分けるように、どんよりと物憂く流れて居た。小さな渡し船は、川幅よりも長そうな荷足りや伝馬が、幾艘も縦に列んでいる間を縫いながら、二た竿三竿ばかりちょろちょろと水底を衝いて往復して居た。

8

渡し【わたし】ferry

渡る【わたる】cross

冬木【ふゆぎ】Fuyugi

米市【こめいち】rice market

名代の【なだいの】famous

そば buckwheat noodles

御馳走する【ごちそうする】treat to a meal

〜てやる do as a favor for (someone of lower social status than oneself)

〜かな particle combination used to express desire

9

云う【いう】say

父【ちち】father

私【わたし】I

境内【けいだい】precincts

社殿【しゃでん】shrine complex

後の方へ【うしろのほうへ】toward the back

連れて行く【つれていく】take (someone somewhere)

〜事がある【〜ことがある】have had the experience of

其処【そこ】there

小網町【こあみちょう】Koami-chō

小舟町【こぶなちょう】Kobuna-chō

〜辺【〜あたり】area, environs

掘割【ほりわり】canal, ditch

全く【まったく】completely

趣【おもむき】appearance, air

違う【ちがう】be different

幅の狭い【はばのせまい】narrow

岸【きし】banks

低い【ひくい】low

"We'll take the ferry across and then I think I'll treat you to some of those famous noodles at the Fuyugi rice market."

Saying this, my father led me off behind the shrine compound. There was a river that felt quite different from the canals around Koami-chō and Kobuna-chō: narrow, low-banked and swollen, it flowed with a sluggish listlessness that seemed to prize apart the eaves of the houses crammed so tightly together on either shore. Weaving its way between any number of lighters and barges anchored nose-to-tail, each looking longer than the river was wide, the tiny ferry made the journey to and fro with no more than two or three thrusts of the pole on the riverbed.

水 【みず】 water

一杯に 【いっぱいに】 full

ふくれ上る 【ふくれあがる】 swell up

川 【かわ】 river

細かく 【こまかく】 closely

建て込む 【たてこむ】 be crowded together (of buildings)

両岸 【りょうぎし】 both banks

家々 【いえいえ】 houses

軒 【のき】 eaves ✲

押し分ける 【おしわける】 push through

どんよりと MIMETIC stagnantly, heavily

物憂く 【ものうく】 languidly, wearily

流れる 【ながれる】 flow

小さな 【ちいさな】 small

渡し船 【わたしぶね】 ferryboat

川幅 【かわはば】 width of the river

長い 【ながい】 long

荷足り 【にたり】 lighter, barge

伝馬 【てんま】 lighter, jollyboat

幾艘も 【いくそうも】 several (boats)

縦に 【たてに】 lengthwise

列ぶ 【ならぶ】 line up

間 【あいだ】 space between, opening

縫う 【ぬう】 weave through

二た竿三竿 【ふたさおみさお】 two or three thrusts of the pole

〜ばかり only

ちょろちょろと MIMETIC with a murmur

水底 【みなそこ】 bottom

衝く 【つく】 thrust

往復する 【おうふくする】 go there and back

10▶

　私はその時まで、たびたび八幡様へお参りをしたが、未だ嘗て境内の裏手がどんなになっているか考えて見たことはなかった。いつも正面の鳥居の方から社殿を拝むだけで、恐らくパノラマの絵のように、表ばかりで裏のない、行き止まりの景色のように自然と考えていたのであろう。現在眼の前にこんな川や渡し場が見えて、その先に広い地面が果てしもなく続いている謎のような光景を見ると、何となく京都や大阪よりももっと東京をかけ離れた、夢の中で屢々出逢うことのある世界の如く思われた。

10

私【わたし】I
その時【そのとき】then, that time
たびたび frequently
八幡様【はちまんさま】Hachiman Shrine
お参りをする【おまいりをする】visit (a holy place)
未だ嘗て〜ない【いまだかつて〜ない】still have not
境内【けいだい】shrine precincts
裏手【うらて】back
考える【かんがえる】think, consider
〜て見る【〜てみる】to see what it is like
正面【しょうめん】front
鳥居【とりい】torii, shrine gateway
〜の方から【〜のほうから】from the direction of
社殿を拝む【しゃでんをおがむ】pay one's respects at a shrine

恐らく【おそらく】perhaps
パノラマ panorama
絵【え】painting
表【おもて】front
〜ばかり only
裏【うら】back
行き止まり【ゆきどまり／いきどまり】dead end
景色【けしき】scene, landscape
自然と【しぜんと】naturally
考える【かんがえる】think
現在【げんざい】now
眼の前【めのまえ】before one's eyes
川【かわ】river
渡し場【わたしば】ferry
見える【みえる】be visible
その先に【そのさきに】ahead of that
広い【ひろい】extensive

I had visited the Hachiman Shrine many times before, but it had never before occurred to me to think what it might be like behind the compound. As I always used to pay my respects to the shrine from the torii gate at the front, perhaps I'd ended up thinking of it as a panorama painting—a scene that was all front and no back and went nowhere. The river and the crossing point right there in front of me, then a broad tract of land stretching off into infinity beyond them—the mysterious vista seemed further from Tokyo than either Kyoto or Osaka: it was more like one of those worlds we so often meet in our dreams.

地面【じめん】piece of land, area
果てしもなく【はてしもなく】limitlessly
続く【つづく】continue
謎【なぞ】riddle, puzzle
光景【こうけい】scene, view
見る【みる】see
何となく【なんとなく】in some way
京都【きょうと】Kyoto
大阪【おおさか】Osaka
もっと more
東京【とうきょう】Tokyo
かけ離れる【かけはなれる】be distant from
夢【ゆめ】dream
〜の中で【〜のなかで】in
屢々【しばしば】often
出逢う【であう】encounter
世界【せかい】world

〜の如く【〜のごとく】just like
思う【おもう】[spontaneous form in text] think

11▶ 　　それから私は、浅草の観音堂の真うしろにはどんな町があったか想像して見たが、仲店の通りから宏大な朱塗りのお堂の甍を望んだ時の有様ばかりが明瞭に描かれ、その外の点はとんと頭に浮かばなかった。だんだん大人になって、世間が広くなるに随い、知人の家を訪ねたり、花見遊山に出かけたり、東京市中は隈なく歩いたようであるが、いまだに子供の時分経験したような不思議な別世界へ、ハタリと行き逢うことがたびたびあった。

12▶ 　　そう云う別世界こそ、身を匿すには究竟であろうと思って、此処彼処といろいろに捜し求めて見れば見る程、今迄通った事のない区域が到る処に発見された。

I then tried to imagine what kind of district there might be immediately behind the Kannon Temple in Asakusa. But although I could clearly picture the sight of the tiled roof of the enormous, vermilion edifice when seen from the shopping promenade, nothing else came to mind. As I grew older and my world gradually widened, it seemed as if I had walked the length and breadth of Tokyo, visiting the houses of acquaintances or going on outings to see the blossoms; and yet, frequently enough, I would still stumble upon marvelous new worlds of the kind I had encountered as a child.

Convinced that such a parallel world would be the ideal place for me to hide, I searched everywhere. And the more I searched, the greater the number of unvisited areas I discovered.

東京市中 【とうきょうしちゅう】 whole city of Tokyo
隈なく 【くまなく】 thoroughly
歩く 【あるく】 walk, journey on foot
いまだに even now
子供 【こども】 child
時分 【じぶん】 time, period
経験する 【けいけんする】 experience
不思議な 【ふしぎな】 extraordinary
別世界 【べっせかい】 other world ⊛
ハタリと MIMETIC out of the blue
行き逢う 【いきあう】 meet on the way
たびたび frequently

12

そう云う 【そういう】 of that kind
〜こそ the very, precisely 〜
身を匿す 【みをかくす】 hide oneself
究竟な 【くっきょうな】 ideal

思う 【おもう】 think
此処彼処 【ここかしこ】 here, there and everywhere
いろいろに variously
捜し求める 【さがしもとめる】 seek, look for
〜ば〜程 【〜ば〜ほど】 the more (one does something) the more . . .
今迄 【いままで】 until now
通る 【とおる】 pass through
〜事のない 【〜ことのない】 have never 〜
区域 【くいき】 district, quarter
到る処 【いたるところ】 everywhere
発見する 【はっけんする】 [passive form in text] discover

浅草橋と和泉橋は幾度も渡って置きながら、その間にある左衛門橋を渡ったことがない。二長町の市村座へ行くのには、いつも電車通りからそばやの角を右へ曲ったが、あの芝居の前を真っ直ぐに柳盛座の方へ出る二三町ばかりの地面は、一度も踏んだ覚えはなかった。昔の永代橋の右岸の袂から、左の方の河岸はどんな工合になって居たか、どうも好く判らなかった。その外八丁堀、越前堀、三味線堀、山谷堀の界隈には、まだまだ知らない所が沢山あるらしかった。

浅草橋【あさくさばし】Asakusa Bridge

和泉橋【いずみばし】Izumi Bridge

幾度も【いくども】numerous times

渡る【わたる】cross ✲

〜て置く【〜ておく】and remain in that state

〜ながら though, while

その間に【そのあいだに】between them

左衛門橋【さえもんばし】Saemon Bridge

二長町【にちょうまち】Nichōmachi

市村座【いちむらざ】Ichimura Theater

行く【いく】go

電車通り【でんしゃどおり】main street with streetcar tracks

そばや buckwheat noodle shop

角【かど】corner

右【みぎ】right

曲る【まがる】turn

芝居【しばい】playhouse

前【まえ】front

真っ直ぐに【まっすぐに】straight

柳盛座【りゅうせいざ】Ryūsei Theater

〜の方へ【〜のほうへ】in the direction of

出る【でる】emerge, come out

二三町【にさんちょう】two or three blocks

〜ばかり roughly

地面【じめん】piece of land, area

一度も〜ない【いちども〜ない】not even once, never

踏む【ふむ】tread

覚え【おぼえ】memory

昔の【むかしの】old, former

永代橋【えいたいばし】Eitai Bridge

右岸【うがん】right bank, east bank

袂【たもと】approach to a bridge

While I had been over the Asakusa and Izumi Bridges countless times, I had never once crossed the Saemon Bridge, which lies between them. To get to the Ichimura Theater in Nichō-machi, I always turned right off the streetcar boulevard at the corner with the noodle shop; but I had no recollection of ever having set foot in the two- or three-block area directly beyond the theater in the direction of the Ryūsei Theater. I had no clear picture of what the waterfront was like if you headed to the left from the east end of the old Eitai Bridge. In addition, it seemed that there remained many places I did not know in the districts of Hatchōbori, Echizenbori, Shamisenbori and Sanyabori.

左の方【ひだりのほう】left side
河岸【かし】riverside
工合【ぐあい】state
どうも really
好く【よく】well
判る【わかる】know, tell
外【ほか】other
八丁堀【はっちょうぼり】Hatchōbori
越前堀【えちぜんぼり】Echizenbori
三味線堀【しゃみせんぼり】Shamisenbori
山谷堀【さんやぼり】Sanyabori
界隈【かいわい】neighborhood
まだまだ still, not yet
知る【しる】know
所【ところ】places
沢山【たくさん】many
〜らしい apparently, it seems

　　松葉町のお寺の近傍は、そのうちでも一番奇妙な町であった。六区と吉原を鼻先に控えてちょいと横丁を一つ曲った所に、淋しい、廃れたような区域を作っているのが非常に私の気に入って了った。今迄自分の無二の親友であった「派手な贅沢なそうして平凡な東京」と云う奴を置いてき堀にして、静かにその騒擾を傍観しながら、こっそり身を隠して居られるのが、愉快でならなかった。

13

松葉町【まつばちょう】Matsuba-chō	所【ところ】place
お寺【おてら】temple	淋しい【さびしい】lonely
近傍【きんぼう】vicinity	廃れた【すたれた】decrepit
そのうち among them	区域【くいき】district, quarter
一番【いちばん】the most	作る【つくる】make
奇妙な【きみょうな】peculiar	非常に【ひじょうに】extremely
町【まち】district, quarter	私【わたし】I
六区【ろっく】Rokku (entertainment district)	気に入る【きにいる】be to one's liking
吉原【よしわら】Yoshiwara (brothel quarter)	～て了う【～てしまう】completely
鼻先【はなさき】in front of one	今迄【いままで】until now
控える【ひかえる】have close by	自分【じぶん】I, myself
ちょいと just a little	無二の親友【むにのしんゆう】dearest friend
横丁【よこちょう】bystreet, alley	派手な【はでな】flashy
一つ【ひとつ】one	贅沢な【ぜいたくな】extravagant
曲る【まがる】turn (and go down)	平凡な【へいぼんな】ordinary
	東京【とうきょう】Tokyo
	～と云う【～という】by the name of

The area near the temple in Matsuba-chō was the most curious of them all. The way that, just when Rokku and the Yoshiwara were right there in front of your nose, a quick dive down an alley brought you to this zone of melancholy and dilapidation pleased me exceedingly. It was pleasant beyond measure to sneak away from my erstwhile bosom friend—a chap by the name of "Flashy, Luxurious and Commonplace Tokyo"—and be able to secrete myself and observe all the commotion in tranquility.

奴【やつ】fellow
置いてき堀にする【おいてきぼりにする】
　give (someone) the slip
静かに【しずかに】quietly
騒擾【そうじょう】commotion
傍観する【ぼうかんする】observe as a
　spectator
こっそり secretly, stealthily
身を隠す【みをかくす】hide oneself
居る【いる】[potential form in text] be
愉快な【ゆかいな】pleasant
～でならない be so ~

　隠遁をした目的は、別段勉強をする為めではない。その頃私の神経は、刃の擦り切れたやすりのように、鋭敏な角々がすっかり鈍って、余程色彩の濃い、あくどい物に出逢わなければ、何の感興も湧かなかった。微細な感受性の働きを要求する一流の芸術だとか、一流の料理だとかを翫味するのが、不可能になっていた。下町の粋と云われる茶屋の板前に感心して見たり、仁左衛門や鴈治郎の技巧を賞美したり、凡べて在り来たりの都会の歓楽を受け入れるには、あまり心が荒んでいた。惰力の為めに面白くもない懶惰な生活を、毎日々々々繰り返して居るのが、堪えられなくなって、全然旧套を擺脱した、物好きな、アーティフィシャルな、Mode of lifeを見出して見たかったのである。

14

隠遁をする【いんとんをする】seclude oneself
目的【もくてき】purpose, aim
別段【べつだん】in particular
勉強をする【べんきょうをする】study
〜為め【〜ため】for
その頃【そのころ】at that time
私【わたし】I
神経【しんけい】nerves
刃【は】blade
擦り切れた【すりきれた】worn-down
やすり file
鋭敏な【えいびんな】sharp, sensitive
角々【かどかど】every corner
すっかり completely
鈍る【にぶる】grow blunt, go dull
余程【よほど】to a great extent

色彩【しきさい】color
濃い【こい】deep, strong
あくどい gaudy, showy
物【もの】thing
出逢う【であう】encounter
何の〜も〜ない【なんの〜も〜ない】not at all
感興【かんきょう】interest
湧く【わく】surge up
微細な【びさいな】fine, subtle
感受性【かんじゅせい】sensitivity
働き【はたらき】working, function
要求する【ようきゅうする】require
一流の【いちりゅうの】top-class ⊛
芸術【げいじゅつ】art
料理【りょうり】cooking, food
翫味する【がんみする】appreciate
不可能な【ふかのうな】impossible

Study was not the goal of my seclusion. At that time, my nerves were like the blade of a file that has been worn smooth—its sharp edges all utterly blunted—and it took an encounter with the most intense and lurid things to even arouse my interest. It was impossible for me to appreciate things like top-notch art or cuisine that depend upon the workings of a fine sensitivity. I was just too world-weary to respond to any of the commonplace pleasures of the metropolis, whether admiring a restaurant cook said to be the *dernier cri* of Tokyo, or appreciating the technique of Nizaemon and Ganjirō. Through inertia I was spending day after day in a life of tedious idleness and I could no longer bear it; I was desperate to discover a new *façon de vivre*—curious, artificial and completely divested of convention.

下町【したまち】low town
粋【すい／いき】chic, fashionable
云う【いう】[passive form in text] say, call
茶屋【ちゃや】tea shop, restaurant
板前【いたまえ】cook
感心する【かんしんする】admire
〜て見る【〜てみる】to see what it is like ⊛
仁左衛門【にざえもん】Nizaemon (Kabuki actor's name)
鴈治郎【がんじろう】Ganjirō (Kabuki actor's name)
技巧【ぎこう】technique
賞美する【しょうびする】appreciate
凡べて【すべて】all
在り来たりの【ありきたりの】commonplace, ordinary
都会【とかい】metropolis
歓楽【かんらく】pleasures

受け入れる【うけいれる】respond to, accept
あまり excessively
心が荒む【こころがすさむ】become jaded
惰力【だりょく】inertia
〜の為めに【〜のために】because of
面白い【おもしろい】enjoyable
懶惰な【らんだな】idle
生活【せいかつ】life
毎日々々【まいにちまいにち】every day
繰り返す【くりかえす】repeat
堪える【たえる】[potential form in text] endure, bear
全然【ぜんぜん】entirely
旧套【きゅうとう】convention
擺脱する【はいだつする】reject
物好きな【ものずきな】curious
見出す【みいだす】discover

15▶　普通の刺戟に馴れて了った神経を顫い戦かすような、何か不思議な、奇怪な事はないであろうか。現実をかけ離れた野蛮な荒唐な夢幻的な空気の中に、棲息することは出来ないであろうか。こう思って私の魂は遠くバビロンやアッシリヤの古代の伝説の世界にさ迷ったり、コナンドイルや涙香の探偵小説を想像したり、光線の熾烈な熱帯地方の焦土と緑野を恋い慕ったり、腕白な少年時代のエクセントリックな悪戯に憧れたりした。

16▶　賑かな世間から不意に韜晦して、行動を唯徒らに秘密にして見るだけでも、すでに一種のミステリアスな、ロマンチックな色彩を自分の生活に賦与することが出来ると思った。

15

普通【ふつう】ordinary
刺戟【しげき】stimulation
馴れる【なれる】become tamed
〜て了う【〜てしまう】thoroughly
神経【しんけい】nerves
顫い戦かす【ふるいおののかす】shake up
何か【なにか】something
不思議な【ふしぎな】extraordinary
奇怪な【きかいな】weird
事【こと】act, experience
現実【げんじつ】reality
かけ離れる【かけはなれる】be distant (from)
野蛮な【やばんな】barbarous
荒唐な【こうとうな】fabulous, fantastical
夢幻的な【むげんてきな】hallucinatory
空気【くうき】atmosphere

〜の中に【〜のなかに】inside
棲息する【せいそくする】inhabit
出来る【できる】be able to do
思う【おもう】think ⊛
私【わたし】I
魂【たましい】soul
遠く【とおく】far
バビロン Babylon
アッシリヤ Assyria
古代【こだい】ancient times
伝説【でんせつ】legends
世界【せかい】worlds
さ迷う【さまよう】wander, roam
コナンドイル Sir Arthur Conan Doyle: creator of Sherlock Holmes
涙香【るいこう】Kuroiwa Ruikō: novelist who adapted works by Alexandre Dumas and Victor Hugo

Was there anything sufficiently extraordinary and bizarre to set my nerves—overaccustomed to all run-of-the-mill stimulation—aquiver? Could I not dwell in a dreamlike ambience, barbarous, fantastical and remote from reality? As I pondered thus, my soul wandered to the faraway world of ancient Babylonian and Assyrian legend; conjured up the detective stories of Conan Doyle and Ruikō; yearned for the burned earth and green grasslands of the sun-scorched tropics; recalled fondly the ingenious practical jokes of my mischievous boyhood.

It occurred to me that to suddenly abstract myself from the busy world and make all my actions secret out of pure whim would be quite enough to endue my life with the hues of mystery and romance.

探偵小説【たんていしょうせつ】detective story
想像する【そうぞうする】imagine
光線【こうせん】light, beam of light
熾烈な【しれつな】intense
熱帯地方【ねったいちほう】tropic
焦土【しょうど】burned earth
緑野【りょくや】green field
恋い慕う【こいしたう】yearn for
腕白な【わんぱくな】naughty, unruly
少年時代【しょうねんじだい】boyhood
エクセントリックな eccentric
悪戯【あくぎ】practical joke
憧れる【あこがれる】feel drawn (to)

16

賑かな【にぎやかな】lively
世間【せけん】society
不意に【ふいに】abruptly

韜晦する【とうかいする】hide
行動【こうどう】action
唯【ただ】just, only
徒らに【いたずらに】to no purpose
秘密【ひみつ】secret
〜て見る【〜てみる】to see what it is like
すでに already
一種の【いっしゅの】a kind of
ミステリアスな mysterious
ロマンチックな romantic
色彩【しきさい】color, tinge
自分【じぶん】I, myself
生活【せいかつ】life
賦与する【ふよする】endue, endow
出来る【できる】be able to do
思う【おもう】think

私は秘密と云う物の面白さを、子供の時分からしみじみと味わって居た。かくれんぼ、宝さがし、お茶坊主のような遊戯——殊に、それが闇の晩、うす暗い物置小屋や、観音開きの前などで行われる時の面白味は、主としてその間に「秘密」と云う不思議な気分が潜んで居るせいであったに違いない。

17▶　私はもう一度幼年時代の隠れん坊のような気持を経験して見たさに、わざと人の気の附かない下町の曖昧なところに身を隠したのであった。そのお寺の宗旨が「秘密」とか「禁厭」とか、「呪詛」とか云うものに縁の深い真言宗であることも、私の好奇心を誘うて、妄想を育ませるには恰好であった。

私【わたし】I ⊛
秘密【ひみつ】secret ⊛
〜と云う【〜という】that is ⊛
物【もの】thing
面白さ【おもしろさ】fun, interest
子供【こども】child
時分【じぶん】time, period
しみじみと keenly, deeply
味わう【あじわう】taste, enjoy
かくれんぼ hide-and-seek
宝さがし【たからさがし】treasure hunt
お茶坊主【おちゃぼうず】blindman's buff
遊戯【ゆうぎ】game
殊に【ことに】especially
闇【やみ】darkness
晩【ばん】evening
うす暗い【うすぐらい】dim, dark
物置小屋【ものおきごや】little storehouse

観音開き【かんのんびらき】double-leafed hinged door
〜の前【〜のまえ】in front of
行う【おこなう】[passive form in text] conduct, do
時【とき】times
面白味【おもしろみ】enjoyment, excitement
主として【しゅとして】mainly
その間に【そのあいだに】at such times
不思議な【ふしぎな】marvelous
気分【きぶん】mood, feeling
潜む【ひそむ】lurk, be latent
〜せい because of, due to
〜に違いない【〜にちがいない】definitely be

17
もう一度【もういちど】one more time
幼年時代【ようねんじだい】childhood

Ever since childhood, I had possessed a keen relish for the pleasure of so-called "secrets." Doubtless the unique enjoyment of games like hide-and-seek, treasure hunt and blindman's buff—particularly when played on a dark evening, or inside a gloomy storage shed or in front of its double doors—was mainly due to the marvelous sense of the "secrets" that they involved.

It was out of a desire to once again experience emotions like those I'd had playing hide-and-seek as a child, that I had deliberately concealed myself in a limbolike part of the low town unknown to anyone. And the fact that the temple's doctrine was that of the Shingon sect, with its profound association with "secrets," "charms" and "maledictions," inevitably stimulated my curiosity and nourished my fantasies.

隠れん坊【かくれんぼう】hide-and-seek
気持【きもち】feelings
経験して見たさ【けいけんしてみたさ】 desire to experience
わざと deliberately
人【ひと】person
気の附く【きのつく】notice
下町【したまち】low town
曖昧な【あいまいな】obscure
ところ place
身を隠す【みをかくす】hide oneself
お寺【おてら】temple
宗旨【しゅうし】doctrine
禁厭【まじない】spell
呪詛【じゅそ】incantation
もの thing
縁【えん】affinity, link
深い【ふかい】deep

真言宗【しんごんしゅう】Shingon sect
好奇心【こうきしん】curiosity
誘う【さそう】invite, entice
妄想【もうそう】fantasy
育む【はぐくむ】[causative form in text] foster
恰好な【かっこうな】suitable, perfect

部屋は新らしく建て増した庫裡の一部で、南を向いた八畳敷きの、日に焼けて少し茶色がかっている畳が、却って見た眼には安らかな暖かい感じを与えた。昼過ぎになると和やかな秋の日が、幻燈の如くあかあかと縁側の障子に燃えて、室内は大きな雪洞のように明るかった。

18▶ それから私は、今迄親しんで居た哲学や芸術に関する書類を一切戸棚へ片附けて了って、魔術だの、催眠術だの、探偵小説だの、化学だの、解剖学だのの奇怪な説話と挿絵に富んでいる書物を、さながら土用干の如く部屋中へ置き散らして、寝ころびながら、手あたり次第に繰りひろげては耽読した。

部屋【へや】room
新らしく【あたらしく】newly
建て増す【たてます】build onto, expand
庫裡【くり】monk's living quarters
一部【いちぶ】a part
南【みなみ】south
向く【むく】face
八畳敷き【はちじょうじき】eight mats (in size)
日に焼ける【ひにやける】get burned by the sun
少し【すこし】slightly
茶色がかる【ちゃいろがかる】turn brown
畳【たたみ】tatami mat
却って【かえって】on the contrary
見た眼【みため】appearance
安らかな【やすらかな】peaceful
暖かい【あたたかい】warm

感じ【かんじ】feeling
与える【あたえる】impart
昼過ぎ【ひるすぎ】early afternoon
和やかな【なごやかな】mellow, mature
秋【あき】autumn
日【ひ】day
幻燈【げんとう】magic lantern
〜の如く【〜のごとく】just like ✿
あかあかと redly
縁側【えんがわ】veranda
障子【しょうじ】shoji, paper screen
燃える【もえる】burn
室内【しつない】interior (of a room)
大きな【おおきな】big
雪洞【ぼんぼり】small paper lamp
明るい【あかるい】bright

18

私【わたし】I

My room was in a newly built addition to the monks' quarters, and as it faced south, its eight tatami mats had been slightly browned by the sun, which actually produced an atmosphere of tranquil warmth. In the early afternoon, the mellow autumn sun would glow red upon the shoji of the veranda like a magic lantern, and the interior of the room shone like an enormous paper lamp.

I put away in the cabinet all the documents on philosophy and art that had until then been my favorites, and instead littered the room—as if spreading things out for a summer airing—with books that overflowed with weird illustrations and tales: books on magic and hypnotism, detective novels and chemistry and anatomy texts. Sprawling on the floor, I would then open up whatever volume came to hand and immerse myself in it.

今迄【いままで】until now

親しむ【したしむ】be fond of

哲学【てつがく】philosophy

芸術【げいじゅつ】art

〜に関する【〜にかんする】connected with

書類【しょるい】documents

一切【いっさい】all

戸棚【とだな】cabinet

片附ける【かたづける】put away

〜て了う【〜てしまう】thoroughly

魔術【まじゅつ】magic

〜だの〜だの indicates a non-exhaustive list ⊛

催眠術【さいみんじゅつ】hypnotism

探偵小説【たんていしょうせつ】detective story

化学【かがく】chemistry

解剖学【かいほうがく】anatomy

奇怪な【きかいな】weird

説話【せつわ】tales

挿絵【さしえ】illustration

富む【とむ】abound (in)

書物【しょもつ】book

さながら just like

土用干【どようほし】summer airing of clothes, books, etc., to guard against damage from insects

部屋中【へやじゅう】throughout the room

置き散らす【おきちらす】litter (things) about

寝ころぶ【ねころぶ】lie about

手あたり次第【てあたりしだい】whatever comes to hand

繰りひろげる【くりひろげる】spread open, unfold

耽読する【たんどくする】read avidly

その中には、コナンドイルの The Sign of Four や、ドキン
シイの Murder, Considered as one of the fine arts や、アラ
ビアンナイトのようなお伽噺から、仏蘭西の不思議なSex-
uology の本なども交っていた。

19▶ 　此処の住職が秘していた地獄極楽の図を始め、須弥山図
だの涅槃像だの、いろいろの、古い仏画を強いて懇望し
て、丁度学校の教員室に掛っている地図のように、所嫌わ
ず部屋の四壁へぶら下げて見た。床の間の香炉からは、始
終紫色の香の煙が真っ直ぐに静かに立ち昇って、明るい暖
かい室内を焚きしめて居た。私は時々菊屋橋際の舗へ行っ
て白檀や沈香を買って来てはそれを燻べた。

その中に【そのなかに】among them

コナンドイル Sir Arthur Conan Doyle

ドキンシイ Thomas De Quincey: English author best known for his *Confessions of an English Opium-Eater.*

アラビアンナイト *Arabian Nights*

お伽噺【おとぎばなし】fairy tales

仏蘭西【フランス】France

不思議な【ふしぎな】strange, curious

Sexuology misspelling of "sexologie"

本【ほん】book

交る【まじる】be mixed (among)

19

此処【ここ】here

住職【じゅうしょく】chief priest

秘する【ひする】keep secret

地獄極楽【じごくごくらく】Heaven and
Hell

図【ず】print, painting

〜を始め【〜をはじめ】including

須弥山図【しゅみせんず】picture of
Mount Sumeru

〜だの〜だの indicates a non-exhaustive list ❀

涅槃像【ねはんぞう】reclining Buddha

いろいろの various

古い【ふるい】old

仏画【ぶつが】paintings of Buddha

強いて【しいて】insistently

懇望する【こんもうする／こんぼうする】
beg for, entreat

丁度【ちょうど】exactly

学校【がっこう】school

教員室【きょういんしつ】teachers' room

掛る【かかる】hang

地図【ちず】map

Among them were Conan Doyle's *The Sign of Four*, De Quincey's *On Murder Considered as One of the Fine Arts* and fairy tales like *Arabian Nights*—they even included an extraordinary French book on "sexologie."

I had been shameless in begging the chief priest for various old religious paintings, such as a picture of Heaven and Hell that he had been keeping to himself, as well as a Mount Sumeru and a reclining Buddha. I hung them arbitrarily on the four walls of my room like the maps we had in the staff room at school. A vertical plume of violet smoke always floated silently up from the incense burner in the alcove, impregnating the bright, warm room with its fragrance. Sometimes I would go to a shop by the Kikuya Bridge and buy some sandalwood or aloes to burn.

所嫌わず 【ところきらわず】 indiscriminately
部屋 【へや】 room
四壁 【しへき】 four walls
ぶら下げる 【ぶらさげる】 hang
〜て見る 【〜てみる】 to see what it is like
床の間 【とこのま】 alcove
香炉 【こうろ】 incense burner
始終 【しじゅう】 always
紫色 【むらさきいろ】 purple
香 【こう】 incense
煙 【けむり】 smoke
真っ直ぐに 【まっすぐに】 straight
静かに 【しずかに】 quietly
立ち昇る 【たちのぼる】 rise up
明るい 【あかるい】 bright
暖かい 【あたたかい】 warm
室内 【しつない】 interior (of a room)

焚きしめる 【たきしめる】 perfume (by burning incense)
私 【わたし】 I
時々 【ときどき】 sometimes
菊屋橋 【きくやばし】 Kikuya Bridge
〜際 【〜ぎわ】 by, beside
舗 【みせ】 shop
行く 【いく】 go
白檀 【びゃくだん】 sandalwood
沈香 【じんこう】 aloeswood
買って来る 【かってくる】 go out to buy (and come back)
燻べる 【くべる】 burn

天気の好い日、きらきらとした真昼の光線が一杯に障子
へあたる時の室内は、眼の醒めるような壮観を呈した。絢
爛な色彩の古画の諸仏、羅漢、比丘、比丘尼、優婆塞、優
婆夷、象、獅子、麒麟などが四壁の紙幅の内から、ゆたか
な光の中に泳ぎ出す。畳の上に投げ出された無数の書物か
らは、惨殺、麻酔、魔薬、妖女、宗教——種々雑多の傀儡
が、香の煙に溶け込んで、朦朧と立ち罩める中に、二畳ば
かりの緋毛氈を敷き、どんよりとした蛮人のような瞳を据
えて、寝ころんだ儘、私は毎日々々幻覚を胸に描いた。

20

天気【てんき】weather

好い【よい】good

日【ひ】day

きらきらとした MIMETIC gleaming

真昼【まひる】midday

光線【こうせん】beams of light

一杯に【いっぱいに】plentifully

障子【しょうじ】shoji, paper screen

あたる strike

〜時【〜とき】when

室内【しつない】interior (of a room)

眼の醒めるような【めのさめるような】dazzling

壮観【そうかん】grand spectacle

呈する【ていする】present

絢爛な【けんらんな】gorgeous, gaudy

色彩【しきさい】color

古画【こが】old picture

諸仏【しょぶつ】various Buddhas

羅漢【らかん】 *arhat* (monk who has attained nirvana)

比丘【びく】 *bhiksu* (Buddhist priest)

比丘尼【びくに】 *bhikṣuṇī* (Buddhist priestess)

優婆塞【うばそく】 *upāsaka* (male lay devotee)

優婆夷【うばい】 *upāsikā* (female lay devotee)

象【ぞう】elephant

獅子【しし】lion

麒麟【きりん】 *qilin* (mythical beast)

四壁【しへき】four walls

紙幅【しふく】picture mount

〜の内から【〜のうちから】from within

ゆたかな rich

光【ひかり】light

On days when the weather was fine and the bright rays of the midday sun fell directly on the shoji, the interior of the room presented a spectacle of the most impressive grandeur. From the gorgeously colored old paintings decorating the four walls, all the various Buddhas, monks who had achieved enlightenment, priests, priestesses, *upāsaka*s and *upāsikā*s, elephants, lions and qilins would detach themselves from their picture mounts and float forth in the lush radiance. And from the countless books flung across the tatami—treating of vicious murders, anesthesia, narcotics, witchcraft and religion—a myriad of figures melted into the incense smoke that shrouded everything in a haze. In the midst of this, I conjured up visions for myself, day after day, as I lounged upon a red fur rug about two tatami in size, my eyes as dull and glassy as those of a savage.

~の中に 【~のなかに】 inside, amidst ⊛
泳ぎ出す 【およぎだす】 swim forth
畳 【たたみ】 tatami mat
~の上に 【~のうえに】 on
投げ出す 【なげだす】 [passive form in text] throw out
無数 【むすう】 countless
書物 【しょもつ】 book
惨殺 【ざんさつ】 cruel murder
麻酔 【ますい】 anesthetic
魔薬 【まやく】 narcotic
妖女 【ようじょ】 witch, enchantress
宗教 【しゅうきょう】 religion
種々雑多の 【しゅじゅざったの】 all sorts of
傀儡 【かいらい】 marionette, figure
香 【こう】 incense
煙 【けむり】 smoke
溶け込む 【とけこむ】 melt into

朦朧と 【もうろうと】 mistily
立ち罩める 【たちこめる】 spread throughout, shroud
二畳 【にじょう】 two tatami mats
~ばかり just
緋毛氈 【ひもうせん】 red fur rug
敷く 【しく】 spread out
どんよりとした MIMETIC stagnant, heavy
蛮人 【ばんじん】 savage, barbarian
瞳を据える 【ひとみをすえる】 stare fixedly
寝ころぶ 【ねころぶ】 lie about
~儘 【~まま】 unchanged
私 【わたし】 I
毎日々々 【まいにちまいにち】 every day
幻覚 【げんかく】 hallucination, vision
胸に描く 【むねにえがく】 imagine, conjure up

21▶　夜の九時頃、寺の者が大概寝静まって了うとウヰスキーの角壜を呷って酔いを買った後、勝手に縁側の雨戸を引き外し、墓地の生け垣を乗り越えて散歩に出かけた。成る可く人目にかからぬように毎晩服装を取り換えて公園の雑沓の中を潜って歩いたり、古道具屋や古本屋の店先を漁り廻ったりした。頬冠りに唐桟の半纏を引っ掛け、綺麗に研いた素足へ爪紅をさして雪駄を穿くこともあった。金縁の色眼鏡に二重廻しの襟を立てて出ることもあった。着け髭、ほくろ、痣と、いろいろに面体を換えるのを面白がったが、或る晩、三味線堀の古着屋で、

21

夜【よる】evening, night	墓地【ぼち】cemetery
九時頃【くじごろ】around nine o'clock	生け垣【いけがき】hedge
寺の者【てらのもの】staff of the temple	乗り越える【のりこえる】climb over
大概【たいがい】mostly	散歩【さんぽ】walk
寝静まる【ねしずまる】be fast asleep	出かける【でかける】go out
〜て了う【〜てしまう】completely	成る可く【なるべく】as much as possible
ウヰスキー【ウイスキー】whiskey	人目にかからぬ【ひとめにかからぬ】not be seen
角壜【かくびん】square-shaped bottle	毎晩【まいばん】every evening
呷る【あおる】quaff	服装【ふくそう】clothes, outfit
酔いを買う【よいをかう】incur drunkenness	取り換える【とりかえる】change
〜後【〜のち／〜あと】after	公園【こうえん】park
勝手に【かってに】without reference to anyone else	雑沓【ざっとう】hustle and bustle
縁側【えんがわ】veranda	〜の中を【〜のなかを】through
雨戸【あまど】shutters	潜る【くぐる】slip through
引き外す【ひきはずす】pull open	歩く【あるく】walk
	古道具屋【ふるどうぐや】antique shop

About nine o'clock at night, with most of the residents of the temple fast asleep, I'd get myself drunk by swigging from a square bottle of whiskey before making bold to slide open the veranda shutters, clamber over the cemetery hedge and set out for a stroll. Wearing a different outfit every night to minimize the chance of being spotted, I would slink through all the hustle and bustle of the park, or forage through the shop fronts of the antique dealers and secondhand bookshops. Some nights I would throw on a scarf and a short, striped coat and paint the toenails of my well-scrubbed feet red before slipping them into a pair of leather-soled sandals. Other times I would go out wearing tinted, gold-framed glasses and a cape with the collar turned up. I also enjoyed changing my appearance with tricks like false beards, moles and birthmarks. But one evening, at a secondhand clothing shop in Shamisenbori,

---

古本屋 【ふるほんや】 secondhand book-shop
店先 【みせさき】 shop front
漁り廻る 【あさりまわる】 walk around
頬冠り 【ほおかむり／ほおかぶり】 cloth tied around the face
唐桟 【とうざん】 shiny striped cotton
半纏 【はんてん】 short coat
引っ掛ける 【ひっかける】 throw on
綺麗に 【きれいに】 beautifully
研く 【みがく】 clean, brush
素足 【すあし】 bare feet
爪紅 【つまべに】 red nail polish
さす apply
雪駄 【せった】 leather-soled sandals
穿く 【はく】 put on (shoes)
金縁 【きんぶち】 gold frames
色眼鏡 【いろめがね】 dark glasses

二重廻し 【にじゅうまわし】 inverness (kind of cape)
襟 【えり】 collar
立てる 【たてる】 put up
出る 【でる】 go out
着け髭 【つけひげ】 false beard
ほくろ mole
痣 【あざ】 birthmark
いろいろに in various ways
面体 【めんてい】 features, looks
換える 【かえる】 change
面白がる 【おもしろがる】 enjoy
或る 【ある】 a certain, one
晩 【ばん】 evening
三味線堀 【しゃみせんぼり】 Shamisenbori
古着屋 【ふるぎや】 old clothing shop

藍地に大小あられの小紋を散らした女物の袷が眼に附いてから、急にそれが着て見たくてたまらなくなった。

22 ▶ 　一体私は衣服反物に対して、単に色合いが好いとか柄が粋だとかいう以外に、もっと深く鋭い愛着心を持って居た。女物に限らず、凡べて美しい絹物を見たり、触れたりする時は、何となく顫い附きたくなって、丁度恋人の肌の色を眺めるような快感の高潮に達することが屢々であった。殊に私の大好きなお召や縮緬を、世間憚らず、恋に着飾ることの出来る女の境遇を、嫉ましく思うことさえあった。

藍地【あいじ】blue background
大小【だいしょう】large and small
あられ hail, small cubes
小紋【こもん】fine pattern
散らす【ちらす】scatter about, distribute about
女物【おんなもの】women's clothing ⊛
袷【あわせ】lined kimono
眼に附く【めにつく】catch one's eye
急に【きゅうに】suddenly
着る【きる】put on, wear
〜て見る【〜てみる】to see what it is like
（したくて）たまらない have an irresistible urge (to do)

22
一体【いったい】originally
私【わたし】I ⊛

衣服反物【いふくたんもの】clothing and fabrics
〜に対して【〜にたいして】with regard to
単に【たんに】merely
色合い【いろあい】colors
好い【よい】pleasing
柄【がら】pattern
粋【いき】fashionable, chic
〜以外に【〜いがいに】beyond
もっと more
深い【ふかい】deep
鋭い【するどい】acute
愛着心【あいちゃくしん】affection, attachment
持つ【もつ】have
〜に限らず【〜にかぎらず】not limited to
凡べて【すべて】all

I caught sight of a woman's lined kimono, blue with a delicate pattern of dots large and small, and was overcome with an irresistible urge to try it on.

Truth be told, I had a deep and keen attachment to clothing and fabrics that went beyond simply liking certain colors or elegant patterns. It wasn't limited to women's clothing; every time I looked at or handled a beautiful bolt of silk, I wanted to bury my face in it, and often my sensations of pleasure would reach a peak as if I were gazing at the tones of a lover's flesh. I even felt jealous of women who were fortunate enough to be able to dress up in my favorite fabrics—crepe and silk crepe—whenever they wanted without fear of public censure.

美しい 【うつくしい】 beautiful

絹物 【きぬもの】 silk

見る 【みる】 see, look at

触れる 【ふれる】 touch

〜時 【〜とき】 when

何となく 【なんとなく】 somehow

顫い附く 【ふるいつく】 hug affectionately in a burst of emotion

丁度 【ちょうど】 exactly, just

恋人 【こいびと】 lover

肌 【はだ】 skin

色 【いろ】 color

眺める 【ながめる】 gaze at

快感 【かいかん】 pleasure

高潮 【たかしお】 high tide, climax

達する 【たっする】 reach, attain

屢々 【しばしば】 often

殊に 【ことに】 especially

大好きな 【だいすきな】 favorite

お召 【おめし】 abbr. of お召縮緬 【おめしちりめん】 high-grade silk crepe kimono

縮緬 【ちりめん】 silk crepe kimono

世間憚らず 【せけんはばからず】 indifferent to public opinion

恣に 【ほしいままに】 self-indulgently

着飾る 【きかざる】 dress up

出来る 【できる】 be able to do

女 【おんな】 woman

境遇 【きょうぐう】 situation

嫉ましく思う 【ねたましくおもう】 be jealous of

〜さえ even

23 ▶　あの古着屋の店にだらりと生々しく下って居る小紋縮緬の袷——あのしっとりした、重い冷たい布が粘つくように肉体を包む時の心好さを思うと、私は思わず戦慄した。あの着物を着て、女の姿で往来を歩いて見たい。……こう思って、私は一も二もなくそれを買う気になり、ついでに友禅の長襦袢や、黒縮緬の羽織迄も取りそろえた。

24 ▶　大柄の女が着たものと見えて、小男の私には寸法も打ってつけであった。夜が更けてがらんとした寺中がひっそりした時分、私はひそかに鏡台に向って化粧を始めた。

23

古着屋【ふるぎや】old clothes dealer

店【みせ】shop

だらりと limply, loosely

生々しく【なまなましく】vividly

下る【さがる】hang

小紋縮緬【こもんちりめん】finely patterned silk crepe

袷【あわせ】lined kimono

しっとりした moist

重い【おもい】heavy

冷たい【つめたい】cold

布【きれ】cloth, fabric

粘つく【ねばつく】stick

肉体【にくたい】flesh, body

包む【つつむ】envelop

〜時【〜とき】when

心好さ【こころよさ】pleasant feeling

思う【おもう】think about ❀

私【わたし】I ❀

思わず【おもわず】involuntarily

戦慄する【せんりつする】shiver

着物【きもの】kimono

着る【きる】put on, wear ❀

女【おんな】woman ❀

姿【すがた】form, figure

往来【おうらい】street

歩く【あるく】walk

〜て見る【〜てみる】to see what it is like

一も二もなく【いちもにもなく】without hesitation

買う気になる【かうきになる】get in the mood to buy

ついでに at the same time

友禅【ゆうぜん】Yūzen silk kimono

That intricately designed silk-crepe kimono that hung so limp and tempting in the old clothing shop—and the delightful sensation of its smooth, heavy, cool fabric enveloping my body in its viscous folds—the mere thought of it sent a shiver down my spine. *I want to put that kimono on and experience walking the streets as a woman.* Such were my thoughts, and without a moment's hesitation I made up my mind to buy it, picking up a set of long Yūzen undergarments and a haori of black silk crepe while I was at it.

It seemed likely that the kimono had been worn by a large-set woman, as it was a perfect fit for a small man like me. When the night had deepened and the temple grounds were empty and silent, I stealthily sat down in front of the mirror and set about making myself up.

長襦袢【ながじゅばん】long undergarment

黒縮緬【くろちりめん】black silk crepe

羽織【はおり】haori, half-coat

〜迄も【〜までも】even

取りそろえる【とりそろえる】gather together

24

大柄【おおがら】large frame, big build

見える【みえる】seem, appear

小男【こおとこ】small man

寸法【すんぽう】measurement

打ってつけな【うってつけな】most suitable, best adapted

夜が更ける【よがふける／よるがふける】grow late, the night deepens

がらんとした MIMETIC empty, deserted

寺中【てらじゅう】the whole temple

ひっそりした MIMETIC quiet, still

時分【じぶん】time, period

ひそかに secretly

鏡台【きょうだい】dresser (with a mirror), vanity table

向う【むかう】face

化粧【けしょう】make-up

始める【はじめる】start

黄色い生地の鼻柱へ先ずベットリと練りお白粉をなすり着けた瞬間の容貌は、少しグロテスクに見えたが、濃い白い粘液を平手で顔中へ万遍なく押し拡げると、思ったよりものりが好く、甘い匂いのひやひやとした露が、毛孔へ沁み入る皮膚のよろこびは、格別であった。紅やとのこを塗るに随って、石膏の如く唯徒らに真っ白であった私の顔が、潑剌とした生色ある女の相に変って行く面白さ。文士や画家の芸術よりも、俳優や芸者や一般の女が、日常自分の体の肉を材料として試みている化粧の技巧の方が、遥かに興味の多いことを知った。

黄色い【きいろい】yellow

生地【きじ】unmade-up skin

鼻柱【はなばしら】bridge of the nose

先ず【まず】first of all

ベットリと MIMETIC thickly

練りお白粉【ねりおしろい】geisha make-up

なすり着ける【なすりつける】rub on, apply

瞬間【しゅんかん】moment

容貌【ようぼう】look, appearance

少し【すこし】slightly

グロテスクな grotesque

見える【みえる】appear, look

濃い【こい】thick

白い【しろい】white

粘液【ねんえき】viscous liquid

平手【ひらて】palms

顔中【かおじゅう】whole face

万遍なく【まんべんなく】evenly

押し拡げる【おしひろげる】smear over

思ったよりも【おもったよりも】more than one thought

のりが好い【のりがよい】spread well

甘い【あまい】sweet

匂い【におい】smell

ひやひやとした cool

露【つゆ】dew

毛孔【けあな】pores

沁み入る【しみいる】penetrate into

皮膚【ひふ】skin

よろこび pleasure, delight

格別な【かくべつな】special, exceptional

紅【べに】rouge

とのこ powder

塗る【ぬる】apply, spread on

～に随って【～にしたがって】as

Initially, when I first applied gobs of the white paste to the yellow skin around the bridge of my nose, my appearance was rather grotesque; but as I used my palms to smear the thick white substance all over my face, it spread much better than I'd expected and I found the sensation extraordinarily delightful as the cool, sweetly scented dew seeped into the pores of my skin. It was amusing how my face, which had just been of a plasterlike whiteness, gradually turned into the blooming countenance of a lively woman as I applied rouge and powder. It dawned on me that the make-up techniques which actors, geisha and ordinary women try out on a daily basis with their own flesh as their medium, are of far greater interest than the works of the man of letters or the painter.

石膏 【せっこう】 plaster
〜の如く 【〜のごとく】 just like
唯 【ただ】 just, only
徒らに 【いたずらに】 to no purpose
真っ白な 【まっしろな】 pure-white
私 【わたし】 I
顔 【かお】 face
潑剌とした 【はつらつとした】 frisky
生色ある 【せいしょくある】 lively looking
女 【おんな】 woman ⊛
相 【そう】 countenance
変る 【かわる】 change
〜て行く 【〜ていく】 indicates an increase in tendency
面白さ 【おもしろさ】 enjoyment
文士 【ぶんし】 man of letters
画家 【がか】 painter
芸術 【げいじゅつ】 art

俳優 【はいゆう】 actor
芸者 【げいしゃ】 geisha
一般の 【いっぱんの】 ordinary
日常 【にちじょう】 every day
自分 【じぶん】 oneself
体 【からだ】 body
肉 【にく】 flesh
材料 【ざいりょう】 material
〜として as
試みる 【こころみる】 test, try out
化粧 【けしょう】 make-up
技巧 【ぎこう】 technique
〜の方が 【〜のほうが】 [followed by an adjective] rather
遥かに 【はるかに】 by a long shot
興味 【きょうみ】 interest
多い 【おおい】 much, many
知る 【しる】 learn, realize

25 ▶ 　長襦袢、半襟、腰巻、それからチュッチュッと鳴る紅絹裏の袂、——私の肉体は、凡べて普通の女の皮膚が味わうと同等の触感を与えられ、襟足から手頸まで白く塗って、銀杏返しの鬘の上にお高祖頭巾を冠り、思い切って往来の夜道へ紛れ込んで見た。

26 ▶ 　雨曇りのしたうす暗い晩であった。千束町、清住町、龍泉寺町——あの辺一帯の溝の多い、淋しい街を暫くさまよって見たが、交番の巡査も、通行人も、一向気が附かないようであった。甘皮を一枚張ったようにぱさぱさ乾いている顔の上を、夜風が冷やかに撫でて行く。

25

長襦袢【ながじゅばん】long undergarment

半襟【はんえり】replaceable kimono collar

腰巻【こしまき】underskirt, waistcloth

チュッチュッと鳴る【チュッチュッとなる】 ONOMATOPOEIC rustle

紅絹裏【もみうら】red silk lining

袂【たもと】sleeve

私【わたし】I

肉体【にくたい】body

凡べて【すべて】all

普通の【ふつうの】normal

女【おんな】woman

皮膚【ひふ】skin

味わう【あじわう】taste, savor

同等の【どうとうの】the same

触感【しょっかん】feeling, sensation

与える【あたえる】[passive form in text] impart

襟足【えりあし】nape of the neck

手頸【てくび】wrists

白く【しろく】white

塗る【ぬる】apply, spread on

銀杏返し【いちょうがえし】butterfly coiffure

鬘【かつら】wig

〜の上に【〜のうえに】above

お高祖頭巾【おこそずきん】hood

冠る【かぶる】wear (on the head)

思い切って【おもいきって】daringly

往来【おうらい】comings and goings

夜道【よみち】nighttime streets

紛れ込む【まぎれこむ】mingle into

The long undergarment, the replaceable collar, the underskirt, the rustling sleeves lined with red silk—my body was having conferred upon it all the sensations that the skin of a normal woman knows. Painting both the nape of neck and my wrists white, I put a hood over my butterfly-coiffure wig and boldly plunged into the busy nighttime streets.

It was a gloomy, overcast night. Senzoku-chō, Kiyosumi-chō and Ryūsenji-chō—I wandered for a while through those neighborhoods with their melancholy streets and numerous canals, but neither the constable at the police box nor the passers-by appeared to pay me any attention. The evening breeze coolly caressed my face, which, dry and brittle, felt as though another layer of skin had been stretched over it.

〜て見る 【〜てみる】 to see what it was like ⊛

26

雨曇り 【あまぐもり】 overcast sky
うす暗い 【うすぐらい】 gloomy
晩 【ばん】 evening
千束町 【せんぞくちょう】 Senzoku-chō
清住町 【きよすみちょう】 Kiyosumi-chō
龍泉寺町 【りゅうせんじちょう】 Ryūsenji-chō
辺 【あたり】 area
一帯 【いったい】 whole neighborhood
溝 【みぞ】 canal
多い 【おおい】 numerous
淋しい 【さびしい】 lonely
街 【まち】 quarter, street
暫く 【しばらく】 for a while
さまよう wander

交番 【こうばん】 police box
巡査 【じゅんさ】 police officer
通行人 【つうこうにん】 passer-by
一向〜ない 【いっこう〜ない】 not at all
気が附く 【きがつく】 notice
甘皮 【あまかわ】 epidermis, skin
一枚 【いちまい】 one layer
張る 【はる】 stretch taut
ぱさぱさ乾く 【ぱさぱさかわく】 dry out
顔 【かお】 face
〜の上を 【〜のうえを】 upon
夜風 【よかぜ】 evening breeze
冷やかに 【ひややかに】 coolly
撫でる 【なでる】 stroke, massage
〜て行く 【〜ていく】 indicates an increase in tendency

口辺を蔽うて居る頭巾の布が、息の為めに熱く湿って、歩くたびに長い縮緬の腰巻の裾は、じゃれるように脚へ纏れる。みぞおちから肋骨の辺を堅く緊め附けている丸帯と、骨盤の上を括っている扱帯の加減で、私の体の血管には、自然と女のような血が流れ始め、男らしい気分や姿勢はだんだんとなくなって行くようであった。

27 ▶　　友禅の袖の蔭から、お白粉を塗った手をつき出して見ると、強い頑丈な線が闇の中に消えて、白くふっくらと柔かに浮き出ている。私は自分で自分の手の美しさに惚れ惚れとした。このような美しい手を、実際に持っている女と云う者が、羨ましく感じられた。

口辺【こうへん】around the mouth
蔽う【おおう】cover
頭巾【ずきん】hood
布【きれ】cloth, fabric
息【いき】breath, breathing
〜の為めに【〜のために】because of
熱く【あつく】hotly
湿う【うるおう】be moist
歩く【あるく】walk
〜たびに every time
長い【ながい】long
縮緬【ちりめん】silk crepe
腰巻【こしまき】underskirt, waistcloth
裾【すそ】hem
じゃれる be playful, gambol about
脚【あし】legs
纏れる【もつれる】get tangled up
みぞおち pit of the stomach

肋骨【あばら】ribs
辺【あたり】region
堅く【かたく】tightly, firmly
緊め附ける【しめつける】bind tight
丸帯【まるおび】one-piece sash
骨盤【こつばん】pelvis
〜の上を【〜のうえを】above
括る【くくる】bind, tie
扱帯【しごき】undergirdle
加減【かげん】degree
私【わたし】I ❀
体【からだ】body
血管【けっかん】veins
自然と【しぜんと】naturally
女【おんな】woman ❀
血【ち】blood
流れ始める【ながれはじめる】start to flow
男らしい【おとこらしい】manly

The cloth of the hood that covered my mouth grew hot and moist with my breath, and at every step I took, the hem of my long crepe underskirt would get tangled up in my legs in an almost playful manner. What with a one-piece sash wrapped tightly from my solar plexus to my ribs and an undergirdle bound around my pelvis, it felt as though the blood of a woman had naturally started coursing through the veins of my body, and my male emotions and posture were gradually starting to disappear.

When I thrust out my white-painted hands from under my muslin sleeves, their strong, solid outlines faded away in the darkness, and they appeared white, plump and soft. I was enchanted by their beauty. I envied women for genuinely possessing beautiful hands like these.

気分 【きぶん】 mood
姿勢 【しせい】 posture
なくなる disappear
〜て行く 【〜ていく】 indicates an increase in tendency

27
友禅 【ゆうぜん】 Yūzen silk kimono
袖 【そで】 sleeve
〜の蔭から 【〜のかげから】 from underneath
お白粉 【おしろい】 make-up
塗る 【ぬる】 apply, spread on
手 【て】 hand ⊛
つき出す 【つきだす】 stick out
〜て見る 【〜てみる】 to see what it is like
強い 【つよい】 strong
頑丈な 【がんじょうな】 solid, firm
線 【せん】 line

闇 【やみ】 darkness
消える 【きえる】 disappear
白い 【しろい】 white
ふっくらと plump
柔かに 【やわらかに】 tenderly, softly
浮き出る 【うきでる】 stand out
自分 【じぶん】 oneself, myself ⊛
美しさ 【うつくしさ】 beauty
惚れ惚れとする 【ほれぼれとする】 be captivated (by)
美しい 【うつくしい】 beautiful
実際に 【じっさいに】 truly
持つ 【もつ】 have
〜と云う 【〜という】 that is called
者 【もの】 person
羨ましい 【うらやましい】 jealous
感じる 【かんじる】 [spontaneous form in text] feel

芝居の弁天小僧のように、こう云う姿をして、さまざまの罪を犯したならば、どんなに面白いであろう。……探偵小説や、犯罪小説の読者を始終喜ばせる「秘密」「疑惑」の気分に髣髴とした心持で、私は次第に人通りの多い、公園の六区の方へ歩みを運んだ。そうして、殺人とか、強盗とか、何か非常な残忍な悪事を働いた人間のように、自分を思い込むことが出来た。

28 ▶ 　十二階の前から、池の汀について、オペラ館の四つ角へ出ると、イルミネーションとアーク燈の光が厚化粧をした私の顔にきらきらと照って、着物の色合いや縞目がはッきりと読める。

芝居【しばい】play, drama
弁天小僧【べんてんこぞう】Benten Kozō (Robin Hood–type hero)
こう云う【こういう】this kind of
姿【すがた】figure, appearance
さまざまの various
罪【つみ】crimes
犯す【おかす】commit
〜ならば if, supposing
面白い【おもしろい】enjoyable
探偵小説【たんていしょうせつ】detective story
犯罪小説【はんざいしょうせつ】crime story
読者【どくしゃ】reader
始終【しじゅう】always
喜ばせる【よろこばせる】make happy
秘密【ひみつ】secret

疑惑【ぎわく】doubt, suspicion
気分【きぶん】mood
髣髴とする【ほうふつとする】closely resemble
心持【こころもち】frame of mind
私【わたし】I ⊛
次第に【しだいに】gradually
人通りの多い【ひとどおりのおおい】with many passers-by
公園【こうえん】park
六区【ろっく】Rokku (entertainment quarter)
〜の方へ【〜のほうへ】in the direction of
歩みを運ぶ【あゆみをはこぶ】walk
殺人【さつじん】murder
とか〜とか particle combination used for desultory lists
強盗【ごうとう】robbery

What fun it would be to commit all sorts of crimes while dressed like this, just like Benten Kozō in the play! In a state of mind akin to the mood of "secrecy" and "suspicion" that provides such endless delight to the readers of detective and crime stories, I ambled over to the busy Rokku end of the park. There I was fully able to imagine myself as someone who had perpetrated a barbarous act of evil—a murder perhaps, or a robbery.

From the Twelve Story Tower I followed the edge of the pond and emerged at the crossing near the Opera House, where the glinting light of the illuminations and arc lamps lit up my heavily made-up face and revealed the colors and striped pattern of my kimono.

何か【なにか】in one form or another
非常な【ひじょうな】remarkable, extreme
残忍な【ざんにんな】cruel
悪事を働く【あくじをはたらく】do a wicked deed
人間【にんげん】person
自分【じぶん】oneself
思い込む【おもいこむ】get (an idea) into one's head
出来る【できる】be able to do, succeed

28

十二階【じゅうにかい】Twelve Story Tower
前【まえ】front
池の汀【いけのみぎわ】edge of a pond
〜について following
オペラ館【おぺらかん】the Opera House (a motion-picture theater)

四つ角【よっかど】crossroads
出る【でる】emerge, come out
イルミネーション decorative lighting
アーク燈【アークとう】arc lamps (street lights)
光【ひかり】light
厚化粧をする【あつげしょうをする】wear thick make-up
顔【かお】face
きらきらと MIMETIC brilliantly
照る【てる】shine
着物【きもの】kimono
色合い【いろあい】color
縞目【しまめ】striped pattern
はッきりと clearly
読める【よめる】be possible to make out

常磐座の前へ来た時、突き当りの写真屋の玄関の大鏡へ、ぞろぞろ雑沓する群集の中に交って、立派に女と化け終せた私の姿が映って居た。

29 ▶　こってり塗り附けたお白粉の下に、「男」と云う秘密が悉く隠されて、眼つきも口つきも女のように動き、女のように笑おうとする。甘いへんのうの匂いと、囁くような衣摺れの音を立てて、私の前後を擦れ違う幾人の女の群も、皆私を同類と認めて訝しまない。そうしてその女達の中には、私の優雅な顔の作りと、古風な衣裳の好みとを、羨ましそうに見ている者もある。

常磐座【ときわざ】Tokiwa Theater
前【まえ】front
来る【くる】come
〜時【〜とき】when
突き当り【つきあたり】end of a street
写真屋【しゃしんや】photographer's shop
玄関【げんかん】vestibule
大鏡【おおかがみ】big mirror
ぞろぞろ MIMETIC in droves
雑沓する【ざっとうする】bustle about
群集【ぐんしゅう】crowd
〜の中に【〜のなかに】among ⊛
交る【まじる】mingle, mix in
立派に【りっぱに】splendidly
女【おんな】woman ⊛
化け終せる【ばけおおせる】completely transform
私【わたし】I ⊛

姿【すがた】figure, form
映る【うつる】be reflected

29

こってり MIMETIC thickly
塗り附ける【ぬりつける】paint on
お白粉【おしろい】make-up
〜の下に【〜のしたに】beneath
男【おとこ】man
〜と云う【〜という】that is, namely
秘密【ひみつ】secret
悉く【ことごとく】entirely
隠す【かくす】[passive form in text] hide
眼つき【めつき】expression in the eyes
口つき【くちつき】expression of the mouth
動く【うごく】move
笑う【わらう】[volitional form in text] smile, laugh

Arriving in front of the Tokiwa Theater, I saw my reflection in a huge mirror in the doorway of a photographer's shop at the end of the street: surrounded by a milling horde of people, there I was, miraculously and completely transformed into a woman.

The secret of my maleness was utterly concealed beneath the thick make-up I wore. My eyes and mouth started to move more like a woman's and even sought to smile like a woman. Redolent of the sweet fragrance of camphor and emitting a whisper of rustling garments, the clusters of women who passed before and behind me suspected nothing; all accepted me as one of their own. There were even some among them who seemed to look with envy at my elegant features and admire my taste in old-fashioned clothes.

〜（お）うとする try to 〜
甘い 【あまい】 sweet
へんのう camphor oil
匂い 【におい】 smell
囁く 【ささやく】 whisper
衣摺れ 【きぬずれ】 rustling of clothes
音を立てる 【おとをたてる】 make a sound
前後 【ぜんご】 before and behind
擦れ違う 【すれちがう】 pass by
幾人 【いくにん】 several people
群 【むれ】 group
皆 【みな】 everyone
同類 【どうるい】 same species
認める 【みとめる】 accept
訝しむ 【あやしむ】 be suspicious
女達 【おんなたち】 women
優雅な 【ゆうがな】 elegant

顔 【かお】 face
作り 【つくり】 form, make-up
古風な 【こふうな】 old-fashioned
衣裳 【いしょう】 clothes
好み 【このみ】 taste, preference
羨ましい 【うらやましい】 envious
見る 【みる】 look
者 【もの】 person

30 ▶　　いつも見馴れて居る公園の夜の騒擾も、「秘密」を持って居る私の眼には、凡べてが新しかった。何処へ行っても、何を見ても、始めて接する物のように、珍しく奇妙であった。人間の瞳を欺き、電燈の光を欺いて、濃艶な脂粉とちりめんの衣裳の下に自分を潜ませながら、「秘密」の帷を一枚隔てて眺める為めに、恐らく平凡な現実が、夢のような不思議な色彩を施されるのであろう。

31 ▶　　それから私は毎晩のようにこの仮装をつづけて、時とすると、宮戸座の立ち見や活動写真の見物の間へ、平気で割って入るようになった。

30

いつも all the time, usually

見馴れる【みなれる】get used to seeing, come to know

公園【こうえん】park

夜【よる】evening, night

騒擾【そうじょう】commotion

秘密【ひみつ】secret ❀

持つ【もつ】have

私【わたし】I ❀

眼【め】eyes

凡べて【すべて】everything

新しい【あたらしい】new, fresh

何処へ〜も【どこへ〜も】wherever

行く【いく】go

何を〜も【なにを〜も】whatever

見る【みる】see

始めて【はじめて】for the first time

接する【せっする】come into contact

物【もの】things

珍しい【めずらしい】rare, curious

奇妙な【きみょうな】peculiar

人間【にんげん】human

瞳【ひとみ】eye

欺く【あざむく】deceive, trick ❀

電燈【でんとう】electric light

光【ひかり】light

濃艶な【のうえんな】bewitching, charming

脂粉【しふん】cosmetics

ちりめん silk crepe

衣装【いしょう】clothes

〜の下に【〜のしたに】beneath

自分【じぶん】oneself

潜む【ひそむ】[causative form in text] conceal

帷【とばり】curtain

Though I was used to the bustle of the park at night, every-thing about it felt new to my eyes, now that I had my "secret." Wherever I went and whatever I saw, everything was novel and bizarre, as if I were encountering it for the first time in my life. Everyday reality was endowed with a mysterious, dreamlike tinge, perhaps because I was contemplating it at one remove through secrecy's gauze curtain—deceiving people's eyes, deceiving the light from the electric lamps—as I hid deep beneath alluring make-up and garments of silk crepe.

From then onward I continued to dress up on most nights, at times unabashedly slipping in among the spectators in the gallery at the Miyato Theater or audiences in motion-picture theaters.

一枚【いちまい】one (thin, flat object)
隔てる【へだてる】interpose
眺める【ながめる】gaze
〜為めに【〜ために】because
恐らく【おそらく】perhaps
平凡な【へいぼんな】ordinary
現実【げんじつ】reality
夢【ゆめ】dream
不思議な【ふしぎな】extraordinary
色彩【しきさい】tinge, coloring
施す【ほどこす】[passive form in text] add

31

毎晩のように【まいばんのように】almost every evening
仮装【かそう】masquerade
つづける【つづける】continue
時とすると【ときとすると】sometimes
宮戸座【みやとざ】Miyato Theater

立ち見【たちみ】watching a play from the gallery; the gallery itself
活動写真【かつどうしゃしん】motion picture
見物【けんぶつ】audience
〜の間へ【〜のあいだへ】among
平気で【へいきで】indifferently
割って入る【わってはいる】slip in

寺へ帰るのは十二時近くであったが、座敷に上ると早速空気ランプをつけて、疲れた体の衣裳も解かず、毛氈の上へぐったり嫌らしく寝崩れた儘、残り惜しそうに絢爛な着物の色を眺めたり、袖口をちゃらちゃらと振って見たりした。剝げかかったお白粉が肌理の粗いたるんだ頬の皮へ滲み着いて居るのを、鏡に映して凝視して居ると、廃頽した快感が古い葡萄酒の酔いのように魂をそそった。地獄極楽の図を背景にして、けばけばしい長襦袢のまま、遊女の如くなよなよと蒲団の上へ腹這って、例の奇怪な書物のページを夜更くる迄繙すこともあった。

寺【てら】temple
帰る【かえる】return
十二時【じゅうにじ】twelve o'clock
〜近く【〜ちかく】nearly 〜
座敷【ざしき】tatami-mat room
上る【あがる】enter (by mounting a step)
早速【さっそく】immediately
空気ランプ【くうきランプ】kerosene lamp
つける【つける】turn on
疲れた【つかれた】tired
体【からだ】body
衣裳【いしょう】clothes
解かず【とかず】without loosening
毛氈【もうせん】carpet
〜の上へ【〜のうえへ】on ✤
ぐったり MIMETIC limply, exhaustedly

嫌らしく【いやらしく】with no self-restraint
寝崩れる【ねくずれる】sprawl, collapse
〜儘【〜まま】unchanged, as is
残り惜しい【のこりおしい】wistful
絢爛な【けんらんな】gaudy
着物【きもの】kimono
色【いろ】color
眺める【ながめる】gaze at
袖口【そでぐち】sleeve end
ちゃらちゃらと MIMETIC blithely, vainly
振る【ふる】shake, flap
〜て見る【〜てみる】to see what it is like
剝げかかる【はげかかる】start to peel off
お白粉【おしろい】make-up
肌理の粗い【きめのあらい】coarse (of skin texture)
たるんだ sagging

By the time I returned to the temple it would be nearly midnight, and no sooner had I got back to my room than I would light the kerosene lamp, and without loosening the clothes on my tired body, sprawl wantonly on the rug, gazing wistfully at the gorgeous colors of my kimono or flapping my sleeve ends to and fro. When I stared at my reflection in the mirror and the peeling white make-up sunk deep into the coarse, sagging skin of my cheeks, the decadent pleasure would thrill my soul like the intoxication of vintage wine. With the painting of Heaven and Hell behind me, I would sometimes lie indolently on my belly on the futon like a courtesan, still dressed in my garish undergarments, and flip back and forth through the pages of those weird books of mine until deep into the night.

頬【ほお】cheek
皮【かわ】skin
滲み着く【しみつく】penetrate and stick to
鏡【かがみ】mirror
映す【うつす】reflect
凝視する【ぎょうしする】stare
廃頹した【はいたいした】decadent
快感【かいかん】pleasure
古い【ふるい】old
葡萄酒【ぶどうしゅ】wine
酔い【よい】drunkenness
魂【たましい】soul
そそる stimulate, excite
地獄極楽【じごくごくらく】Heaven and Hell
図【ず】print, picture
背景【はいけい】background

けばけばしい showy, gaudy
長襦袢【ながじゅばん】long undergarment
〜のまま in the unchanged state of
遊女【ゆうじょ】courtesan
〜の如く【〜のごとく】just like
なよなよと MIMETIC languidly, effeminately
蒲団【ふとん】futon
腹這う【はらばう】lie on one's stomach
例の【れいの】the previously mentioned
奇怪な【きかいな】weird
書物【しょもつ】book
夜更くる【よるふくる】RARE USAGE grow late (of night)
〜迄【〜まで】until
飜す【ひるがえす】flip through

次第に扮装も巧くなり、大胆にもなって、物好きな聯想を醸させる為めに、匕首だの麻酔薬だのを、帯の間へ挿んでは外出した。犯罪を行わずに、犯罪に附随して居る美しいロマンチックの匂いだけを、十分に嗅いで見たかったのである。

32▶ そうして、一週間ばかり過ぎた或る晩の事、私は図らずも不思議な因縁から、もッと奇怪なもッと物好きな、そうしてもッと神秘な事件の端緒に出会した。

33▶ その晩私は、いつもよりも多量にウヰスキーを呷って、三友館の二階の貴賓席に上り込んで居た。

次第に【しだいに】gradually

扮装【ふんそう】masquerade

巧い【うまい】skillfull

大胆な【だいたんな】bold

物好きな【ものずきな】curious, fanciful ⊛

聯想【れんそう】association (of ideas)

醸す【かもす】[causative form in text] give rise to

〜為めに【〜ために】in order to

匕首【あいくち】dagger

〜だの〜だの indicates a non-exhaustive list

麻酔薬【ますいやく】narcotic, opiate

帯【おび】sash

〜の間へ【〜のあいだへ】between

挿む【はさむ】insert, slip in

〜では no sooner would one 〜 than . . .

外出する【がいしゅつする】go out

犯罪【はんざい】crime ⊛

行わずに【おこなわずに】without doing

附随する【ふずいする】accompany, be incidental

美しい【うつくしい】beautiful

ロマンチックの romantic

匂い【におい】smell

十分に【じゅうぶんに】fully, enough

嗅ぐ【かぐ】smell

〜て見る【〜てみる】to see what it is like

32

一週間【いっしゅうかん】one week

〜ばかり about

過ぎる【すぎる】pass (of time)

或る【ある】a certain, one

晩【ばん】evening ⊛

事【こと】experience, happening, thing

With time, becoming more skilled at disguise, I also became bolder, and would sally forth with a dagger or an opiate slipped into my sash in order to evoke bizarre associations. I wanted to inhale deeply of the beautiful, romantic perfume that accompanies crime, without actually committing any criminal act.

Then, one evening about a week later, through an extraordinary twist of fate, I chanced upon the beginnings of a stranger, more fanciful and more mysterious episode.

That evening, having drunk whiskey in even greater quantities than usual, I had gone up to the reserved seats on the second floor of the Sanyūkan Motion Picture Theater.

私【わたし】I ⊛
図らずも【はからずも】unexpectedly, by chance
不思議な【ふしぎな】extraordinary
因縁【いんねん】karma, fate
もッと more ⊛
奇怪な【きかいな】weird
神秘な【しんぴな】mysterious
事件【じけん】incident
端緒【たんしょ／たんちょ】beginning
出会す【でくわす】encounter by chance

33
いつもより more than usual
多量に【たりょうに】in large amounts
ウヰスキー【ウイスキー】whiskey
呷る【あおる】quaff
三友館【さんゆうかん】Sanyū Theater
二階【にかい】second floor

貴賓席【きひんせき】seats of honor
上り込む【あがりこむ】go up into

何でももう十時近くであったろう、恐ろしく混んでいる場内は、霧のような濁った空気に充たされて、黒く、もくもくとかたまって蠢動している群衆の生温かい人いきれが、顔のお白粉を腐らせるように漂って居た。暗中にシャキシャキ軋みながら目まぐるしく展開して行く映画の光線の、グリグリと瞳を刺す度毎に、私の酔った頭は破れるように痛んだ。時々映画が消えてぱっと電燈がつくと、渓底から沸き上る雲のように、階下の群衆の頭の上を浮動して居る煙草の烟の間を透かして、私は真深いお高祖頭巾の蔭から、場内に溢れて居る人々の顔を見廻した。

何でも【なんでも】probably

十時【じゅうじ】ten o'clock

〜近く【〜ちかく】nearly 〜

〜であったろう＝〜であったであろう

恐ろしく【おそろしく】frightfully

混む【こむ】be crowded

場内【じょうない】within the hall, the interior (of a theater) ✿

霧【きり】mist, fog

濁った【にごった】thick, turbid

空気【くうき】air

充たす【みたす】[passive form in text] fill

黒い【くろい】black

もくもくと MIMETIC wriggling and writhing

かたまる cluster together

蠢動する【しゅんどうする】writhe, squirm

群衆【ぐんしゅう】crowd ✿

生温かい【なまあたたかい】unpleasantly warm

人いきれ【ひといきれ】stuffiness, smell of humanity

顔【かお】face ✿

お白粉【おしろい】make-up

腐る【くさる】[causative form in text] spoil

漂う【ただよう】float, drift

暗中【あんちゅう】in the darkness

シャキシャキ ONOMATOPOEIC indicates a sharp sound

軋む【きしむ】squeak

目まぐるしく【めまぐるしく】dizzyingly

展開する【てんかいする】unfold

〜て行く【〜ていく】indicates an increase in tendency

It must have been almost ten o'clock; inside it was fearfully crowded and filled with a fog of muggy air. The hot stench of humanity floated up from the black, restless, densely packed, squirming crowd as if to wreck my face make-up. Every time the bright light of the film—which was unfolding at a dizzying speed with a series of grating squeaks in the darkness—stabbed my eyes, my drunken head ached fit to burst. Sometimes when the film stopped and the lights came up abruptly, then from the deep shadow of my hood, through the tobacco smoke that floated over the heads of the crowd below like a cloud seething up the bottom of a valley, I would inspect the faces of the people who filled the place.

映画【えいが】film ⊛
光線【こうせん】light, beam of light
グリグリと MIMETIC sparklingly, brightly
瞳【ひとみ】eye
刺す【さす】pierce
〜度毎に【〜たびごとに】every time
私【わたし】I ⊛
酔った【よった】drunk
頭【あたま】head ⊛
破れる【やぶれる】split, crack
痛む【いたむ】hurt
時々【ときどき】sometimes
消える【きえる】go out
ぱッと MIMETIC suddenly
電燈【でんとう】electric light
つく go on
渓底【たにそこ】bottom of a ravine
沸き上る【わきあがる】seethe up
雲【くも】cloud
階下【かいか】downstairs
〜の上を【〜のうえを】above
浮動する【ふどうする】float, waft
煙草【タバコ】cigarettes
烟【けむり】smoke
〜の間を透かして【〜のあいだをすかして】through
真深い【まぶかい】very deep
お高祖頭巾【おこそずきん】hood
〜の蔭から【〜のかげから】from behind
溢れる【あふれる】overflow, brim
人々【ひとびと】people
見廻す【みまわす】look around

そうして私の旧式な頭巾の姿を珍しそうに窺って居る男や、粋な着附けの色合いを物欲しそうに盗み視ている女の多いのを、心ひそかに得意として居た。見物の女のうちで、いでたちの異様な点から、様子の婀娜っぽい点から、乃至器量の点からも、私ほど人の眼に着いた者はないらしかった。

34▶　始めは誰も居なかった筈の貴賓席の私の側の椅子が、いつの間に塞がったのか能くは知らないが、二三度目に再び電燈がともされた時、私の左隣りに二人の男女が腰をかけて居るのに気が附いた。

私【わたし】I ⊛

旧式な【きゅうしきな】old-fashioned

頭巾【ずきん】hood

姿【すがた】figure, appearance

珍しい【めずらしい】curious

窺う【うかがう】look at furtively

男【おとこ】man

粋な【いきな】fashionable

着附け【きつけ】being accustomed to wearing

色合い【いろあい】color, hue

物欲しそうに【ものほしそうに】longingly

盗み視る【ぬすみみる】steal a glance at

女【おんな】woman

多い【おおい】numerous

心ひそかに【こころひそかに】inwardly, secretly

得意とする【とくいとする】feel proud of oneself

見物の女【けんぶつのおんな】female spectator

〜のうちで【〜のうちで】among

いでたち outfit, attire

異様な【いような】outlandish, bizarre

点【てん】point, regard ⊛

様子【ようす】appearance, air

婀娜っぽい【あだっぽい】seductive

乃至【ないし】or

器量【きりょう】good looks

〜ほど to the extent of

人【ひと】person

眼に着く【めにつく】stand out, attract attention

者【もの】person

In my heart I was gratified by the number of men who looked with furtive amazement at my old-fashioned hood, and the women who stole covetous glances at the chic colors of my outfit. Whether for unusual attire, sexual allure, or good looks, among the women in the audience it seemed that no one was getting as much attention as me.

I don't know when the deluxe seats beside me—empty at first, I was certain—came to be occupied; but when the lights came up for the second or third time, I realized that a man and woman were sitting directly to my left.

34

始め 【はじめ】 at first
誰も〜ない 【だれも〜ない】 no one
〜筈 【〜はず】 I am certain that 〜
貴賓席 【きひんせき】 seat of honor
〜の側の 【〜のそばの】 beside
椅子 【いす】 chair, seat
いつの間に 【いつのまに】 at some point
塞がる 【ふさがる】 become occupied
能く 【よく】 well
知る 【しる】 realize, understand
二三度目に 【にさんどめに】 second or third time
再び 【ふたたび】 again
電燈 【でんとう】 electric light
ともす turn on
〜時 【〜とき】 when

左隣りに 【ひだりどなりに】 beside one on the left
二人の男女 【ふたりのだんじょ】 couple
腰をかける 【こしをかける】 sit down
気が附く 【きがつく】 notice

35 ▶ 　女は二十二三と見えるが、その実六七にもなるであろう。髪を三つ輪に結って、総身をお召の空色のマントに包み、くっきりと水のしたたるような鮮やかな美貌ばかりを、これ見よがしに露わにして居る。芸者とも令嬢とも判断のつき兼ねる所はあるが、連れの紳士の態度から推して、堅儀の細君ではないらしい。

36 ▶ 「……Arrested at last.……」

37 ▶ 　と、女は小声で、フィルムの上に現れた説明書を読み上げて、土耳古巻のM. C. C.の薫りの高い烟を私の顔に吹き附けながら、指に嵌めて居る宝石よりも鋭く輝く大きい瞳を、闇の中できらりと私の方へ注いだ。

35

女【おんな】woman ⊛
二十二三【にじゅうにさん】22 or 23
見える【みえる】appear
その実【そのじつ】in fact
六七【ろくしち】26 or 27
髪【かみ】hair
三つ輪【みつわ】three rings, the *mitsuwa* style
結う【ゆう】tie up
総身【そうみ】whole body
お召【おめし】silk crepe
空色【そらいろ】sky blue
マント cloak, cape
包む【つつむ】wrap up (in)
くッきりと MIMETIC distinctly
水【みず】water
したたる drip

鮮やかな【あざやかな】fresh, delightful
美貌【びぼう】good looks
〜ばかり only
これ見よがしに【これみよがしに】ostentatiously
露わにする【あらわにする】expose
芸者【げいしゃ】geisha
〜とも〜とも whether . . . or
令嬢【れいじょう】young lady
判断のつき兼ねる【はんだんのつきかねる】be difficult to judge
所【ところ】case, instance
連れ【つれ】companion
紳士【しんし】gentleman
態度【たいど】attitude, bearing
推す【おす】deduce
堅儀の【かたぎの】respectable
細君【さいくん】wife

The woman looked around twenty-two or -three, but in fact was probably twenty-six or -seven. Her hair was done up in the *mitsuwa* style, and a sky blue cape of silk crepe enveloped her entire body; only her beautiful face—as fresh as a drop of water—was clearly visible, for this she was exposing ostentatiously. It was hard to say whether she was a geisha or a respectable young lady, but hazarding a guess based on the demeanor of the gentleman accompanying her, it seemed unlikely that she was a proper little wife.

". . . Arrested at last. . . ."

In a whisper, the woman read a title card that came up in the film, and as she exhaled the fragrant smoke of a Turkish M.C.C. cigarette into my face, cast me a glance. In the dark, her big eyes sparkled more brightly than the jewels upon her fingers.

37

小声 【こごえ】 murmur, whisper
〜の上に 【〜のうえに】 on top of
現れる 【あわれる】 appear
説明書 【せつめいしょ】 title, title card
読み上げる 【よみあげる】 read aloud
土耳古巻 【トルコまき】 rolled in Turkey (of cigarettes)
M. C. C. brand of cigarette
薫りの高い 【かおりのたかい】 fragrant
烟 【けむり】 smoke
私 【わたし】 I ⊛
顔 【かお】 face
吹き附ける 【ふきつける】 blow at
指 【ゆび】 finger
嵌める 【はめる】 wear (on the fingers)
宝石 【ほうせき】 jewel
〜よりも more than even 〜

鋭く 【するどく】 keenly
輝く 【かがやく】 shine
大きい 【おおきい】 big
瞳 【ひとみ】 eye, glance
闇 【やみ】 darkness
〜の中で 【〜のなかで】 in
きらりと MIMETIC with a gleam
〜の方へ 【〜のほうへ】 in the direction of
注ぐ 【そそぐ】 direct

38 ▶ 　あでやかな姿に似合わぬ太棹の師匠のような皺嗄れた声、――その声は紛れもない、私が二三年前に上海へ旅行する航海の途中、ふとした事から汽船の中で暫く関係を結んで居たT女であった。

39 ▶ 　女はその頃から、商売人とも素人とも区別のつかない素振りや服装を持って居たように覚えて居る。船中に同伴して居た男と、今夜の男とはまるで風采も容貌も変っているが、多分はこの二人の男の間を連結する無数の男が女の過去の生涯を鎖のように貫いて居るのであろう。兎も角その婦人が、始終一人の男から他の男へと、胡蝶のように飛んで歩く種類の女であることは確かであった。

38

あでやかな seductive

姿【すがた】figure, appearance

似合わぬ【にあわぬ】not suit, not match

太棹【ふとざお】thick-necked samisen

師匠【ししょう】master, expert

皺嗄れた【しわがれた】husky

声【こえ】voice ⊛

紛れもない【まぎれもない】unmistakable

私【わたし】I

二三年前【にさんねんまえ】two or three years ago

上海【シャンハイ】Shanghai

旅行する【りょこうする】travel

航海【こうかい】voyage

〜の途中【〜のとちゅう】in the middle of

ふとした unlooked-for, casual

事【こと】happening, event

汽船【きせん】steamboat

〜の中で【〜のなかで】in, on

暫く【しばらく】for a (short) while

関係を結ぶ【かんけいをむすぶ】have a relationship

T女【ティーじょ】Miss T.

39

女【おんな】woman ⊛

その頃【そのころ】that time

商売人【しょうばいにん】professional

〜とも〜とも whether . . . or

素人【しろうと】nonprofessional, ordinary person

区別のつかない【くべつのつかない】be indistinguishable

素振り【そぶり】manner

服装【ふくそう】dress, clothes

持つ【もつ】have

Gravelly like a samisen singer's, the voice hardly matched the woman's charming appearance—quite unmistakably, it was the voice of Miss T., a woman with whom I'd had a brief and spur-of-the-moment relationship on board ship during a voyage to Shanghai some two or three years before.

I seemed to recall that even in those days, she had dressed and behaved in a manner that made it difficult to tell whether she was a "professional" or just an ordinary woman. The man escorting her on the ship and the man of this evening were entirely different in bearing and countenance. To link up the interval between these two men, there were probably countless other men who ran like a chain through the woman's past. At all events, it was certain that she was the kind of lady who flits constantly, like a butterfly, from one man to another.

覚える 【おぼえる】 remember
船中 【せんちゅう】 on board ship
同伴する 【どうはんする】 accompany
男 【おとこ】 man ⊛
今夜 【こんや】 this evening
まるで completely
風采 【ふうさい】 mien, bearing
容貌 【ようぼう】 appearance, face
変る 【かわる】 be different
多分 【たぶん】 probably
二人 【ふたり】 two people
間 【あいだ】 gap
連結する 【れんけつする】 connect, link
無数 【むすう】 countless
過去 【かこ】 past
生涯 【しょうがい】 lifetime, career
鎖 【くさり】 chain
貫く 【つらぬく】 run through

兎も角 【ともかく】 anyway
婦人 【ふじん】 woman, lady
始終 【しじゅう】 always
一人 【ひとり】 one person
他の 【ほかの】 other
胡蝶 【こちょう】 butterfly
飛んで歩く 【とんであるく】 flit
種類 【しゅるい】 type
確かな 【たしかな】 certain, sure

二年前に船で馴染みになった時、二人はいろいろの事情から本当の氏名も名乗り合わず、境遇も住所も知らせずにいるうちに上海へ着いた。そうして私は自分に恋い憧れている女を好い加減に欺き、こッそり跡をくらまして了った。以来太平洋上の夢の中なる女とばかり思って居たその人の姿を、こんな処で見ようとは全く意外である。あの時分やや小太りに肥えて居た女は、神々しい迄に痩せて、すッきりとして、睫毛の長い潤味を持った円い眼が、拭うが如くに冴え返り、男を男とも思わぬような凜々しい権威さえ具えている。

二年前【にねんまえ】two years ago
船【ふね】ship
馴染みになる【なじみになる】become intimate
～時【～とき】when
二人【ふたり】two people
いろいろの【いろいろの】various
事情【じじょう】circumstances, reasons
本当【ほんとう】real, true
氏名【しめい】full name
名乗り合わず【なのりあわず】without introducing ourselves to each other
境遇【きょうぐう】situation, circumstance
住所【じゅうしょ】address
知らせず【しらせず】without revealing
～うちに [preceded by a negative] before
上海【シャンハイ】Shanghai
着く【つく】reach
私【わたし】I
自分【じぶん】oneself, myself
恋い憧れる【こいあこがれる】become infatuated (with)
女【おんな】woman ⊛
好い加減に【いいかげんに】irresponsibly, in a slapdash way
欺く【あざむく】deceive, trick
こッそり MIMETIC secretly, stealthily
跡をくらます【あとをくらます】cover one's tracks, vanish
～て了う【～てしまう】throughly
以来【いらい】since then
太平洋上【たいへいようじょう】on the Pacific Ocean
夢の中【ゆめのなか】in a dream
ばかり just, only
思う【おもう】think ⊛
人【ひと】person

After becoming intimate on board ship two years ago, for a variety of reasons we reached Shanghai without having revealed our real names to one another, or told each other of our circumstances in life or where we lived. The woman was infatuated with me, but I fed her some story and gave her the slip. To see this woman whom I had ever since thought of as "a dream of the Pacific" here in a place like this was totally unexpected. She had been somewhat plump in those days, but was now sublimely slender and streamlined, and her round, moist eyes with their long lashes were as clear as if they had been polished and had a devil-may-care superiority as if men were not men to her.

姿 【すがた】 figure, form
処 【ところ】 place
見る 【みる】 [volitional form in text] see
全く 【まったく】 completely
意外な 【いがいな】 unexpected
時分 【じぶん】 time, period
やや somewhat, rather
小太りに 【こぶとりに】 plumply
肥える 【こえる】 grow fat
神々しい 【こうごうしい】 divine, heavenly
〜迄に 【〜までに】 to the point of
痩せる 【やせる】 lose weight, grow thin
すッきりとする MIMETIC be neat, be trim
睫毛 【まつげ】 eyelash
長い 【ながい】 long
潤味 【うるみ】 moisture
持つ 【もつ】 have
円い 【まるい】 round

眼 【まなこ】 eye
拭う 【ぬぐう】 wipe, polish
〜が如くに 【〜がごとくに】 just like
冴え返る 【さえかえる】 be very clear
男 【おとこ】 man ⊛
思わぬ 【おもわぬ】 not think of, not
  regard
凛々しい 【りりしい】 dignified, gallant,
  commanding
権威 【けんい】 authority, power
〜さえ even
具える 【そなえる】 have, possess

触るるものに紅の血が濁染むかと疑われた生々しい唇と、耳朶の隠れそうな長い生え際ばかりは昔に変らないが、鼻は以前よりも少し嶮しい位に高く見えた。

40 ▶ 　女は果して私に気が附いて居るのであろうか。どうも判然と確かめることが出来なかった。明りがつくと連れの男にひそひそ戯れて居る様子は、傍に居る私を普通の女と蔑んで、別段心にかけて居ないようでもあった。実際その女の隣りに居ると、私は今迄得意であった自分の扮装を卑しまない訳には行かなかった。表情の自由な、如何にも生き生きとした妖女の魅力に気圧されて、技巧を尽した化粧も着附けも、醜く浅ましい化物のような気がした。

触るる 【ふるる】 ARCHAIC touch
もの thing
紅 【くれない】 crimson
血 【ち】 blood
濁染む 【にじむ】 blot, smudge
疑う 【うたがう】 [passive form in text] suspect
生々しい 【なまなましい】 vivid, fresh
唇 【くちびる】 lip
耳朶 【みみたぶ】 earlobe
隠れる 【かくれる】 be concealed
長い 【ながい】 long
生え際 【はえぎわ】 hairline
〜ばかり only
昔 【むかし】 the old days
変る 【かわる】 change
鼻 【はな】 nose
以前 【いぜん】 before
少し 【すこし】 slightly

嶮しい 【けわしい】 severe, sharp, fierce
〜位 【〜ぐらい／〜くらい】 to the extent of
高い 【たかい】 prominent
見える 【みえる】 appear

40

女 【おんな】 woman ⊛
果たして 【はたして】 possibly (used to emphasize a doubt)
私 【わたし】 I ⊛
気が附く 【きがつく】 find (someone) out
どうも just, by any means
判然と 【はんぜんと】 clearly
確かめる 【たしかめる】 make certain
出来る 【できる】 be able to do
明り 【あかり】 light
つく go on (of lights)
連れ 【つれ】 companion
男 【おとこ】 man

Only the moist, fleshy lips looking as though they might ooze bloody crimson onto anything they touched and the low hairline almost covering her earlobes were unchanged from the old days. Her nose seemed more prominent than before—a little sharp even.

Did the woman recognize me? I had no means of making sure, one way or the other. The flirtatious way she whispered to her male escort when the lights came on suggested she had dismissed me as an ordinary woman who just happened to be near her, and was not taking any special notice of me. The truth was, sitting next to that woman, I couldn't help but feel ashamed of the disguise about which I'd been so smug until then. I was crushed by the beauty of this enchantress with her expressive features and vitality, and despite all the ingenuity I'd expended on my make-up and clothing, I felt like a hideous, contemptible monster.

ひそひそ in whispers
戯れる 【たわむれる】 flirt, joke
様子 【ようす】 manner, appearance
傍に居る 【そばにいる】 be next to
普通の 【ふつうの】 normal
蔑む 【さげすむ】 look down on, dismiss
別段 【べつだん】 particularly
心にかける 【こころにかける】 be conscious of
実際 【じっさい】 in fact
隣りに居る 【となりにいる】 be next to
今迄 【いままで】 until now
得意である 【とくいである】 be proud, be self-satisfied
自分 【じぶん】 oneself, myself
扮装 【ふんそう】 disguise, costume
卑しむ 【いやしむ】 despise
～ない訳には行かない 【～ないわけにはいかない】 cannot help but ~

表情 【ひょうじょう】 expression
自由な 【じゆうな】 free
如何にも 【いかにも】 truly
生き生きとした 【いきいきとした】 lively
妖女 【ようじょ】 witch, enchantress
魅力 【みりょく】 attractiveness
気圧される 【けおされる】 be overawed, be overwhelmed
技巧 【ぎこう】 technique
尽す 【つくす】 use up, exhaust
化粧 【けしょう】 make-up
着附け 【きつけ】 dressing
醜い 【みにくい】 ugly
浅ましい 【あさましい】 wretched, despicable
化物 【ばけもの】 monster
～のような気がする 【～のようなきがする】 feel as though

女らしいと云う点からも、美しい器量からも、私は到底彼女の競争者ではなく、月の前の星のように果敢なく萎れて了うのであった。

41▶　朦々と立ち罩めた場内の汚れた空気の中に、曇りのない鮮明な輪郭をくッきりと浮かばせて、マントの蔭からしなやかな手をちらちらと、魚のように泳がせているあでやかさ。男と対談する間にも時々夢のような瞳を上げて、天井を仰いだり、眉根を寄せて群衆を見下ろしたり、真っ白な歯並みを見せて微笑んだり、その度毎に全く別趣の表情が、溢れんばかりに湛えられる。

女らしい【おんならしい】womanly

〜と云う【〜という】that is to say

点【てん】point, regard

美しい【うつくしい】beautiful

器量【きりょう】good looks

私【わたし】I

到底〜ない【とうてい〜ない】by no possibility

彼女【かのじょ】she

競争者【きょうそうしゃ】competitor

月【つき】the moon

〜の前の【〜のまえの】in front of

星【ほし】star

果敢なく【はかなく】vainly

萎れる【しおれる】lose vitality

〜て了う【〜てしまう】completely, utterly

41

朦々と【もうもうと】thickly, turbidly

立ち罩める【たちこめる】envelop, shroud

場内【じょうない】within the hall, the interior

汚れた【よごれた】dirty

空気【くうき】air

〜の中に【〜のなかに】in, amidst

曇りのない【くもりのない】clear (lit., "cloudless")

鮮明な【せんめいな】vivid, distinct

輪郭【りんかく】outline (of the face)

くッきりと MIMETIC distinctly

浮かぶ【うかぶ】[causative form in text] stand out

マント cloak, cape

〜の蔭から【〜のかげから】from behind

しなやかな supple, lithe

I was no competitor to this woman for femininity or good looks, and I just faded hopelessly away to nothing like a star before the moon.

There was something captivating about the sight of her profile—unclouded, fresh and clear-cut—and the way her supple hands swam forth from her cape to shimmer like fish in the muggy, foul air that enveloped the place. As she chatted with the man, from time to time she would raise her dreamy eyes and gaze up at the ceiling, knit her brows as she looked down at the crowd below, or display her pure white teeth in a smile; and each time she did so, her face was flooded with a succession of wholly different expressions.

手 【て】 hand
ちらちらと MIMETIC shimmeringly, flutteringly
魚 【さかな】 fish
泳がせる 【およがせる】 cause to swim, release (into water)
あでやかさ charm
男 【おとこ】 man
対談する 【たいだんする】 converse, chat
〜間 【〜あいだ】 while
時々 【ときどき】 sometimes
夢 【ゆめ】 dream
瞳 【ひとみ】 eye
上げる 【あげる】 raise
天井 【てんじょう】 ceiling
仰ぐ 【あおぐ】 look up at
眉根を寄せる 【まゆねをよせる】 knit one's brows, frown

群衆 【ぐんしゅう】 crowd
見下ろす 【みおろす】 look down at
真っ白な 【まっしろな】 pure-white
歯並み 【はなみ】 row of teeth
見せる 【みせる】 show
微笑む 【ほほえむ】 smile
その度毎に 【そのたびごとに】 every time
全く 【まったく】 completely
別趣 【べっしゅ】 different tone
表情 【ひょうじょう】 expression
溢れんばかりに 【あふれんばかりに】 as if about to brim over
湛える 【たたえる】 [passive form in text] show on one's face

如何なる意味をも鮮かに表わし得る黒い大きい瞳は、場内の二つの宝石のように、遠い階下の隅からも認められる。顔面の凡べての道具が単に物を見たり、嗅いだり、聞いたり、語ったりする機関としては、あまりに余情に富み過ぎて、人間の顔と云うよりも、男の心を誘惑する甘味ある餌食であった。

42 ▶　もう場内の視線は、一つも私の方に注がれて居なかった。愚かにも、私は自分の人気を奪い去ったその女の美貌に対して、嫉妬と憤怒を感じ始めた。嘗ては自分が弄んで恋に棄ててしまった女の容貌の魅力に、忽ち光を消されて踏み附けられて行く口惜しさ。

如何なる【いかなる】what kind of

意味【いみ】meaning

をも　even, no matter

鮮かに【あざやかに】vividly, skillfully, beautifully

表わし得る【あらわしうる】able to express

黒い【くろい】black

大きい【おおきい】big

瞳【ひとみ】eye

場内【じょうない】within the hall ⊛

二つ【ふたつ】two

宝石【ほうせき】jewel

遠い【とおい】far

階下【かいか】downstairs

隅【すみ】corner, remote place

認める【みとめる】[passive form in text] see, notice

顔面【がんめん】face

凡べて【すべて】all

道具【どうぐ】part of the body

単に【たんに】simply

物【もの】thing

見る【みる】see

嗅ぐ【かぐ】smell

聞く【きく】hear

語る【かたる】speak

機関【きかん】organ, means

あまりに　excessively

余情【よじょう】lingering charm

富み過ぎる【とみすぎる】be too rich (in)

人間【にんげん】human

顔【かお】face

～と云うよりも【～というよりも】even more than a ~

男【おとこ】man

Her enormous black eyes, able to express any point with eloquence, were like twin jewels in the auditorium and captured people's attention in the furthest corners of the gallery floor. The various components of her face were too rich in evocative charm to be mere organs for seeing, smelling, hearing and speaking; no, more than a human face, it was a sweet-tasting bait to entrap men's hearts.

Nobody in the picture house was directing their gaze at me anymore. Foolish it might have been, but I began to feel jealousy and anger toward the beauty of the woman who had snatched my popularity away from me. It was mortifying that, from one moment to the next, my light should be snuffed out and trampled underfoot by the charms of a woman I'd at one time toyed with and tossed aside as I pleased.

心 【こころ】 heart, mind
誘惑する 【ゆうわくする】 tempt
甘味 【かんみ】 sweet
餌食 【えじき】 bait

42

視線 【しせん】 gaze
私 【わたし】 I ⊛
〜の方に 【〜のほうに】 in the direction of
注ぐ 【そそぐ】 [passive form in text] direct
愚かにも 【おろかにも】 ridiculously enough
自分 【じぶん】 oneself, myself ⊛
人気 【にんき】 popularity
奪い去る 【うばいさる】 snatch away
女 【おんな】 woman
美貌 【びぼう】 good looks
〜に対して 【〜にたいして】 in regard to
嫉妬 【しっと】 jealousy

憤怒 【ふんぬ】 rage
感じ始める 【かんじはじめる】 start to feel
嘗ては 【かつては】 previously
弄ぶ 【もてあそぶ】 trifle with
恣に 【ほしいままに】 arbitrarily, at will, as one sees fit
棄てる 【すてる】 get rid of
〜てしまう expresses with regret the completion of an action
容貌 【ようぼう】 looks, appearance
魅力 【みりょく】 attractiveness, charm
忽ち 【たちまち】 in an instant
光 【ひかり】 light
消す 【けす】 [passive form in text] extinguish
踏み附ける 【ふみつける】 [passive form in text] trample underfoot
〜て行く 【〜ていく】 indicates an increase in tendency
口惜しさ 【くちおしさ】 mortification

事に依ると女は私を認めて居ながら、わざと皮肉な復讐をして居るのではないであろうか。

43 ▶ 　私は美貌を羨む嫉妬の情が、胸の中で次第々々に恋慕の情に変って行くのを覚えた。女としての競争に敗れた私は、今一度男として彼女を征服して勝ち誇ってやりたい。こう思うと、抑え難い欲望に駆られてしなやかな女の体を、いきなりむずと鷲摑みにして、揺す振って見たくもなった。

44 ▶ 　　君は予の誰なるかを知り給うや。今夜久し振りに君を見て、予は再び君を恋し始めたり。今一度、予と握手し給うお心はなきか。明晩もこの席に来て、予を待ち給うお心はなきか。

事に依ると【ことによると】maybe
女【おんな】woman ❋
私【わたし】I ❋
認める【みとめる】recognize
わざと deliberately
皮肉な【ひにくな】ironic
復讐をする【ふくしゅうをする】take revenge

43

美貌【びぼう】good looks
羨む【うらやむ】be envious of
嫉妬【しっと】jealousy
情【じょう】feelings ❋
胸【むね】chest, heart
〜の中で【〜のなかで】inside
次第々々に【しだいしだいに】very gradually
恋慕【れんぼ】love, yearning

変る【かわる】change
〜て行く【〜ていく】indicates an increase in tendency
覚える【おぼえる】feel
〜として as ❋
競争【きょうそう】competition
敗れる【やぶれる】be defeated, lose
今一度【いまいちど】once again ❋
男【おとこ】man
彼女【かのじょ】she
征服する【せいふくする】subjugate, dominate
勝ち誇る【かちほこる】crow over, exult in victory
〜てやる and teach her a lesson (expresses the narrator's eagerness)
思う【おもう】think
抑え難い【おさえがたい】hard to suppress
欲望【よくぼう】desire

Could the woman have recognized me and be knowingly extracting an ironic revenge?

I sensed the jealous emotions I had for her beauty gradually changing into feelings of love within me. As a woman I had been defeated in the contest, but as a man I wanted to subjugate her and exult in my victory once again. Come this thought and I was overcome by the powerful urge to grab hold of her willowy, female frame and shake her violently.

Do you know who I am? Seeing you tonight after all this time, I have fallen in love with you all over again. Do you not feel that you would like us to be reconciled? Tomorrow evening, how about coming back to these seats to wait for me?

駆られる 【かられる】 be driven (by), be moved (by)

しなやかな supple, lithe

体 【からだ】 body

いきなり suddenly, unexpectedly

むずと violently

鷲摑みにする 【わしづかみにする】 clutch, swoop down and grab

揺す振る 【ゆすぶる】 shake

〜て見る 【〜てみる】 to see what it is like

44

君 【きみ】 FAMILIAR you ⊛

予 【よ】 ARCHAIC I ⊛

誰 【だれ】 who

〜なる ＝ 〜である be

知る 【しる】 know, recognize

〜給う 【〜たまう】 ARCHAIC, HONORIFIC auxiliary verb equivalent to modern お〜になります ⊛

〜や ARCHAIC interrogative particle

今夜 【こんや】 tonight

久し振りに 【ひさしぶりに】 for the first time in a long time

見る 【みる】 see

再び 【ふたたび】 again

恋し始めたり 【こいしはじめたり】 ARCHAIC started to fall in love

握手す 【あくしゅす】 ARCHAIC reconcile

お心はなきか 【おこころはなきか】 ARCHAIC do you not feel disposed to . . . ? ⊛

明晩 【みょうばん】 tomorrow evening

席 【せき】 seat, place

来る 【くる】 come

待つ 【まつ】 wait for

予は予の住所を何人にも告げ知らす事を好まねば、唯願わくは明日の今頃、この席に来て予を待ち給え。

45▶ 闇に紛れて私は帯の間から半紙と鉛筆を取出し、こんな走り書きをしたものをひそかに女の袂へ投げ込んだ、そうして、又じッと先方の様子を窺っていた。

46▶ 十一時頃、活動写真の終るまでは女は静かに見物していた。観客が総立ちになってどやどやと場外へ崩れ出す混雑の際、女はもう一度、私の耳元で、

47▶ 「……Arrested at last.……」

48▶ と囁きながら、前よりも自信のある大胆な凝視を、私の顔に暫く注いで、やがて男と一緒に人ごみの中へ隠れてしまった。

49▶ 「……Arrested at last.……」

予【よ】ARCHAIC I ⊛
住所【じゅうしょ】address
何人にも【なんぴとにも】[followed by a negative in text] ARCHAIC to nobody
告げ知らす【つげしらす】tell, reveal
事【こと】act
好まねば【このまねば】not like to do
唯【ただ】just, only
願わくは【ねがわくは】what I wish for is . . .
明日【あした／あす】tomorrow
今頃【いまごろ】about this time
席【せき】seat
来る【くる】come
待つ【まつ】wait ⊛
〜給え【〜たまえ】[imperative form] ARCHAIC, POLITE would you please

45
闇【やみ】darkness

紛れる【まぎれる】disappear (into), blend (into)
私【わたし】I ⊛
帯【おび】sash
〜の間から【〜のあいだから】from between
半紙【はんし】writing paper
鉛筆【えんぴつ】pencil
取出す【とりだす】take out
走り書きをする【はしりがきをする】write in a hurry, scribble off
ひそかに secretly
女【おんな】woman ⊛
袂【たもと】sleeve
投げ込む【なげこむ】throw into
又【また】and, again
じッと MIMETIC fixedly
先方【せんぽう】the other party

As I do not like to reveal my address to anybody, tomorrow at this same time, come, I pray you, to these seats and wait for me.

Under cover of darkness, I had taken a piece of paper and a pencil from my sash and discreetly tossed this hastily scrawled note into the woman's sleeve. Then once again I scrutinized her out of the corner of my eye.

The woman quietly watched the motion picture until it finished at around eleven o'clock. Then, in the confusion as the audience stood up en masse and headed outside in noisy groups, the woman once more whispered into my ear, ". . . Arrested at last. . . ." At the same time, she stared right at me for a while with even more self-assurance than before, until eventually she and the man were swallowed up in the crowd.

". . . Arrested at last. . . ."

様子 【ようす】 behavior, manner
窺う 【うかがう】 look at furtively

46

十一時頃 【じゅういちじごろ】 around
  eleven o'clock
活動写真 【かつどうしゃしん】 motion
  picture
終る 【おわる】 end
静かに 【しずかに】 quietly
見物する 【けんぶつする】 watch
観客 【かんきゃく】 audience
総立ちになる 【そうだちになる】 all stand
  up
どやどやと ONOMATOPOEIC noisily, in a
  crowd
場外 【じょうがい】 outside the auditorium
崩れ出す 【くずれだす】 break up and go
  out
混雑 【こんざつ】 crowdedness, disorder

際 【さい】 time
もう一度 【もういちど】 once again
耳元 【みみもと】 close to one's ear

48

囁く 【ささやく】 whisper
前よりも 【まえよりも】 more than before
自信のある 【じしんのある】 self-confident
大胆な 【だいたんな】 bold, audacious
凝視 【ぎょうし】 stare, fixed look
顔 【かお】 face
暫く 【しばらく】 for a while
注ぐ 【そそぐ】 direct
〜と一緒に 【〜といっしょに】 together
  with
人ごみ 【ひとごみ】 crowd
〜の中へ 【〜のなかへ】 into
隠れる 【かくれる】 be lost to sight
〜てしまう thoroughly

50▶　　女はいつの間にか自分を見附け出して居たのだ。こう思って私は竦然とした。

51▶　　それにしても明日の晩、素直に来てくれるであろうか。大分昔よりは年功を経ているらしい相手の力量を測らずに、あのような真似をして、却って弱点を握られはしまいか。いろいろの不安と疑惧に挟まれながら私は寺へ帰った。

52▶　　いつものように上着を脱いで、長襦袢一枚になろうとする時、ぱらりと頭巾の裏から四角にたたんだ小さい洋紙の切れが落ちた。

53▶　「Mr. S. K.」

54▶　と書き続けたインキの痕をすかして見ると、玉甲斐絹のように光っている。

50

女【おんな】woman

いつの間にか【いつのまにか】before one
　knows it

自分【じぶん】oneself

見附け出す【みつけだす】find out

思う【おもう】think

私【わたし】I ⊛

竦然とする【しょうぜんとする】shudder

51

それにしても even so

明日【あした／あす】tomorrow

晩【ばん】evening

素直に【すなおに】meekly, compliantly

来る【くる】come

大分【だいぶ】considerably

昔【むかし】the old days

年功【ねんこう】long experience

経る【へる】pass through

〜らしい apparently

相手【あいて】counterpart, opponent

力量【りきりょう】ability, strength

測らずに【はからずに】in not measuring

真似【まね】(foolish) behavior

却って【かえって】all the more

弱点【じゃくてん】weak point

握る【にぎる】[passive form in text] grasp,
　seize

〜はしまいか＝〜てしまうのではな
　いか

いろいろの various

不安【ふあん】anxiety

疑惧【ぎぐ】apprehension

挟む【さしはさむ】[passive form in text] har-
　bor (doubts)

寺【てら】temple

Unbeknownst to me, the woman had found me out. The thought made me shudder.

But would she be amenable and come the following evening? She seemed to be far more experienced than before; in underestimating her strength and behaving as I had, had I ended up exposing my weak points? I returned to the temple full of anxiety and apprehension.

When, in my usual manner, I had taken off my outer kimono and was on the point of stripping down to my undergarments, a small scrap of paper that had been folded into a square fluttered from the back of my hood down onto the floor.

"Mr. S.K."

As I held the flowingly written ink inscription up to the light, it shone like Tamakai silk.

帰る【かえる】return

52

いつものように as usual

上着【うわぎ】outer kimono

脱ぐ【ぬぐ】take off

長襦袢【ながじゅばん】long undergarment

一枚【いちまい】one (thin, flat object)

〜（ろ）うとする be about to 〜

〜時【〜とき】when

ぱらりと ONOMATOPOEIC describes the fall of something light

頭巾【ずきん】hood

裏【うら】back

四角に【しかくに】squarely, in a square

たたむ fold

小さい【ちいさい】small

洋紙【ようし】machine-made paper

切れ【きれ】scrap

落ちる【おちる】fall

54

書き続ける【かきつづける】write in cursive script

インキ ink

痕【あと】mark, trace, imprint

すかして見る【すかしてみる】hold up to the light

玉甲斐絹【たまかいき】Tamakai silk

光る【ひかる】shine

正しく彼女の手であった。見物中、一二度小用に立ったようであったが、早くもその間に、返事をしたためて、人知れず私の襟元へさし込んだものと見える。

55 ▶　思いがけなき所にて思いがけなき君の姿を見申候。たとい装いを変え給うとも、三年このかた夢寐にも忘れぬ御面影を、いかで見逃し候べき。妾は始めより頭巾の女の君なる事を承知仕候。それにつけても相変わらず物好きなる君にておわせしことの可笑しさよ。妾に会わんと仰せらるるも多分はこの物好きのおん興じにやと心許なく存じ候えども、

正しく【まさしく】genuinely

彼女【かのじょ】she, the woman

手【て】hand(writing)

見物中【けんぶつちゅう】while watching

一二度【いちにど】once or twice

小用に立つ【しょうようにたつ】go to the toilet

早く【はやく】quickly

その間に【そのあいだに】during that time

返事【へんじ】answer

したためる write, put down

人知れず【ひとしれず】unbeknownst to anyone

襟元【えりもと】collar

さし込む【さしこむ】insert

もの thing, situation

見える【みえる】seem

55

思いがけなき【おもいがけなき】ARCHAIC
  unexpected ✸

所【ところ】place

～にて in, at

君【きみ】HONORIFIC you ✸

姿【すがた】figure, form

見る【みる】see

～申候【～もうしそうろう】ARCHAIC, HUM-
  BLE auxiliary verb equivalent to modern
  お～申します

たとい = たとえ even though

装い【よそおい】dress, attire

変える【かえる】change

～給う【～たまう】ARCHAIC, HONORIFIC
  auxiliary verb equivalent to modern
  お～になります

～とも even

三年【さんねん】three years

It was definitely her hand. I had the impression she had popped out once or twice during the film, so I suppose she must have quickly written down this reply then, and slipped it discreetly into my collar.

I did not expect to see you, least of all here. Even though you have changed your garb, how could I possibly fail to notice the countenance that, for these three years, I have not forgotten wake or sleep? From the start I knew that the woman in the hood was you. And in this respect it amuses me that you are as eccentric as ever. I feel uneasy that your saying you wish to meet me may be just another way for you to amuse this fancy of yours.

このかた since

夢寐にも忘れぬ【むびにもわすれぬ】not forget even when asleep

御面影【おんおもかげ】ARCHAIC, HONORIFIC face

いかで how

見逃す【みのがす】overlook

〜候べき【〜そうろうべき】POLITE equivalent to modern 〜でしょう

妾【わらわ】HUMBLE, FEMININE I ⊛

始め【はじめ】start, beginning

頭巾【ずきん】hood

女【おんな】woman

〜なる＝〜である be ⊛

事【こと】fact

承知する【しょうちする】know

〜仕候【〜つかまつりそうろう】HUMBLE auxiliary verb equivalent to modern いたします

それにつけても be that as it may

相変わらず【あいかわらず】as usual

物好きな【ものずきな】fanciful

〜にておわせしこと＝〜でいらっしゃること ARCHAIC, HONORIFIC be

可笑しさ【おかしさ】absurdity

会わん【あわん】ARCHAIC let's meet

仰せらるるも【おおせらるるも】ARCHAIC, HONORIFIC although you say

多分【たぶん】probably

物好き【ものずき】fancy, whim

おん興じ【おんきょうじ】ARCHAIC, HONORIFIC fun, diversion

〜にや ARCHAIC is it not?

心許なく【こころもとなく】uneasily, insecurely

存じ候えども【ぞんじそうらえども】ARCHAIC, HUMBLE though I think

あまりの嬉しさに兎角の分別も出でず、唯仰せに従い明夜は必ず御待ち申す可く候。ただし、妾に少々都合もあり、考えも有之候えば、九時より九時半までの間に雷門までお出で下されまじくや。其処にて当方より差し向けたるお迎いの車夫が、必ず君を見つけ出して拙宅へ御案内致す可く候。君の御住所を秘し給うと同様に、妾も今の在り家を御知らせ致さぬ所存にて、車上の君に眼隠しをしてお連れ申すよう取りはからわせ候間、右御許し下され度、若しこの一事を御承引下され候わずば、妾は永遠に君を見ることかなわず、これに過ぎたる悲しみは無之候。

あまりの excessive

嬉しさ【うれしさ】joy, delight

兎角【とかく】this and that

分別も出でず【ふんべつもいでず】without one's wits about one, unable to exercise good judgment

唯【ただ】just

仰せ【おおせ】ARCHAIC, HONORIFIC as/what you say

従う【したがう】obey, comply

明夜【みょうや】tomorrow night

必ず【かならず】without fail ✪

御待ち申す可く候【おんまちもうすべくそうろう】ARCHAIC, HUMBLE will wait

妾【わらわ】HUMBLE, FEMININE I ✪

少々【しょうしょう】a little

都合【つごう】circumstances, convenience

考え【かんがえ】thought

有之候えば【これありそうらえば】ARCHAIC, POLITE because I have

九時【くじ】nine o'clock

九時半【くじはん】9:30

～の間に【～のあいだに】between

雷門【かみなりもん】Kaminari Gate

お出で下されまじくや【おいでくだされまじくや】ARCHAIC, HONORIFIC won't you please come?

其処にて【そこにて】there

当方【とうほう】I, we

差し向けたる【さしむけたる】ARCHAIC have sent around

お迎いの【おむかいの】POLITE to pick you up

車夫【しゃふ】rickshaw driver

君【きみ】HONORIFIC you ✪

見つけ出す【みつけだす】find

拙宅【せったく】my humble abode

Nonetheless, excess of delight renders me incapable of exercising common sense, so I shall do as you say and most definitely wait for you tomorrow night. However, as I have certain reasons of my own, and my own thoughts on the matter, could you kindly make your way to the Kaminari Gate between nine and half-past nine? There, a rickshaw driver, whom I shall dispatch to meet you, will surely find you and bring you to my humble home. Just as you keep secret your address, nor am I of a mind to reveal the house where I live; I shall therefore arrange that you shall be blindfolded whilst in the rickshaw and brought round to me thus. Please permit me to do the above, for if you choose to reject this one condition, then I will never be able to see you again, than which there could be no greater sorrow.

御案内致す可く候 【ごあんないいたすべくそうろう】 ARCHAIC, POLITE will guide you

御住所 【おんじゅうしょ】 ARCHAIC, HONORIFIC address

秘し給う 【ひしたまう】 ARCHAIC, HONORIFIC keep secret

〜と同様に 【〜とどうように】 in the same way

今 【いま】 now

在り家 【ありか】 secret abode, whereabouts

御知らせ致さぬ 【おんしらせいたさぬ】 ARCHAIC, HUMBLE not tell

所存 【しょぞん】 thought, opinion

〜にて = 〜で

車上 【しゃじょう】 in the rickshaw

眼隠しをする 【めかくしをする】 blindfold

お連れ申す 【おつれもうす】 HUMBLE bring (someone somewhere)

〜よう取りはからわせ候間 【〜ようとりはからわせそうろうあいだ】 ARCHAIC, POLITE as I will arrange (for the driver) to 〜

右御許し下され度 【みぎおんゆるしくだされたく】 ARCHAIC, HONORIFIC please accept what is written above

若し 【もし】 if

一事 【いちじ】 one thing

御承引下され候わずば 【ごしょういんくだされそうらわずば】 ARCHAIC, HONORIFIC, POLITE if you do not kindly consent to

永遠に 【えいえんに】 forever

見ることかなわず 【みることかなわず】 unable to see (you)

〜に過ぎたる 【〜にすぎたる】 ARCHAIC has exceeded

悲しみ 【かなしみ】 sadness, sorrow

無之候 【これなくそうろう】 does not exist

56▶ 　私はこの手紙を読んで行くうちに、自分がいつの間にか探偵小説中の人物となり終せて居るのを感じた。不思議な好奇心と恐怖とが、頭の中で渦を巻いた。女が自分の性癖を呑み込んで居て、わざとこんな真似をするのかとも思われた。

57▶ 　明くる日の晩は素晴らしい大雨であった。私はすっかり服装を改めて、対の大島の上にゴム引きの外套を纏い、ざぶん、ざぶんと、甲斐絹張りの洋傘に、滝の如くたたきつける雨の中を戸外へ出た。新堀の溝が往来一円に溢れているので、私は足袋を懐へ入れたが、びしょびしょに濡れた素足が家並みのランプに照らされて、ぴかぴか光って居た。

As I proceeded to read this letter, I felt that at some point I had metamorphosed into a character in a detective story. Wondrous curiosity and fear whirled around in my mind. It occurred to me that the woman might be deliberately going about things in this way because she understood my propensities.

The evening of the morrow there was a tremendous downpour. Changing into a completely different outfit, I put a rubber raincoat over my Ōshima and left the house, the pelting rain hammering down on my silk umbrella like a waterfall. As the Shinbori Canal had flooded all the streets nearby, I had stuffed my tabi into the breast of my kimono; now my soaking-wet bare feet glistened when the lamplight from the houses along the street fell on them.

改める 【あらためる】 change (clothes)

対 【つい】 matching, a pair

大島 【おおしま】 Ōshima (gorgeous, expensive style of kimono)

〜の上に 【〜のうえに】 on top of

ゴム引き 【ゴムびき】 rubberized

外套 【がいとう】 raincoat

纏う 【まとう】 put on

ざぶん、ざぶんと ONOMATOPOEIC describes a pelting sound

甲斐絹張りの 【かいきばりの】 stretched with Kaiki silk

洋傘 【ようがさ】 Western-style umbrella

滝 【たき】 waterfall

〜の如く 【〜のごとく】 just like

たたきつける 【たたきつける】 strike upon

雨 【あめ】 rain

〜の中を 【〜のなかを】 amidst, among

戸外 【おもて】 outside

出る 【でる】 go out

新堀 【しんぼり】 Shinbori

溝 【みぞ】 canal, channel

往来 【おうらい】 street

一円 【いちえん】 the whole place

溢れる 【あふれる】 overflow

足袋 【たび】 tabi sock

懐 【ふところ】 breast (of a garment)

入れる 【いれる】 put in

びしょびしょに MIMETIC sopping

濡れる 【ぬれる】 get wet

素足 【すあし】 bare foot

家並み 【やなみ／いえなみ】 row of houses on a street

照らす 【てらす】 [passive form in text] illuminate

ぴかぴか MIMETIC glisteningly

光る 【ひかる】 shine

夥しい雨量が、天からざあざあと直瀉する喧囂の中に、何もかも打ち消されて、ふだん賑やかな広小路の通りも大概雨戸を締め切り、二三人の臀端折りの男が、敗走した兵士のように駈け出して行く。電車が時々レールの上に溜まった水をほとばしらせて通る外は、ところどころの電柱や広告のあかりが、朦朧たる雨の空中をぼんやり照らしているばかりであった。

58▶ 外套から、手首から、肘の辺まで水だらけになって、漸く雷門へ来た私は、雨中にしょんぼり立ち止りながらアーク燈の光を透かして、四辺を見廻したが、一つも人影は見えない。

夥しい【おびただしい】immense

雨量【うりょう】amount of rain, rainfall

天【てん】sky, heavens

ざあざあと ONOMATOPOEIC describes the heavy fall of rain

直瀉する【ちょくしゃする】strike directly

喧囂【けんごう】noise, din

〜の中に【〜のなかに】amidst

何もかも【なにもかも】anything and everything

打ち消す【うちけす】extinguish

ふだん normally

賑やかな【にぎやかな】lively

広小路の通り【ひろこうじのとおり】boulevard

大概【たいがい】for the most part

雨戸【あまど】shutter

締め切る【しめきる】close tight

二三人【にさんにん】two or three people

臀端折り【しりはしょり】tucking the ends of one's kimono into one's sash at the back

男【おとこ】man

敗走する【はいそうする】flee, be routed

兵士【へいし】soldier

駈け出す【かけだす】scamper, dash off

〜て行く【〜ていく】indicates movement away from the narrator

電車【でんしゃ】streetcar

時々【ときどき】sometimes

〜の上に【〜のうえに】on

溜まる【たまる】collect, accumulate

水【みず】water

ほとばしる [causative form in text] spurt out

通る【とおる】pass

〜外【〜ほか】besides, other than

Everything was drowned out by the fearful quantities of rain that came pouring and crashing down from the heavens; the normally bustling boulevard was all shuttered up, and two or three men were running at full tilt like routed soldiers, their kimonos tucked into their sashes. Apart from the occasional streetcar sending the water that had formed pools in the rails flying as it went by, there was only the light of the occasional telegraph pole or billboard casting a dim glow through the rainy haze.

When I finally got to the Kaminari Gate, I was soaked through—my raincoat, my wrists, even right up to my elbows. As I stood hunched and miserable in the rain, I peered through the glow of the streetlights but could not see a soul.

ところどころ here and there
電柱【でんちゅう】utility pole
広告【こうこく】advertisement
あかり light
朦朧たる【もうろうたる】dim, hazy
雨【あめ】rain
空中【くうちゅう】throughout the air
ぼんやり MIMETIC vaguely, dimly
照らす【てらす】illuminate, shine on
〜ばかり just, only

58

外套【がいとう】raincoat
手首【てくび】wrist
肘【ひじ】elbow
辺【あたり】area, region
水だらけになる【みずだらけになる】
 become drenched
漸く【ようやく】finally

雷門【かみなりもん】Kaminari Gate
来る【くる】come
私【わたし】I
雨中【うちゅう】in the rain
しょんぼり MIMETIC disconsolately
立ち止まる【たちどまる】stand
アーク燈【アークとう】arc lamp (street
 light)
光【ひかり】light
〜を透かして【〜をすかして】through
四辺【あたり】area
見廻す【みまわす】look around
一つも〜ない【ひとつも〜ない】not even
 one
人影【ひとかげ】human figure
見える【みえる】be visible

何処かの暗い隅に隠れて、何物かが私の様子を窺っているのかも知れない。こう思って暫く佇んで居ると、やがて吾妻橋の方の暗闇から、赤い提灯の火が一つ動き出して、がらがらがらと街鉄の鋪き石の上を駛走して来た旧式な相乗りの俥がぴたりと私の前で止まった。

59 ▶ 「旦那、お乗んなすって下さい。」

60 ▶ 　深い饅頭笠に雨合羽を着た車夫の声が、車軸を流す雨の響きの中に消えたかと思うと、男はいきなり私の後へ廻って、羽二重の布を素早く私の両眼の上へ二た廻り程巻きつけて、蟀谷の皮がよじれる程強く緊め上げた。

61 ▶ 「さあ、お召しなさい。」

何処か【どこか】somewhere
暗い【くらい】dark
隅【すみ】nook, corner
隠れる【かくれる】hide
何物か【なにものか】somebody
私【わたし】I ⊛
様子【ようす】behavior, appearance
窺う【うかがう】look furtively
思う【おもう】think ⊛
暫く【しばらく】for a while
佇む【たたずむ】linger
やがて before long
吾妻橋【あづまばし】Azuma Bridge
〜の方の【〜のほうの】in the direction of
暗闇【くらやみ】darkness
赤い【あかい】red
提灯【ちょうちん】lantern
火【ひ】light

動き出す【うごきだす】start to move
がらがらがらと ONOMATOPOEIC with a rattle
街鉄【がいてつ】abbr. of 東京市街鉄道株式会社【とうきょうしがいてつどうかぶしきがいしゃ】Tokyo City Railways: a now defunct company; 街鉄 refers to the trolley line the company ran
鋪き石【しきいし】cobbles
〜の上を【〜のうえを】over, across ⊛
駛走する【しそうする】run at full speed
〜て来る【〜てくる】indicates movement toward the narrator
旧式な【きゅうしきな】old-fashioned
相乗りの【あいのりの】for two passengers
俥【くるま】rickshaw
ぴたりと MIMETIC exactly
〜の前で【〜のまえで】in front of
止まる【とまる】stop

Maybe somebody hidden in a dark nook somewhere was keeping a close eye on me. Thinking such thoughts, I loitered for a while; by and by, the light of a single red lantern began to bob about in the darkness over by the Azuma Bridge, and an old-fashioned, two-seat rickshaw rattled over the cobblestone street on which the trolleys ran before coming to a halt directly in front of me.

"Please get in, sir."

No sooner had the voice of the driver—who wore a broad-brimmed wicker hat and a rain cape—faded into the roar of the torrential rain, than he suddenly slipped around behind me and deftly wrapped a length of silk twice around my eyes. He tied it tight enough to stretch the skin of my temples.

"Come on then, sir, in you get."

59
旦那 【だんな】 master
お乗りなする 【おのりなする】 HONORIFIC
　　get in (a vehicle)
60
深い 【ふかい】 deep
饅頭笠 【まんじゅうがさ】 round wicker hat
雨合羽 【あまがっぱ】 rain cape
着る 【きる】 wear
車夫 【しゃふ】 rickshaw man
声 【こえ】 voice
車軸を流す雨 【しゃじくをながすあめ】
　　torrential rain (lit., "rain that would
　　sweep away a carriage axle")
響き 【ひびき】 noise
消える 【きえる】 disappear
男 【おとこ】 man
いきなり suddenly

～の後へ 【～のうしろへ】 behind
廻る 【まわる】 go around
羽二重 【はぶたえ】 silk
布 【ぬの】 cloth
素早く 【すばやく】 nimbly
両眼 【りょうがん】 both eyes
二た廻り 【ふたまわり】 two circuits
～程 【～ほど】 to the extent of ⊛
巻きつける 【まきつける】 wrap around
蟀谷 【こめかみ】 temple
皮 【かわ】 skin
よじれる be twisted, be pulled
強く 【つよく】 forcefully
緊め上げる 【しめあげる】 tie tight
61
さあ come on, well then
お召しなさい 【おめしなさい】 HONORIFIC
　　get in (a vehicle)

62▶ 　こう云って男のざらざらした手が、私を摑んで、惶しく俥の上へ乗せた。

63▶ 　しめっぽい匂いのする幌の上へ、ぱらぱらと雨の注ぐ音がする。疑いもなく私の隣りには女が一人乗って居る。お白粉の薫りと暖かい体温が、幌の中へ蒸すように罩っていた。

64▶ 　轅を上げた俥は、方向を晦ます為めに一つ所をくるくると二三度廻って走り出したが、右へ曲り、左へ折れ、どうかすると Labyrinth の中をうろついて居るようであった。時々電車通りへ出たり、小さな橋を渡ったりした。

65▶ 　長い間、そうして俥に揺られて居た。隣りに並んでいる女は勿論T女であろうが、黙って身じろぎもせずに腰かけている。

As the man said this, his rough hands grabbed me and hastily bundled me into the rickshaw.

The rain was drumming on the hood, which smelled of damp. There was no doubt that a woman was sitting beside me. Inside the hood, it was airless and muggy with the heat of her body and the fragrance of her make-up.

The shafts had been picked up, but we got going only after the rickshaw had whirled around two or three times on the spot to confuse my sense of direction; and indeed, as we turned to the right, then veered off to the left, it felt almost as though we were meandering through a labyrinth. From time to time we would emerge onto a streetcar route, or go over a small bridge.

We were jolted around in the rickshaw for a long time. Of course, the woman beside me must have been T., but she sat in silence without moving a muscle.

上げる【あげる】lift up
方向【ほうこう】direction
晦ます【くらます】confuse, conceal
〜為めに【〜ために】in order to
一つ所【ひとつところ】the same place
くるくると MIMETIC round and round
二三度【にさんど】two or three times
廻る【まわる】spin around
走り出す【はしりだす】get going
右【みぎ】right
曲る【まがる】turn
左【ひだり】left
折れる【おれる】turn
どうかすると somehow
うろつく wander, roam
時々【ときどき】sometimes
電車通り【でんしゃどおり】street with streetcar tracks

出る【でる】emerge
小さな【ちいさな】small
橋【はし】bridge
渡る【わたる】cross

65

長い間【ながいあいだ】for a long time
揺られる【ゆられる】be shaken
隣りに【となりに】beside ⊛
並ぶ【ならぶ】be side by side
勿論【もちろん】of course
T女【ティーじょ】Miss T.
黙る【だまる】say nothing
身じろぎもせずに【みじろぎもせずに】 without making even the slightest movement
腰かける【こしかける】sit down

多分私の眼隠しが厳格に守られるか否かを監督する為めに同乗して居るものらしい。しかし、私は他人の監督がなくても、決してこの眼かくしを取り外す気はなかった。海の上で知り合いになった夢のような女、大雨の晩の幌の中、夜の都会の秘密、盲目、沈黙――凡べての物が一つになって、渾然たるミステリーの靄の裡に私を投げ込んで了って居る。

66 ▶ 　やがて女は固く結んだ私の唇を分けて、口の中へ巻煙草を挿し込んだ。そうしてマッチを擦って火をつけてくれた。

67 ▶ 　一時間程経って、漸く俥は停った。

多分【たぶん】probably
私【わたし】I ❋
眼隠し【めかくし】blindfold ❋
厳格に【げんかくに】strictly, sternly
守る【まもる】protect, observe (a rule)
〜か否か【〜かいなか】whether or not
監督する【かんとくする】supervise
〜為めに【〜ために】in order to
同乗する【どうじょうする】ride together
もの state, situation
〜らしい apparently
しかし however
他人【たにん】another person
監督【かんとく】supervise
決して〜ない【けっして〜ない／けして〜ない】by no means
取り外す【とりはずす】remove, take off
気【き】mind, intention

海の上で【うみのうえで】at sea
知り合いになる【しりあいになる】get to know
夢【ゆめ】dream
女【おんな】woman ❋
大雨【おおあめ】downpour
晩【ばん】evening
幌【ほろ】hood
〜の中【〜のなか】inside
夜【よる】night
都会【とかい】city, town
秘密【ひみつ】secret
盲目【もうもく】blindness
沈黙【ちんもく】silence
凡べて【すべて】all
物【もの】thing
一つ【ひとつ】one

It seemed likely she was traveling with me to make sure my blind-fold remained firmly in place. Even without anyone there to keep an eye on me though, I would never have wanted to take it off. The dreamlike woman I had met on board ship; being inside this hood on a stormy evening; the secrets of the city at night; the blindness; the silence—all these elements fused together to plunge me deep into a fog of exquisite mystery.

In due course the woman parted my tightly closed lips and slipped a cigarette into my mouth. She then struck a match and lit it for me.

About an hour passed before the rickshaw finally stopped.

渾然たる【こんぜんたる】whole, harmo-
　nious
ミステリー mystery
靄【もや】haze, mist
〜の裡に【〜のうちに】into
投げ込む【なげこむ】fling into
〜て了う【〜てしまう】completely

66

やがて before long
固く【かたく】firmly
結ぶ【むすぶ】close, fasten together
唇【くちびる】lip
分ける【わける】divide, part
口【くち】mouth
〜の中へ【〜のなかへ】in
巻煙草【まきタバコ】cigarette
挿し込む【さしこむ】insert
マッチ match

擦る【する】strike (a match)
火をつける【ひをつける】light

67

一時間【いちじかん】one hour
〜程【〜ほど】about, around
経つ【たつ】elapse
漸く【ようやく】finally
俥【くるま】rickshaw
停る【とまる】stop

再びざらざらした男の手が私を導きながら狭そうな路次を二三間行くと、裏木戸のようなものをギーと開けて家の中へ連れて行った。

68 ▶ 　眼を塞がれながら一人座敷に取り残されて、暫く坐っていると、間もなく襖の開く音がした。女は無言の儘、人魚のように体を崩して擦り寄りつつ、私の膝の上へ仰向きに上半身を靠せかけて、そうして両腕を私の項に廻して羽二重の結び目をはらりと解いた。

69 ▶ 　部屋は八畳位もあろう。

再び【ふたたび】again
ざらざらした MIMETIC rough, coarse
男【おとこ】man
手【て】hand
私【わたし】I ⊛
導く【みちびく】lead, guide
狭い【せまい】narrow
路次【ろじ】lane, alley
二三間【にさんげん】two or three *ken* (1 *ken* = 6 feet)
行く【いく】go
裏木戸【うらきど】backdoor
もの thing
ギーと ONOMATOPOEIC with a creak
開ける【あける】open
家【いえ／うち】house
〜の中へ【〜のなかへ】into

連れて行く【つれていく】take (someone somewhere)

68
眼【め】eye, vision
塞ぐ【ふさぐ】[passive form in text] cover, obstruct
一人【ひとり】alone
座敷【ざしき】tatami-mat room
取り残す【とりのこす】[passive form in text] leave behind
暫く【しばらく】for a while
坐る【すわる】sit
間もなく【まもなく】shortly, before long
襖【ふすま】sliding door
開く【あく／ひらく】open
音がする【おとがする】make a sound
女【おんな】woman
無言【むごん】silence

Steering me once again with his rough hands, the driver took me some four or five yards down an apparently narrow alley, and with a creaking sound he opened what I suspect was a backdoor, and led me into a house.

Left on my own in a tatami room with my eyes still covered, I remained seated for a while. Soon I heard the sound of a sliding door opening. Without a word, the woman went limp and lolled against me like a mermaid. Lying on my lap with her face toward me, she placed her arms around my neck and untied the knot of the silken blindfold.

The room was probably about eight mats.

〜の儘 【〜のまま】 still, in the unchanged state of
人魚 【にんぎょ】 mermaid
体を崩す 【たいをくずす】 relax one's body
擦り寄る 【すりよる】 press up close to
〜つつ while, as
膝 【ひざ】 knee
〜の上へ 【〜のうえへ】 onto, on
仰向きに 【あおむきに】 facing upward
上半身 【じょうはんしん】 upper body
靠せかける 【もたせかける】 lean (something) on
両腕 【りょううで】 both arms
項 【うなじ】 nape of the neck
廻す 【まわす】 encircle
羽二重 【はぶたえ】 silk (material of blindfold)
結び目 【むすびめ】 knot

はらりと MIMETIC lightly, flutteringly
解く 【とく】 undo

69

部屋 【へや】 room
八畳 【はちじょう】 eight mats
〜位 【〜ぐらい／〜くらい】 around

普請と云い、装飾と云い、なかなか立派で、木柄なども選んではあるが、丁度この女の身分が分らぬと同様に、待合とも、妾宅とも、上流の堅気な住まいとも見極めがつかない。一方の縁側の外にはこんもりとした植え込みがあって、その向うは板塀に囲われている。唯これだけの眼界では、この家が東京のどの辺にあたるのか、大凡その見当すら判らなかった。

70▶ 「よく来て下さいましたね。」

71▶ 　こう云いながら、女は座敷の中央の四角な紫檀の机へ身を靠せかけて、白い両腕を二匹の生き物のように、だらりと卓上に匍わせた。

普請【ふしん】construction, building
〜と云い〜と云い【〜といい〜といい】
　　whether . . . or, both . . . and
装飾【そうしょく】decor
なかなか rather, very
立派な【りっぱな】magnificent
木柄【きがら】pattern/quality of wood
選ぶ【えらぶ】choose
丁度【ちょうど】exactly, just
女【おんな】woman ⊛
身分【みぶん】status, social position
分らぬ【わからぬ】not understand
〜と同様に【〜とどうように】in the same
　　way that 〜
待合【まちあい】house of assignation
〜とも〜とも whether . . . or
妾宅【しょうたく】house of a mistress
上流の【じょうりゅうの】upper-class

堅気な【かたぎな】respectable
住まい【すまい】residence
見極めがつかない【みきわめがつかない】
　　hard to ascertain
一方【いっぽう】on one side
縁側【えんがわ】veranda
〜の外に【〜のそとに】outside
こんもりとした MIMETIC thick, dense
植え込み【うえこみ】shrubbery, bush
向う【むこう】other side
板塀【いたべい】wooden fence
囲う【かこう】[passive form in text] surround
唯【ただ】just, only
眼界【がんかい】range of vision
家【いえ／うち】house
東京【とうきょう】Tokyo
辺【あたり】area
あたる lie, be (of a place)

The construction and the decor were both rather splendid, the wood and so forth very choice, but just as I was unable to determine the woman's own position, I simply could not tell if this was a house of assignation, a kept woman's house or the residence of a respectable upper-class lady. Beyond the veranda off to one side was a thick growth of plants enclosed by a wooden fence. My field of vision thus restricted, I could not even make the roughest guess about which part of Tokyo the house might be in.

"I'm so pleased you came."

As the woman said this, she leaned against the rectangular rosewood table in the middle of the room, and sent her limp white arms gliding over its top like a pair of living creatures.

大凡そ【おおよそ】roughly
見当【けんとう】rough direction
～すら even
判る【わかる】judge

70

来る【くる】come
よく～て下さる【よく～てくださる】
　HONORIFIC thank you for (doing)

71

云う【いう】say
座敷【ざしき】tatami-mat room
中央【ちゅうおう】center
四角な【しかくな】square, rectangular
紫檀【したん】rosewood
机【つくえ】desk, table
身を靠せかける【みをもたせかける】lean
　against
白い【しろい】white

両腕【りょううで】both arms
二匹【にひき】two (small animals)
生き物【いきもの】animal, creature
だらりと MIMETIC limply, languidly
卓上【たくじょう】tabletop
匍う【はう】[causative form in text] crawl

襟のかかった渋い縞お召に腹合わせ帯をしめて、銀杏返しに結って居る風情の、昨夜と恐ろしく趣が変っているのに、私は先ず驚かされた。

72▶ 「あなたは、今夜あたしがこんな風をして居るのは可笑しいと思っていらッしゃるんでしょう。それでも人に身分を知らせないようにするには、こうやって毎日身なりを換えるより外に仕方がありませんからね。」

73▶ 卓上に伏せてある洋盃を起して、葡萄酒を注ぎながら、こんな事を云う女の素振りは、思ったよりもしとやかに打ち萎れて居た。

襟のかかった【えりのかかった】with a cloth loosely sewn onto the collar (to protect it from getting stained)

渋い【しぶい】sober, chaste

縞【しま】stripe

お召【おめし】abbr. of お召縮緬【おめしちりめん】high-grade silk crepe kimono

腹合わせ帯【はらあわせおび】women's sash lined with different fabric on front and back (usu. white satin on front and black velvet on back)

しめる fasten, wear (of belts, etc.)

銀杏返し【いちょうがえし】butterfly coiffure

結う【ゆう】do (one's hair)

風情【ふぜい】appearance

昨夜【さくや／ゆうべ】the night before

恐ろしく【おそろしく】incredibly

趣【おもむき】beauty, general effect

変る【かわる】be different

私【わたし】I

先ず【まず】first of all

驚く【おどろく】[causative-passive form in text] be surprised

72

今夜【こんや】this evening, tonight

あたし FEMININE I

こんな風をする【こんなふうをする】have this kind of air

可笑しい【おかしい】funny, odd

思う【おもう】think

〜ていらッしゃる HONORIFIC be ——ing

それでも even so

人【ひと】person

身分【みぶん】social standing, identity

知らせる【しらせる】make known

こうやって in this way

I was first of all astonished at the tremendous change in her appearance from the night before: around a discreetly striped kimono with a cloth loosely sewn onto the collar, she wore a white-satin sash lined with black velvet, while her hair was arranged in a butterfly coiffure.

"I suppose you think it odd that I'm dressed like this tonight. But the only possible way I can keep people from knowing my identity is to alter my appearance every day like this."

The manner in which she said this—she had picked up a cup that stood upended on the table and was pouring wine into it—was more modest and diffident than I had expected.

毎日 【まいにち】 everyday
身なり 【みなり】 attire, dress
換える 【かえる】 change
〜より外に 【〜よりほかに】 other than to
仕方がありません 【しかたがありません】 there's nothing for it but

73

卓上 【たくじょう】 tabletop
伏せる 【ふせる】 place upside down
洋盃 【コップ】 cup
起す 【おこす】 turn over, upturn
葡萄酒 【ぶどうしゅ】 wine
注ぐ 【つぐ】 pour
事 【こと】 thing
云う 【いう】 say
女 【おんな】 woman
素振り 【そぶり】 attitude, bearing

思ったより 【おもったより】 more than one expects
しとやかに in a ladylike manner, modestly
打ち萎れる 【うちしおれる】 get disspirited

74 ▶ 「でも好く覚えて居て下さいましたね。上海でお別れしてから、いろいろの男と苦労もして見ましたが、妙にあなたの事を忘れることが出来ませんでした。もう今度こそは私を棄てないで下さいまし。身分も境遇も判らない、夢のような女だと思って、いつまでもお附き合いなすって下さい。」

75 ▶ 　女の語る一言一句が、遠い国の歌のしらべのように、哀韻を含んで私の胸に響いた。昨夜のような派手な勝気な悧発な女が、どうしてこう云う憂鬱な、殊勝な姿を見せることが出来るのであろう。さながら万事を打ち捨てて、私の前に魂を投げ出しているようであった。

74

好く〜て下さる【よく〜てくださる】
　HONORIFIC thank you for (doing)

覚える【おぼえる】remember

上海【シャンハイ】Shanghai

お別れする【おわかれする】POLITE part

いろいろの various

男【おとこ】man

苦労する【くろうする】have difficulties, suffer

〜て見る【〜てみる】to see what it is like

妙に【みょうに】peculiarly, strangely

あなたの事【あなたのこと】you

忘れる【わすれる】forget

出来る【できる】be able to do ⊛

今度こそ【こんどこそ】this time for sure

私【わたし】I ⊛

棄てる【すてる】throw away, reject

〜ないで下さいまし【〜ないでくださいまし】[imperative form] POLITE, FEMININE
　do not

身分【みぶん】social status, identity

境遇【きょうぐう】situation, circumstances

判る【わかる】understand, know

夢【ゆめ】dream

女【おんな】woman ⊛

思う【おもう】think

いつまでも forever

お附き合いなする【おつきあいなする】
　HONORIFIC have a relationship

〜て下さい【〜てください】please

75

語る【かたる】say, tell

一言一句【いちごんいっく】each word and phrase

遠い【とおい】faraway

"I'm so pleased you remembered me. I have had trying relationships with various men since we parted in Shanghai, but I've been strangely unable to forget you. Please don't abandon me this time, I beg you. Think of me as a woman from a dream whose identity and background you do not know, and stay with me forever."

Every word the woman uttered touched a melancholy chord in my heart, like the melody of a song from a faraway land. How was the flashy, aggressive, razor-sharp woman of the previous night able to reveal this vulnerable and demure side of herself to me? It was as if she had thrown everything aside and was laying her soul before me.

国【くに】country
歌【うた】song
しらべ melody
哀韻【あいいん】note of pathos
含む【ふくむ】contain
胸に響く【むねにひびく】resonate in one's heart
昨夜【さくや／ゆうべ】the night before
派手な【はでな】flashy
勝気な【かちきな】strong-minded, willful
悧発な【りはつな】clever, shrewd
こう云う〜【こういう〜】this kind of
憂鬱な【ゆううつな】gloomy
殊勝な【しゅしょうな】praiseworthy
姿【すがた】form, figure
見せる【みせる】show
さながら just like
万事【ばんじ】everything

打ち捨てる【うちすてる】throw away
〜の前に【〜のまえに】in front of
魂【たましい】soul
投げ出す【なげだす】deliver up, throw down

「夢の中の女」「秘密の女」朦朧とした、現実とも幻覚とも区別の附かない Love adventure の面白さに、私はそれから毎晩のように女の許に通い、夜半の二時頃迄遊んでは、また眼かくしをして、雷門まで送り返された。一と月も二た月も、お互に所を知らず、名を知らずに会見していた。女の境遇や住宅を捜り出そうと云う気は少しもなかったが、だんだん時日が立つに従い、私は妙な好奇心から、自分を乗せた俥が果して東京の何方の方面に二人を運んで行くのか、自分の今眼を塞がれて通って居る処は、浅草から何の辺に方って居るのか、唯それだけを是非とも知って見たくなった。

夢【ゆめ】dream
〜の中の【〜のなかの】inside
女【おんな】woman ⊛
秘密【ひみつ】secret
朦朧とした【もうろうとした】dim, hazy
現実【げんじつ】reality
〜とも〜とも whether . . . or
幻覚【げんかく】illusion, fantasy
区別の附かない【くべつのつかない】impossible to distinguish
面白さ【おもしろさ】enjoyment
私【わたし】I ⊛
毎晩のように【まいばんのように】almost every evening
〜の許に【〜のもとに】to the house of
通う【かよう】go regularly
夜半【よなか】middle of the night

二時頃【にじごろ】around two o'clock
〜迄【〜まで】until
遊ぶ【あそぶ】have fun
また and, also, again
眼かくしをする【めかくしをする】put on a blindfold
雷門【かみなりもん】Kaminari Gate
送り返す【おくりかえす】[passive form in text] send back, take back
一と月【ひとつき】one month
二た月【ふたつき】two months
お互に【おたがいに】mutually
所【ところ】place, address
知らず【しらず】not knowing ⊛
名【な】name
会見する【かいけんする】meet
境遇【きょうぐう】situation, circumstances

Such was the fascination of this nebulous, half-real, half-fantastic *affaire du coeur* with my "dream woman" or "secret woman," I went to visit her almost every subsequent night, when, after having fun until about two in the morning, I would again be blindfolded and driven back to the Kaminari Gate. We met for a month—then two months—without either of us knowing the other's address or name. At first I didn't have the least interest in ferreting out the woman's background or address, but gradually, as time went by, an inexplicable curiosity made me desperate to discover one simple thing: to which part of Tokyo was the rickshaw I was riding in taking us both? And this place I was passing through right now with my eyes covered—where did it lie in relation to Asakusa?

住宅 【じゅうたく】 residence
捜り出す 【さぐりだす】 look for, hunt out
〜と云う 【〜という】 of such a kind
気 【き】 mind, inclination
少しもない 【すこしもない】 none at all
だんだん gradually
時日が立つ 【じじつがたつ】 time passes
〜に従い 【〜にしたがい】 as
妙な 【みょうな】 strange, odd
好奇心 【こうきしん】 curiosity
自分 【じぶん】 myself ⊛
乗せる 【のせる】 put on board
俥 【くるま】 rickshaw
果して 【はたして】 ever, in the world
東京 【とうきょう】 Tokyo
何方の 【どっちの】 which
方面 【ほうめん】 direction
二人 【ふたり】 two people

運ぶ 【はこぶ】 carry, bear
〜て行く 【〜ていく】 indicates movement away from the narrator
今 【いま】 now
眼 【め】 eye, vision
塞ぐ 【ふさぐ】 cover, obstruct
通る 【とおる】 pass through
処 【ところ】 place
浅草 【あさくさ】 Asakusa
何の辺 【どのあたり】 which area
方る 【あたる】 lie, be (of a place)
唯 【ただ】 just, only
是非とも 【ぜひとも】 at all costs
知る 【しる】 find out, learn
〜て見る 【〜てみる】 to see what it is like

三十分も一時間も、時とすると一時間半もがらがらと市街を走ってから、轅を下ろす女の家は、案外雷門の近くにあるのかも知れない。私は毎夜俥に揺す振られながら、此処か彼処かと心の中に憶測を廻らす事を禁じ得なかった。

77▶　或る晩、私はとうとうたまらなくなって、

78▶　「一寸でも好いから、この眼かくしを取ってくれ。」

79▶　と俥の上で女にせがんだ。

80▶　「いけません、いけません。」

81▶　と、女は慌てて、私の両手をしっかり抑えて、その上へ顔を押しあてた。

82▶　「何卒そんな我が儘を云わないで下さい。此処の往来はあたしの秘密です。この秘密を知られればあたしはあなたに捨てられるかも知れません。」

三十分【さんじゅっぷん】thirty minutes
一時間【いちじかん】one hour
時とすると【ときとすると】sometimes
一時間半【いちじかんはん】one hour and a half
がらがらと ONOMATOPOEIC with a rattle
市街【しがい】city, city streets
走る【はしる】run
轅を下ろす【かじをおろす】put down the shafts (= stop)
女【おんな】woman ⊛
家【いえ／うち】house
案外【あんがい】surprisingly
雷門【かみなりもん】Kaminari Gate
〜の近くに【〜のちかくに】near
〜かも知れない【〜かもしれない】maybe, perhaps ⊛
私【わたし】I ⊛

毎夜【まいよ】every night
俥【くるま】rickshaw ⊛
揺す振る【ゆすぶる】[passive form in text] shake, sway
此処【ここ】here ⊛
彼処【かしこ】there
心の中に【こころのなかに】in my mind
憶測【おくそく】guess, conjecture
廻らす【めぐらす】turn (thoughts) in one's mind
事【こと】act
禁じ得ない【きんじえない】not be able to stop

77
或る【ある】a certain
晩【ばん】evening
とうとう finally
たまらない be unbearable

Perhaps the woman's house, where the rickshaw came to a halt after thirty minutes, an hour, sometimes even an hour and a half of trundling through the city streets, was surprisingly close to the Kaminari Gate after all. As I was jolted about in the rickshaw every night, I could not stop myself from speculating internally whether we were in this part of town or that.

Finally one night I could bear it no more.

"Please, take off this blindfold, even for a moment."

In the rickshaw I entreated the woman.

"No, you can't! You can't!"

In a panic, the woman pushed down hard on my hands, pressing her face against them.

"Please don't be so headstrong. Which street we are in is my secret. I'm afraid that if you discover my secret, you may throw me aside."

78

一寸でも 【ちょっとでも】 just a little

好い 【いい】 enough

眼かくし 【めかくし】 blindfold

取る 【とる】 take

～てくれ [imperative form] BLUNT, MASCULINE please

79

～の上で 【～のうえで】 on

せがむ press, pester

80

いけません must not, should not ⊛

81

慌てる 【あわてる】 be flustered, panic

両手 【りょうて】 both hands

シッカリ firmly

抑える 【おさえる】 restrain, force down

その上へ 【そのうえへ】 onto it

顔 【かお】 face

押しあてる 【おしあてる】 press against

82

何卒 【どうぞ】 please

我が儘 【わがまま】 willfullness, selfishness

云う 【いう】 say

～ないで下さい 【～ないでください】 please do not

往来 【おうらい】 street

あたし FEMININE I

秘密 【ひみつ】 secret

知る 【しる】 [passive form in text] know, find out

あたし FEMININE I ⊛

捨てる 【すてる】 [passive form in text] discard ⊛

83 ▶ 「どうして私に捨てられるのだ。」

84 ▶ 「そうなれば、あたしはもう『夢の中の女』ではありません。あなたは私を恋して居るよりも、夢の中の女を恋して居るのですもの。」

85 ▶ いろいろに言葉を尽して頼んだが、私は何と云っても聴き入れなかった。

86 ▶ 「仕方がない、そんなら見せて上げましょう。……その代り一寸ですよ。」

87 ▶ 女は嘆息するように云って、力なく眼かくしの布を取りながら、

"Why would I abandon you?"

"Because in that case, I would no longer be your 'dream woman.' And I know you're in love with the dream woman—not with me."

I begged her, deploying all sorts of arguments, but it made no difference; she was deaf to my request.

"Oh, very well then. If that's how you feel, I'll let you have a look . . . but only for a moment."

The woman sighed as she spoke, and listlessly removing the blindfold, asked me:

88 ▶ 「此処が何処だか判りますか。」

89 ▶ と、心許ない顔つきをした。

90 ▶ 　美しく晴れ渡った空の地色は、妙に黒ずんで星が一面にきらきらと輝き、白い霞のような天の川が果てから果てへ流れている。狭い道路の両側には商店が軒を並べて、燈火の光が賑やかに町を照らしていた。

91 ▶ 　不思議な事には、可なり繁華な通りであるらしいのに、私はそれが何処の街であるか、さっぱり見当が附かなかった。俥はどんどんその通りを走って、やがて一二町先の突き当りの正面に、精美堂と大きく書いた印形屋の看板が見え出した。

88
此処 【ここ】 here, this place
何処 【どこ】 where ✿
判る 【わかる】 understand, know

89
心許ない 【こころもとない】 apprehensive
顔つき 【かおつき】 expression

90
美しく 【うつくしく】 beautifully
晴れ渡った 【はれわたった】 clear and cloudless
空 【そら】 sky
地色 【じいろ】 (back)ground color
妙に 【みょうに】 bizarrely
黒ずむ 【くろずむ】 darken
星 【ほし】 star
一面に 【いちめんに】 across the whole expanse

きらきらと MIMETIC brilliantly
輝く 【かがやく】 shine
白い 【しろい】 white
霞 【かすみ】 haze, mist
天の川 【あまのがわ】 Milky Way
果て 【はて】 end, extremity ✿
流れる 【ながれる】 flow, stream
狭い 【せまい】 narrow
道路 【どうろ】 street
両側 【りょうがわ】 both sides
商店 【しょうてん】 shop
軒を並べる 【のきをならべる】 be crammed together (of shops, so that their eaves are almost touching)
燈火 【とうか】 lamplight
光 【ひかり】 light
賑やかに 【にぎやかに】 in a lively manner
町 【まち】 district, quarter

"So, do you recognize this place?"

Her expression was uneasy.

Stars twinkled across the whole expanse of the sky—a beautifully clear, but unusually black backdrop—while the Milky Way stretched from one end of it to the other like a white mist. Shops crammed both sides of a narrow street, and the light of electric lamps made the area cheerful and bright.

The funny thing was that although it looked like a very bustling street, I had not the faintest idea which part of town it was in. The rickshaw bowled on down the street until, before long, directly in front of me at the end of the street a block or two farther on, I caught sight of a sealmaker's shop sign with the name Seibidō painted on it in large characters.

照らす【てらす】illuminate

91

不思議な【ふしぎな】extraordinary
事【こと】thing
可なり【かなり】considerably
繁華な【はんかな】thriving, bustling
通り【とおり】street ⊛
〜らしい apparently
〜のに although
私【わたし】I
街【まち】street, quarter
さっぱり〜ない not at all
見当が附く【けんとうがつく】guess, have an idea
俥【くるま】rickshaw
どんどん MIMETIC rapidly
走る【はしる】run
やがて in due course, before long

一二町先【いちにちょうさき】one or two blocks ahead
突き当り【つきあたり】end (of a street)
〜の正面に【〜のしょうめんに】in front of
精美堂【せいびどう】Seibidō (shop name)
大きく【おおきく】at a large size
書く【かく】write
印形屋【いんぎょうや】sealmaker's shop
看板【かんばん】signboard
見え出す【みえだす】become visible

　私が看板の横に書いてある細い文字の町名番地を、俥の上で遠くから覗き込むようにすると、女は忽ち気が附いたか、

「あれッ」

と云って、再び私の眼を塞いで了った。

　賑やかな商店の多い小路で突きあたりに印形屋の看板の見える街、——どう考えて見ても、私は今迄通ったことのない往来の一つに違いないと思った。子供時代に経験したような謎の世界の感じに、再び私は誘われた。

「あなた、あの看板の字が読めましたか。」

「いや読めなかった。一体此処は何処なのだか私にはまるで判らない。

92

私【わたし】I ⊛
看板【かんばん】signboard ⊛
横【よこ】side
書く【かく】write
細い【こまかい】fine, small
文字【もじ】characters, letters
町名番地【ちょうめいばんち】area name and lot number
俥【くるま】rickshaw
〜の上で【〜のうえで】on
遠くから【とおくから】from a distance
覗き込む【のぞきこむ】scrutinize, peer
女【おんな】woman
忽ち【たちまち】immediately
気が附く【きがつく】notice

93

あれッ oh! (exclamation of surprise)

94

云う【いう】say
再び【ふたたび】again
眼【め】eye
塞ぐ【ふさぐ】cover
〜で了う【〜でしまう】thoroughly

95

賑やかな【にぎやかな】lively
商店【しょうてん】shop
多い【おおい】numerous
小路【こみち／こうじ】lane, alley
突きあたり【つきあたり】end (of a street)
印形屋【いんぎょうや】sealmaker's shop
見える【みえる】be visible
街【まち】street, quarter
考える【かんがえる】think
〜て見る【〜てみる】to see what it is like
今迄【いままで】until now

From inside the rickshaw I started trying to make out the street name and house number inscribed in small characters at the corner of the sign, but the woman noticed immediately.

"Oh no!"

She exclaimed, and covered my eyes again.

A quarter with a lively little street full of shops and a seal-maker's sign at the corner—I was forced to acknowledge that this was obviously one of those streets I had not yet been down. I was seduced anew by the sense of mystery I had experienced as a child.

"Could you read the characters on the sign?"

"No, I couldn't decipher them. I have absolutely no idea where we are.

通る 【とおる】 pass along

往来 【おうらい】 street

一つ 【ひとつ】 one

〜に違いない 【〜にちがいない】 definitely be

思う 【おもう】 think

子供時代 【こどもじだい】 childhood

経験する 【けいけんする】 experience

謎 【なぞ】 riddle, puzzle

世界 【せかい】 world, sphere

感じ 【かんじ】 feeling, atmosphere

再び 【ふたたび】 again

誘う 【いざなう】 [passive form in text] allure, tempt

96

字 【じ】 character, letter

読む 【よむ】 [potential form in text] read ⊛

97

いや no

一体 【いったい】 (where) on earth

此処 【ここ】 here

何処 【どこ】 where

まるで〜ない absolutely . . . not

判る 【わかる】 understand, know

私はお前の生活に就いては三年前の太平洋の波の上の事ばかりしか知らないのだ。私はお前に誘惑されて、何だか遠い海の向うの、幻の国へ伴れて来られたように思われる。」

98 ▶ 　私がこう答えると、女はしみじみとした悲しい声で、こんな事を云った。

99 ▶ 「後生だからいつまでもそう云う気持で居て下さい。幻の国に住む、夢の中の女だと思って居て下さい。もう二度と再び、今夜のような我が儘を云わないで下さい。」

100 ▶ 　女の眼からは、涙が流れて居るらしかった。

101 ▶ 　その後暫く、私は、あの晩女に見せられた不思議な街の光景を忘れることが出来なかった。

私【わたし】I ❈
お前【おまえ】MASCULINE, FAMILIAR you ❈
生活【せいかつ】life, way of life
〜に就いて【〜について】about
三年前【さんねんまえ】three years ago
太平洋【たいへいよう】Pacific Ocean
波【なみ】wave
〜の上の【〜のうえの】on
事【こと】experience, act, thing ❈
〜ばかり just, only
〜しか other than, besides
知る【しる】know
誘惑する【ゆうわくする】[passive form in text] tempt, seduce
何だか【なんだか】somehow
遠い【とおい】distant
海【うみ】sea
向う【むこう】other side

幻【まぼろし】illusion, phantom ❈
国【くに】country, land ❈
伴れて来る【つれてくる】[passive form in text] bring (someone somewhere)
思う【おもう】[spontaneous form in text] think ❈

98
答える【こたえる】answer
女【おんな】woman ❈
しみじみとした full of feeling
悲しい【かなしい】sad
声【こえ】voice
云う【いう】say ❈

99
後生だから【ごしょうだから】for the love of God
いつまでも forever
そう云う【そういう】that kind of

All I know about your life is what happened three years ago out in the Pacific. I feel as though, seduced by you, I've been carried off to some phantom land beyond the farthest ocean."

After I had thus replied, the woman said in voice heavy with sadness:

"And I pray God that you'll feel that way forever. Think of me as a dream woman who lives in a phantom land, and never again make such an unreasonable request as you did tonight."

I guessed that tears were streaming from the woman's eyes.

For some time after, I was unable to forget the extraordinary sight of the street that the woman had revealed to me that night.

気持【きもち】feeling
〜て下さい【〜てください】please ⊛
住む【すむ】live
夢【ゆめ】dream
〜の中の【〜のなかの】in, inside
もう二度と〜ない【もうにどと〜ない】 never again
再び【ふたたび】again
今夜【こんや】tonight
我が儘【わがまま】willfullness, selfish- ness

100

眼【め】eye
涙【なみだ】tear
流れる【ながれる】flow
〜らしい seemingly

101

その後【そのご】thereafter

暫く【しばらく】for a while
晩【ばん】evening
見せる【みせる】[passive form in text] show
不思議な【ふしぎな】extraordinary
街【まち】street, quarter
光景【こうけい】sight
忘れる【わすれる】forget
出来る【できる】be able to do

燈火のかんかんともっている賑やかな狭い小路の突き当りに見えた印形屋の看板が、頭にはッきりと印象されて居た。何とかして、あの町の在りかを捜し出そうと苦心した揚句、私は漸く一策を案じ出した。

102 ▶

　長い月日の間、毎夜のように相乗りをして引き擦り廻されて居るうちに、雷門で俥がくるくると一つ所を廻る度数や、右に折れ左に曲る回数まで、一定して来て、私はいつともなくその塩梅を覚え込んでしまった。或る朝、私は雷門の角へ立って眼をつぶりながら二三度ぐるぐると体を廻した後、この位だと思う時分に、俥と同じ位の速度で一方へ駈け出して見た。

燈火【とうか】lamplight

かんかん MIMETIC brightly and hotly

ともる burn

賑やかな【にぎやかな】lively

狭い【せまい】narrow

小路【こみち／こうじ】lane, alley

突き当り【つきあたり】end (of a street)

見える【みえる】be visible

印形屋【いんぎょうや】sealmaker's shop

看板【かんばん】signboard

頭【あたま】head, brain

はッきりと clearly

印象する【いんしょうする】[passive form in text] print, impress

何とかして【なんとかして】somehow or other

町【まち】district, quarter

在りか【ありか】whereabouts

捜し出す【さがしだす】[volitional form in text] find, discover

苦心する【くしんする】rack one's brains

〜揚句【あげく】after (a difficult process)

私【わたし】I ⊛

漸く【ようやく】finally

一策【いっさく】plan, scheme

案じ出す【あんじだす】hatch a plan

102

長い【ながい】long

月日【つきひ】months and days, time

間【あいだ】interval

毎夜【まいよ】every night

相乗りをする【あいのりをする】ride together

引き擦り廻す【ひきずりまわす】[passive form in text] drag around

雷門【かみなりもん】Kaminari Gate ⊛

The sealmaker's sign, which I had glimpsed at the crossroads of that narrow, bustling lane all ablaze with lamplight, was clearly imprinted on my mind. After racking my brains thinking how I could pinpoint the location of the street, I finally came up with a scheme.

In the course of being pulled around together with the woman every night for months, the number of times we would spin on the spot at the Kaminari Gate—even the number of turns we made to right and left—had settled into a pattern of which I had memorized the sequence. One morning, I stood at the corner by the Kaminari Gate, shut my eyes and spun myself around two or three times. Then, when I reckoned I'd got it about right, I tried dashing off in one direction at about the same speed as the rickshaw.

俥【くるま】rickshaw ⊛
くるくると MIMETIC round and round
一つ所【ひとつところ】one place
廻る【まわる】turn around
度数【どすう】number of times
右【みぎ】right
折れる【おれる】turn
左【ひだり】left
曲る【まがる】turn
回数【かいすう】number of times
一定する【いっていする】be fixed
〜て来る【〜てくる】indicates a situation
　or phenomenon emerging
いつともなく without one being aware
塩梅【あんばい】pattern
覚え込む【おぼえこむ】commit to
　memory
或る【ある】a certain, one

朝【あさ】morning
角【かど】corner
立つ【たつ】stand
眼をつぶる【めをつぶる】shut one's eyes
二三度【にさんど】two or three times
ぐるぐると MIMETIC round and round
体【からだ】body
廻す【まわす】turn around
〜後【〜のち／〜あと】after
この位【このぐらい】about this much
思う【おもう】think
時分【じぶん】time, point
〜と同じ位の【〜とおなじぐらいの】
　about the same
速度【そくど】speed
一方【いっぽう】one direction
駈け出す【かけだす】scamper off

唯好い加減に時間を見はからって彼方此方の横町を折れ曲るより外の方法はなかったが、丁度この辺と思う所に、予想の如く、橋もあれば、電車通りもあって、確かにこの道に相違ないと思われた。

103 ▶ 　道は最初雷門から公園の外郭を廻って千束町に出て、龍泉寺町の細い通りを上野の方へ進んで行ったが、車坂下で更に左へ折れ、お徒町の往来を七八町も行くとやがて又左へ曲り始める。私は其処でハタとこの間の小路にぶつかった。

104 ▶ 　成る程正面に印形屋の看板が見える。

All I could do was duck off into side streets here and there by estimating the time rather haphazardly, but it felt like I was on the right track because no sooner had I thought "It must be about here" than up would pop a bridge, or a road with streetcar tracks, just where I expected them to be.

From the Kaminari Gate, the route first followed the line of the park coming out at Senzoku-chō, then proceeded along a narrow street in Ryūsenji-chō heading toward Ueno; but at the bottom of Kurumazaka it veered left again and advanced seven or eight blocks through Okachimachi, before soon starting to curve off to the left once more. It was there that, quite suddenly, I chanced upon the lane of that night.

Sure enough, I could see the sign of the sealmaker directly in front of me.

上野【うえの】Ueno
〜の方へ【〜のほうへ】in the direction of
進む【すすむ】advance, progress
〜て行く【〜ていく】indicates movement away from the narrator
車坂【くるまざか】Kurumazaka
〜下【した】beneath, at the foot of
更に【さらに】further, more
左【ひだり】left ✪
折れる【おれる】turn
お徒町【おかちまち】Okachimachi
往来【おうらい】street
七八町【しちはちちょう／しちはっちょう】seven or eight blocks
行く【いく】go
やがて in due course, before long
又【また】and, also, again

曲り始める【まがりはじめる】start to turn
私【わたし】I
其処で【そこで】there
ハタと MIMETIC all of a sudden
この間【このあいだ】a short time ago
小路【こみち／こうじ】lane, alley
ぶつかる come upon by chance

104

成る程【なるほど】sure enough
正面に【しょうめんに】in front
印形屋【いんぎょうや】sealmaker's shop
看板【かんばん】signboard
見える【みえる】be visible

　それを望みながら、秘密の潜んでいる巌窟の奥を究めで
もするように、つかつかと進んで行ったが、つきあたりの
通りへ出ると、思いがけなくも、其処は毎晩夜店の出る下
谷竹町の往来の続きであった。いつぞや小紋の縮緬を買っ
た古着屋の店もつい二三間先に見えて居る。不思議な小路
は、三味線堀と仲お徒町の通りを横に繋いで居る街路であ
ったが、どうも私は今迄其処を通った覚えがなかった。
散々私を悩ました精美堂の看板の前に立って、私は暫く佇
んで居た。

105

望む【のぞむ】gaze at

秘密【ひみつ】secret

潜む【ひそむ】lie concealed, lurk

巌窟【がんくつ】cave, cavern

奥【おく】depths

究める【きわめる】investigate thoroughly

つかつかと MIMETIC directly, without ceremony

進む【すすむ】advance, progress

〜て行く【〜ていく】indicates an increase in tendency

つきあたり end (of a street)

通り【とおり】street ❀

出る【でる】come out, emerge ❀

思いがけなくも【おもいがけなくも】to-
tally unexpectedly

其処【そこ】there, that place ❀

毎晩【まいばん】every evening

夜店【よみせ】night stall

下谷竹町【したやたけちょう】Shitayatake-
chō

往来【おうらい】street, thoroughfare

続き【つづき】continuation

いつぞや the other day

小紋【こもん】fine pattern

縮緬【ちりめん】silk crepe

買う【かう】buy

古着屋の店【ふるぎやのみせ】old cloth-
ing shop

つい only

二三間【にさんげん】two or three *ken* (1
ken = 6 feet)

先【さき】ahead

見える【みえる】be visible

不思議な【ふしぎな】extraordinary

Keeping my eyes on the sign, I continued to advance in a straight line as if exploring the depths of a cave where a secret lay concealed. Coming out into the transverse street, I was amazed to find that it was the continuation of a street in Shitayatake-chō where market stalls are put out every night. Just five or six yards away I could see the old clothing shop where I had bought the delicately patterned kimono of silk crepe not so long ago. My "wondrous lane" was a street that ran crosswise between the streets of Shamisenbori and Naka-Okachimachi, though for the life of me I couldn't recall ever having been that way before. I stood and lingered for a while in front of the Seibidō sign that had preoccupied me so.

小路【こみち／こうじ】lane, alley
三味線堀【しゃみせんぼり】Shamisenbori
仲お徒町【なかおかちまち】Naka-Okachi-machi
横に【よこに】crosswise
繋ぐ【つなぐ】connect, join
街路【がいろ】street
どうも somehow, by any means
私【わたし】I ⊛
今迄【いままで】until now
通る【とおる】pass
覚え【おぼえ】memory
散々【さんざん】terribly, severely
悩ます【なやます】torment, make anxious
精美堂【せいびどう】Seibidō
看板【かんばん】signboard
〜の前に【〜のまえに】in front of

立つ【たつ】stand
暫く【しばらく】for a while
イむ【たたずむ】linger, loiter

燦爛とした星の空を戴いて夢のような神秘な空気に蔽われながら、赤い燈火を湛えて居る夜の趣とは全く異り、秋の日にかんかん照り附けられて乾涸びて居る貧相な家並を見ると、何だか一時にがっかりして興が覚めて了った。

106 ▶ 　抑え難い好奇心に駆られ、犬が路上の匂いを嗅ぎつつ自分の棲み家へ帰るように、私は又其処から見当をつけて走り出した。

107 ▶ 　道は再び浅草区へ這入って、小島町から右へ右へと進み、菅橋の近所で電車通りを越え、代地河岸を柳橋の方へ曲って、遂に両国の広小路へ出た。

燦爛とした【さんらんとした】radiant
星【ほし】star
空【そら】sky
戴く【いただく】have above one
夢【ゆめ】dream
神秘な【しんぴな】mysterious
空気【くうき】air, atmosphere
蔽う【おおう】[passive form in text] cover, sheathe
赤い【あかい】red
燈火【とうか】lamplight
湛える【たたえる】fill
夜【よる】night
趣【おもむき】beauty, general effect
全く【まったく】completely
異る【ことなる】be different
秋【あき】evening
日【ひ】day

かんかん MIMETIC brightly and hotly
照り附ける【てりつける】[passive form in text] blaze down on
乾涸びる【ひからびる】become parched
貧相な【ひんそうな】seedy-looking
家並【いえなみ／やなみ】row of houses
見る【みる】see
何だか【なんだか】somehow
一時に【いちじに／いちどきに】instantaneously
がっかりする be disappointed
興が覚める【きょうがさめる】lose interest
〜て了う【〜てしまう】thoroughly

106
抑え難い【おさえがたい】hard to suppress
好奇心【こうきしん】curiosity
駆られる【かられる】be impelled
犬【いぬ】dog

Looking at the stretch of seedy houses all parched under the fierce autumn sun, it was so utterly unlike the splendor of that night—clad in an atmosphere of dreamlike mystery, crowned with a radiant starry sky and ablaze with red lamplight—that I was disillusioned and felt my interest dry up on the spot.

Driven by an inexorable curiosity, I started running again, guessing the way like a dog sniffing at the street to find its way home.

My route went back into Asakusa Ward, proceeded east for some while from Kojima-chō, crossed the streetcar avenue near Suga Bridge, turned toward Yanagi Bridge along the Daichi Riverbank and finally emerged into Ryōgoku Boulevard.

路上 【ろじょう】 on the street
匂い 【におい】 smell
嗅ぐ 【かぐ】 sniff, smell
〜つつ while, as
自分 【じぶん】 oneself
棲み家 【すみか】 dwelling
帰る 【かえる】 return
私 【わたし】 I
又 【また】 again
其処から 【そこから】 from there
見当をつける 【けんとうをつける】 make a guess
走り出す 【はしりだす】 start to run

107
道 【みち】 route, way
再び 【ふたたび】 again
浅草区 【あさくさく】 Asakusa Ward
這入る 【はいる】 go into

小島町 【こじまちょう】 Kojima-chō
右 【みぎ】 right, east ✪
進む 【すすむ】 advance, progress
菅橋 【すがばし】 Suga Bridge
近所 【きんじょ】 neighborhood, vicinity
電車通り 【でんしゃどおり】 main road with streetcar tracks
越える 【こえる】 cross, go over
代地河岸 【だいちがし】 Daichi Riverbank
柳橋 【やなぎばし】 Yanagi Bridge
〜の方へ 【〜のほうへ】 in the direction of
曲る 【まがる】 turn
遂に 【ついに】 at length
両国の広小路 【りょうごくのひろこうじ】 Ryōgoku Boulevard
出る 【でる】 come out, emerge

女が如何に方角を悟らせまいとして、大迂廻をやって居たかが察せられる。薬研堀、久松町、浜町と来て蠣浜橋を渡った処で、急にその先が判らなくなった。

108 ▶ 何でも女の家は、この辺の路次にあるらしかった。一時間ばかりかかって、私はその近所の狭い横町を出つ入りつした。

109 ▶ 丁度道了権現の向い側の、ぎっしり並んだ家と家との庇間を分けて、殆ど眼につかないような、細い、ささやかな小路のあるのを見つけ出した時、私は直覚的に女の家がその奥に潜んで居ることを知った。

女【おんな】woman ✸

如何に【いかに】very, truly

方角【ほうがく】direction, orientation

悟らせまいとする【さとらせまいとする】keep from figuring out

大迂廻をやる【だいうかいをやる】make a major detour

察する【さっする】[spontaneous form in text] guess, judge

薬研堀【やげんぼり】Yagenbori

久松町【ひさまつちょう】Hisamatsu-chō

浜町【はまちょう】Hama-chō

来る【くる】come

蠣浜橋【かきはまばし】Kakihama Bridge

渡る【わたる】cross

処【ところ】time, moment

急に【きゅうに】suddenly

先【さき】ahead

判る【わかる】understand, know

108

何でも【なんでも】probably, likely

家【うち】house ✸

辺【あたり】area

路次【ろじ】road

～らしい apparently

一時間【いちじかん】one hour

～ばかり about

かかる take (of time)

私【わたし】I ✸

近所【きんじょ】vicinity, neighborhood

狭い【せまい】narrow

横町【よこちょう】bystreet, alley

出つ入りつする【いでついりつする】go in and out of

109

丁度【ちょうど】exactly, just

It was clear that the woman had taken an extremely roundabout route in an effort to stop me figuring out the way. At the point when I had gone through Yagenbori, Hisamatsu-chō and Hama-chō and crossed Kakihama Bridge, I suddenly had no idea where to go.

The woman's house was probably down an alley around here. I spent about an hour going in and out of the narrow side streets in the quarter.

When I discovered that there was an almost unnoticeable narrow little lane squeezed between the tightly packed houses immediately opposite the Dōryō Gongen Temple, I knew instinctively that the woman's house was hidden at the end of it.

道了権現【どうりょうごんげん】Dōryō Gongen Temple
向い側【むかいがわ】opposite side
ぎっしり MIMETIC tightly
並ぶ【ならぶ】be side by side
家【いえ】house ⊕
庇間【ひあわい】narrow space between houses (lit., "space between the eaves")
分ける【わける】divide, part
殆ど【ほとんど】almost
眼につく【めにつく】catch one's eye
細い【ほそい】narrow
ささやかな small
小路【こみち／こうじ】lane, alley
見つけ出す【みつけだす】find, discover
〜時【〜とき】when
直覚的に【ちょっかくてきに】intuitively
奥【おく】innermost part

潜む【ひそむ】lie concealed
知る【しる】know

中へ這入って行くと右側の二三軒目の、見事な洗い出しの板塀に囲まれた二階の欄干から、松の葉越しに女は死人のような顔をして、じっと此方を見おろして居た。

110▶　思わず嘲けるような瞳を挙げて、二階を仰ぎ視ると、寧ろ空惚けて別人を装うものの如く、女はにこりともせずに私の姿を眺めて居たが、別人を装うても訝しまれぬくらい、その容貌は夜の感じと異って居た。たった一度、男の乞いを許して、眼かくしの布を弛めたばかりに、秘密を発かれた悔恨、失意の情が見る見る色に表われて、やがて静かに障子の蔭へ隠れて了った。

中へ【なかへ】in, inside

這入る【はいる】go in, enter

〜て行く【〜ていく】indicates movement away from the narrator

右側【みぎがわ】right-hand side

二三軒目【にさんげんめ】second or third house

見事な【みごとな】splendid, fine

洗い出しの【あらいだしの】scrubbed

板塀【いたべい】wooden fence

囲む【かこむ】[passive form in text] surround

二階【にかい】two stories, second story ✳

欄干【らんかん】handrail, railing

松【まつ】pine tree

葉越しに【はごしに】through the leaves

女【おんな】woman ✳

死人【しにん】corpse

顔【かお】face

じっと MIMETIC fixedly

此方【こちら】this way

見おろす【みおろす】look down

110

思わず【おもわず】involuntarily

嘲ける【あざける】scoff, mock

瞳【ひとみ】eye

挙げる【あげる】raise

仰ぎ視る【あおぎみる】look up

寧ろ【むしろ】rather

空惚ける【そらとぼける】feign ignorance

別人【べつじん】different person ✳

装う【よそおう】pose as, pretend to be ✳

もの person

〜の如く【〜のごとく】just like

にこりともせず without even smiling

私【わたし】I

姿【すがた】figure, form

I went in. The second or third house on the right was surrounded by a magnificently scrubbed wooden fence. From the handrail in the second-floor window, the woman stared down at me through the pine branches. Her face was like a corpse.

As I looked up at the second floor, I could not keep the sneer out of my eyes. The woman looked at me without the hint of smile, as if feigning ignorance and pretending to be someone else. So different did she look from her nighttime self that one might not even have suspected her regardless of these efforts. Just once she had yielded to a man's request and loosened his blindfold, and her secret had been revealed. Emotions of regret and despair clearly visible in her face, she soundlessly vanished behind the shoji.

眺める【ながめる】gaze at
訝しまれぬ【あやしまれぬ】not be looked at suspiciously
〜くらい to the extent of
容貌【ようぼう】appearance, looks
夜【よる】night
感じ【かんじ】feeling, mood
異る【ことなる】be different
たッた just
一度【いちど】one time, once
男【おとこ】man
乞い【こい】request, wishes
許す【ゆるす】grant, yield to
眼かくし【めかくし】blindfold
布【ぬの】cloth
弛める【ゆるめる】loosen
〜ばかりに simply because
秘密【ひみつ】secret

発く【あばく】[passive form in text] disclose
悔恨【かいこん】regret, remorse
失意【しつい】despair
情【じょう】feeling, emotion
見る見る【みるみる】visibly
色に表われる【いろにあらわれる】appear on one's face
やがて before long
静かに【しずかに】quietly
障子【しょうじ】shoji, paper screen
〜の蔭へ【〜のかげへ】behind
隠れる【かくれる】be lost to sight
〜て了う【〜てしまう】completely

111▶ 　女は芳野と云うその界隈での物持の後家であった。あの印形屋の看板と同じように、凡べての謎は解かれて了った。私はそれきりその女を捨てた。

112▶ 　二三日過ぎてから、急に私は寺を引き払って田端の方へ移転した。私の心はだんだん「秘密」などと云う手ぬるい淡い快感に満足しなくなって、もっと色彩の濃い、血だらけな歓楽を求めるように傾いて行った。

111

女【おんな】woman ⊛
芳野【よしの】Yoshino
〜と云う【〜という】called, so-called ⊛
界隈【かいわい】neighborhood
物持【ものもち】wealthy person
後家【ごけ】widow
印形屋【いんぎょうや】sealmaker's shop
看板【かんばん】signboard
〜と同じように【〜とおなじように】in the same fashion as
凡べて【すべて】all
謎【なぞ】riddle, puzzle
解く【とく】[passive form in text] solve
〜て了う【〜てしまう】expresses with regret the completion of a process
私【わたし】I ⊛

それきり that was the last of it, that was that
捨てる【すてる】abandon, throw away

112

二三日【にさんにち】two or three days
過ぎる【すぎる】pass
急に【きゅうに】suddenly
寺【てら】temple
引き払う【ひきはらう】leave, vacate
田端【たばた】Tabata
〜の方へ【〜のほうへ】in the direction of
移転する【いてんする】move
心【こころ】heart, mind
だんだん gradually
秘密【ひみつ】secret
手ぬるい【てぬるい】mild, lukewarm
淡い【あわい】faint, superficial
快感【かいかん】pleasure

She was the widow of a man called Yoshino who had been wealthy for that neighborhood. Like the sealmaker's sign, all her mystery had evaporated. I discarded her—and that was that.

Two or three days later, I abruptly left the temple and moved to Tabata. My heart no longer found satisfaction in the insipid, anemic pleasure of "secrets." I was disposed to pursue more intense, blood-soaked delights.

満足する【まんぞくする】be satisfied
もッと more
色彩【しきさい】color
濃い【こい】strong, heavy
血だらけな【ちだらけな】blood-covered
歓楽【かんらく】pleasure
求める【もとめる】seek, pursue
傾く【かたむく】incline to
〜て行く【〜ていく】indicates an increase in tendency

WORKS CITED

Cabell, Charles. 2001. Kawabata Yasunari. In Rubin, 149–67.

Gessel, Van C. 1993. *Three Modern Novelists: Sōseki, Tanizaki, Kawabata.* Tokyo: Kodansha International.

Nathan, John. 1974. *Mishima: A Biography.* Boston: Little, Brown and Company.

Österling, Anders. 1968. Presentation speech. http://nobelprize.org/nobel_prizes/literature/laureates/1968/press.html

Ross, Christopher. 2006. *Mishima's Sword: Travels in Search of a Samurai Legend.* London: Harper Perennial.

Rubin, Jay, ed. 2001. *Modern Japanese Writers.* New York: Charles Scribner's Sons.

Seidensticker, Edward G. 1957. Introd. to *Snow Country,* by Yasunari Kawabata. Trans. Edward G. Seidensticker. Tokyo: Tuttle Publishing.

———. 1973. Introd. to *The Master of Go,* by Yasunari Kawabata. Trans. Edward G. Seidensticker. Tokyo: Tuttle Publishing.

Vidal, Gore. 1971. Mr. Japan. *The New York Review of Books* 16, no. 11 (June 17). http://www.nybooks.com/archives/

Washburn, Dennis. 2001. Mishima Yukio. In Rubin, 213–26.